# THE PATRIOT ACT

## A Documentary and Reference Guide

*Herbert N. Foerstel*

Foreword by *Sanford Berman*

Greenwood Press

Westport, Connecticut • London

**Library of Congress Cataloging-in-Publication Data**

Foerstel, Herbert N.
    The Patriot Act : a documentary and reference guide / Herbert N.
Foerstel ; foreword by Sanford Berman.
        p. cm.
    Includes bibliographical references and index.
    ISBN: 978-0-313-34142-7 (alk. paper)
1. United States. Uniting and Strengthening America by Providing
Appropriate Tools Required to Intercept and Obstruct Terrorism (USA
PATRIOT ACT) Act of 2001. 2. War on Terrorism, 2001– —Law and
legislation—United States. 3. Terrorism—United States—Prevention.
4. Library surveillance—United States. 5. Domestic surveillance—United
States. I. Title.
KF9430.F64 2008
345.73'02—dc22        2007029292

British Library Cataloguing in Publication Data is available.

Library of Congress Catalog Card Number: 2007029292
ISBN: 978-0-313-34142-7

First published in 2008

Greenwood Press, 88 Post Road West, Westport, CT 06881
An imprint of Greenwood Publishing Group, Inc.
www.greenwood.com

Printed in the United States of America

The paper used in this book complies with the
Permanent Paper Standard issued by the National
Information Standards Organization (Z39.48–1984).

10  9  8  7  6  5  4  3  2  1

# Contents

# Contents

# Reader's Guide to Documents and Sidebars

# Foreword

At a May 16, 2005, conference in St. Paul, Minnesota, titled "Libraries and the Patriot Act: Your Loss of Privacy?" I remarked:

> Several years of speeches, columns, editorials, panel discussions, books, and press releases, and hundreds of municipal, state, and county resolutions, declare unmistakably that Section 215 of the Patriot Act (if not the entire law) is Bad News. Bad for the First Amendment. Bad for privacy. Bad for libraries and bookstores dedicated to the Freedom to Read, whose users expect their reading and viewing to remain confidential.

Two years later, it's still true. The Patriot Act represents a severe and continuing assault on individual privacy and free speech. And nowhere is that assault better or more systematically documented than in this volume.

Herb Foerstel has assembled all the relevant data associated with the Act's genesis, passage, and reauthorization. Beyond that, he has incisively analyzed that data, persuasively explaining what they mean. There may be many ways to respond to the material in this handbook. Some—indeed, most—of it is simply frightening, a stunning documentation of how "it *can* happen here" in terms of sudden and draconian limitations or abrogation of basic rights. It is frankly appalling in its account of how our elected representatives passed legislation as a direct result of hysteria, not solemn deliberation. However, the story also inspires, because these speeches, draft bills, and statements equally highlight the depth, passion, and determination of resistance to the Act and its repressive provisions. While they have not yet prevailed in wholly undoing or reforming that grotesquely Orwellian law and its later permutations, such courageous persons and groups as Representatives Dennis Kucinich, Ron Paul, and Bernie Sanders, Senator Russ Feingold, and the five Connecticut librarians who successfully challenged a National Security Letter gag order deserve our praise and thanks. They are models of outspoken, fearless dissent in defense of liberty. (See especially Feingold's sterling declaration, quoted in Chapter 2, that begins: "There is no doubt that if we lived in a police state, it would be easier to catch terrorists.")

It would be a serious mistake to simply recoil in paralysis at the wealth of First Amendment-wrecking evidence Foerstel has compiled. Rather, the facts and interpretation should spur all of us to renewed efforts to dismantle this odious legislation and ensure that it never re-emerges.

Sanford Berman
Honorary Member, American Library Association
Author, "Fighting the USA Patriot Act," *Unabashed Librarian*

# Preface

The catastrophic events of September 11, 2001, are said to have permanently changed the American political and social fabric. Indeed, one frequently hears criticism of "pre-9/11 thinking," as if that terrible day was a time for sober thought and reflection. It was instead a day of emotion and determination. Post-9/11 thinking came later. The political representation of the "new thinking" was undoubtedly the USA PATRIOT Act, signed into law on October 26, 2001. As will be seen in the documents and analyses presented in this reference work, the congressional debate on the Patriot Act could hardly be characterized as sober deliberation, but, in a spirit of bipartisan solidarity, Congress codified the new national priorities on everything from national security to criminal justice to personal privacy. The nation has constructed new rules for pursuing terrorists, recalibrating the balance between individual rights and public safety in ways that make public speech and private property legitimate targets in the war on terror.

The 342-page Patriot Act was approved overwhelmingly by Congress. Just one senator voted against it. There was bipartisan support for the broad new surveillance authorities in the Act, as a spirit of action-oriented patriotism swept Capitol Hill. But, on some level, our political leaders knew they were acting hastily, in the heat of the moment. One of the more conservative members of Congress, Representative Dick Armey (R-TX), insisted that "sunsets" be applied to some of the more controversial sections of the Patriot Act, ensuring that they would be re-examined four years later when cooler heads might take a different view of the massive new powers ceded by Congress to the executive branch.

The drama and significance of the post-9/11 transformation of our political culture make for a compelling story. The documents presented and analyzed in this book provide a view of the federal government's rationale for domestic surveillance and the political and public response to the unprecedented federal powers acquired through the USA PATRIOT Act. Beginning with the September 11, 2001, terrorist attacks on New York's World Trade Center and the Pentagon, this book takes us through the feverish urgency to take action, the hasty congressional passage of the Patriot Act, its often controversial implementation, the legal and legislative challenges to its authority, and its contentious reauthorization in 2006.

The sixty-four documents that form the basis for the book include federal statutes, congressional hearings and floor debates, White House press conferences, interviews with politicians and constitutional scholars, and position papers from the American Library Association, the American Civil Liberties Union, and other civil liberties organizations. Each document was chosen to provide an authoritative and illuminating insight into the germination and development of the massive legislative package called the Uniting and

Strengthening America by Providing Appropriate Tools Required to Intercept and Obstruct Terrorism Act (USA PATRIOT Act).

Each document, or group of documents, is introduced by a bulleted paragraph providing a capsule description, the date of its origin or publication, the location of its creation, and its significance in the continuing Patriot Act drama. Then follows the actual document or document set, usually in full text, but sometimes excerpted or edited, and with complete source provided. The document is followed by a detailed analysis of its importance and implications, examining its relevance to significant events or decisions in the five and one-half years between 9/11 and the post-reauthorization scandals revolving around the Patriot Act. The analysis will often include explanatory sidebars, which reveal background information or other relevant matters of interest.

In the tradition of major reference books, this work provides "Further Readings" following each document's analysis. In addition, at the conclusion of the book there is a comprehensive listing of "Patriot Act Resources," including electronic, print, and video references.

There is, our course, a standard alphabetical index at the conclusion of the book, but there is also a "Reader's Guide to Documents and Sidebars" preceding the body of the book. The Reader's Guide divides the book's documents and sidebars into about 40 subject headings, arranged alphabetically. Within each subject, documents and sidebars are listed alphabetically by their titles, followed by the page number on which they appear. A particular document or sidebar may be listed under more than one subject.

This is a substantial, heavily-researched reference work, but an attempt has been made to make it readable as well as informative. Together, the documents, analyses, sidebars, and bibliographic resources will provide the reader with all the information necessary for a proper understanding of the USA PATRIOT Act, its origins and applications. Grounded in authoritative documents, this reference work will be invaluable to students, scholars, and the general public.

# Introduction

The USA PATRIOT Act may be the longest, broadest, most sweeping piece of legislation in American history. The legislation itself is so massive and technical that both supporters and critics have been free to interpret it loosely and in partisan fashion. This book will not silence the raging controversy over the Patriot Act, but by presenting relevant source documents, analyzed and placed in context, it may provide a more reliable basis for the ongoing debate.

Chapter 1, The Library Awareness Program: Precursor to the USA PATRIOT Act, examines the Library Awareness Program (LAP) conducted secretly by the Federal Bureau of Investigation (FBI) during the 1970s and 1980s. It was a narrowly-defined surveillance program, targeting foreign agents in America's libraries, but its tactics were quite similar to those used today under the Patriot Act's most controversial provisions. Unlike the surveillance conducted under the Patriot Act, the Library Awareness Program had no statutory basis. FBI agents simply visited libraries around the country, flashed a badge, warned of spies who might read the library's unclassified scientific journals, and asked librarians to report anyone who had a foreign-sounding name or foreign-sounding accent. Once exposed to public scrutiny, the Library Awareness Program was ridiculed and rejected as a crude and misguided threat to the freedom to read.

The relevant documents presented in Chapter 1 include previously secret FBI memos, acquired through the Freedom of Information Act, and congressional hearings on the Library Awareness Program. The first document is a letter from a Columbia University librarian describing the FBI's unwelcome visit there. Additional documents include: congressional testimony by an FBI assistant director describing the Library Awareness Program; testimony by the chairman of a congressional subcommittee deploring the program; a declassified FBI memo indicating that librarians who opposed the FBI's program had been subject to government investigations; excerpts from a typical state confidentiality law making it illegal to comply with the Library Awareness Program; and letters to Representative Don Edwards, Chairman of the House Subcommittee on Civil and Constitutional Rights, asking him to investigate the FBI's actions.

Chapter 2, The Legislative Response to 9/11: Conceived under Siege, Passed in Haste, analyzes the quick passage of the Patriot Act and its minimal debate, remarkable for a bill of such size and significance. Documents include President Bush's stirring address to the nation after the 9/11 attacks; Majority Leader Tom Daschle's 9/11 comments; President Carter's signing statement for the Foreign Intelligence Surveillance Act of 1978 (FISA), legislation that would be significantly altered by the Patriot Act; Representative John Edwards' comments on revising FISA; Representative John Conyers' description of Attorney General John

Ashcroft's surreptitious replacement of the original Patriot Act bill with one of his own making; Senator Patrick Leahy's description of an agreement with Attorney General John Ashcroft on civil liberties improvements to the Patriot Act bill, an agreement that the Attorney General would later break; congressional testimony warning that the undue haste and inadequate debate on the Patriot Act would jeopardize its constitutionality; Senator Russ Feingold's complaints about the suppression of his amendments to the Patriot Act; and descriptions of the new powers requested by the executive branch.

Chapter 3, The USA PATRIOT Act: The Bill That Defined America's Domestic War on Terrorism, introduces the text of the USA PATRIOT Act. The first document displayed is President Bush's signing statement accompanying the USA PATRIOT Act. Other documents include an outline of the entire Patriot Act identifying all ten titles and their numerous sections; Section 203 of the Act, the crucial information-sharing provision; Section 213, the delayed-notice warrant or "sneak and peek" provision; Section 215, the so-called "library provision," which became the primary target of civil liberties advocates; Section 412, authorizing indefinite detention of suspected terrorists; and Section 802, which defines the new crime of domestic terrorism, a broad definition that includes the politically motivated civil disobedience of groups like Greenpeace.

Chapter 4, Domestic Surveillance under the Patriot Act, examines incidents of domestic surveillance conducted under the Patriot Act since its passage in 2001. Documents include Attorney General John Ashcroft's testimony before Congress on the use of Section 215 to seize library and business records; FBI counsel Chuck Rosenberg's defense of gag orders under the Patriot Act; a national survey of library surveillance conducted under the Patriot Act; a speech by Attorney General John Ashcroft describing library reaction to the Patriot Act as "hysterical"; American Library Association guidelines on how to deal with surveillance visits; and FBI counsel Chuck Rosenberg's address to librarians on the kinds of warrants that may be served on libraries.

Chapter 5, Detention, Deportation, Exclusion, and Expropriation, examines the use of the Patriot Act to detain aliens and suspected terrorists and to seize charitable assets. Documents include testimony by Senator Russ Feingold about the abuses of aliens under the Patriot Act; a speech by constitutional scholar David Cole on deportation and exclusion under the Patriot Act; congressional questions to and responses from the Department of Justice concerning treatment of aliens; comments by David Cole on the seizure of assets from aliens under the Patriot Act; and statements on the controversial Sami al-Arian case from the Department of Justice and the American Civil Liberties Union.

Chapter 6, Congressional Oversight of the Patriot Act, examines the limits of congressional oversight of the Patriot Act. Documents analyzed include oversight requirements in Sections 215, 411, 412, and 1001 of the Patriot Act; FBI Director Robert Mueller's testimony to Congress on the need for strong oversight of the Patriot Act; a congressional report on oversight that notes a lack of support from the Bush Administration; letters from the House Judiciary Committee to Attorney General Ashcroft and letters from Assistant Attorney General Daniel Bryant to the Judiciary Committee; Attorney General Ashcroft's testimony before Congress in June 2003; and questions from Represenatative Linda Chavez to the Justice Department on abuses revealed in the Inspector General's report.

Chapter 7, Amendments and Legal Challenges to the Patriot Act, documents the legislative and legal actions taken to improve the civil liberties protections in the Patriot Act. Documents include text of the most significant amendment proposed to the Patriot Act, the Freedom to Read Protection Act; the text of the Benjamin Franklin True Patriot Act; excerpts from the decision by the secret Foreign Intelligence Surveillance Court that challenged surveillance procedures under the Patriot Act; legal briefs from plaintiffs (American Civil Liberties Union [ACLU]) and defendants (Department of Justice) in the Freedom of Information Act (FOIA) suit seeking Patriot Act documents; District Court Judge Heuvel's ruling in the FOIA case; and court rulings in *Doe v. Ashcroft* and *Doe v. Gonzales*, the suits brought anonymously against the Justice Department, challenging the constitutionality of Patriot Act gag orders.

Chapter 8, Reauthorization and Beyond: The New and Improved Patriot Act, examines the contentious process of amending and reauthorizing the Patriot Act during 2005 and early 2006, and describes two national scandals that arose directly from the Patriot Act reauthorization. Documents include the table of contents and list of titles in the USA PATRIOT Act Improvement and Reauthorization Act of 2005 (H.R.3199); the text of S.2271, the Additional Reauthorizing Amendments Act that amended FISA orders, National Security Letters, and gag orders under the Patriot Act; Sections 108 and 114 of H.R.3199, which made changes to the "roving wiretap" and "sneak and peek" authorities of the Patriot Act; Section 102 of H.R.3199, which makes permanent 14 of the 16 "sunsetted" provisions of the Patriot Act; Section 109 of H.R.3199, which mandates additional congressional oversight of the Patriot Act; Senator Dianne Feinstein's statement introducing S.214, which successfully repealed a provision in the Patriot Act reauthorization; the conclusions of the Inspector General's report documenting FBI abuses of National Security Letters; and the statement of Senator Patrick Leahy on the need to reexamine the Patriot Act in light of the Inspector General's report.

These eight chapters provide the descriptive and analytic basis for evaluating the USA PATRIOT Act. Recent public opinion polls have revealed a growing concern over government intrusion on privacy rights. In September 2003, a *Washington Post-ABC News* poll asked: "In investigating terrorism do you think the federal agencies like the FBI are or are not intruding on some Americans' privacy rights?" At that time, 33 percent of respondents said the government was not intruding, while 58 percent said it was intruding. Among those who said the government was intruding, only 29 percent said this was unjustified, while 63 percent said the intrusions were justified. Just three years later in December 2006, the same poll asked the same questions, but this time only 30 percent said the government was not intruding on privacy, while 66 percent said it was, and, most significant, a bare 51 percent said the intrusions were justified. The 2006 poll also found that 52 percent favored congressional hearings on "how the Bush administration has handled surveillance, treatment of prisoners, and related issues in the U.S. campaign against terrorism."

Bruce Hoffman, a terrorism expert at Georgetown University's Security Studies Program, said the poll results could spell trouble for the expanded anti-terrorism powers granted in the Patriot Act. "I don't think you can view these polling results in isolation from an overall phenomenon, which is that people are more skeptical of the government's conduct of the war on terrorism," said Hoffman ("66% Think U.S. Spies on Its Citizens," *Washington Post*, December 13, 2006, p. A19).

Given such poll results, we can anticipate increased congressional and public scrutiny of the Patriot Act. Hopefully, this book will contribute to an informed public debate and appropriate congressional oversight.

# CHAP**1**TER

## The Library Awareness Program: Precursor to the USA PATRIOT Act

Figure 1. A 1988 Herblock cartoon. Copyright 1988 by Herblock in the *Washington Post*.

# FBI Visit to Columbia University Makes Front-Page News

- **Document:** Letter from librarian Paula Kaufman to American Library Association
- **Date:** September 18, 1987
- **Where:** New York University (NYU), New York, NY
- **Significance:** The FBI visits to NYU, as described by Paula Kaufman in her letter to the American Library Association (reprinted in the *New York Times*) sent shock waves through academia and raised public doubts about the confidentiality of library records. The FBI's secret program of library surveillance was now front-page news, and it soon found its way to national TV as well.

---

## DOCUMENT

### Letter from Paula Kaufman to American Library Association

"On July 7, 1987, when I was the Director of the Academic Information Services Group at the Columbia Libraries, two New York-based FBI agents attempted to gain the coopera-tion of a support staff member in our Mathematics/Science Library to report to them on the activities of foreigners who use that facility....I met with them on June 11, at which time they explained to me that they were conducting a Library Awareness Program in New York City, the purpose of which was to alert the librarians to the possibilities that foreigners from countries hostile to the United States were using our library resources to piece together data which would yield information dangerous to our national security....They asked us to report on who was reading what, and I refused to cooperate with them.... Subsequent investigations indicate that this program has been carried on for many years throughout the country....The FBI's request to me to report on foreigners using our libraries is one with which I could not practically comply, even if our institution supported such cooperation, which it does not; even if such a request did not contravene my professional ethics, which it does; even if it did not infringe upon the First Amendment and privacy rights of all library patrons, which it does; and even if it does not violate the laws of the State of New York, which it does."

*SOURCE*: U.S. Congress, House Committee on the Judiciary, *FBI Counterintelligence Visits to Libraries*, 100th Cong., 2d Session, June 20 and July 13, 1988 (Washington, DC: GPO, 1989), pp. 77, 81.

---

## ANALYSIS

Paula Kaufman's congressional testimony describing the FBI's visit to her Columbia University library summarized her earlier letter to the American Library Association (ALA), reprinted in *The New York Times* on September 18, 1987. The letter, splashed across the front page of the *Times*, gave the public its first view of the FBI's Cold War surveillance

Figure 2. A 1988 Herblock cartoon. Copyright 1988 by Herblock in the *Washington Post*.

program in America's libraries. The FBI agent who spoke with Kaufman had referred to "a program in the city," suggesting that there were other New York City libraries involved.

Because the FBI conducted its Library Awareness Program (LAP) in secret, its origin and extent were unknown, even to those librarians who were contacted by federal agents. As it turned out, many other libraries around the country had been visited before Columbia University. For librarians working at those institutions, the *Times* article had been a revelation. For the FBI, it marked the beginning of unwelcome criticism and public ridicule (see Figure 2).

In 1986, my own libraries at the University of Maryland (College Park) were visited by agents who asked library staff to "report anyone with a foreign-sounding name or foreign-sounding accent" to the Bureau. I directed my staff to maintain the confidentiality of all library records and wrote some articles about the FBI visits for the Maryland Library Association newspaper. I assumed that the visits were an anomaly, perhaps the work of a loose cannon at the FBI.

At that time, nothing had been published in the mainstream media about library surveillance, and no reports of FBI visits to libraries had been received by the ALA. After notifying

**TABLE 1.1 Libraries Visited by the FBI**

| Institution | Library | Contact |
|---|---|---|
| *Academic Institutions* | | |
| Columbia University | Math/Science Library | Paula Kaufman |
| New York University | Courant Institute of Mathematical Sciences | Nancy Gubman |
| University of Maryland* | Engineering and Physical Sciences Library | Herb Foerstel |
| George Mason University* | | Charlene Hurt |
| University of Kansas* | OIF has documentation, but library has requested confidentiality on details of visit. | |
| University of California at Los Angeles* | Engineering and Mathematical Sciences Library | Ruth B. Gibbs |
| Pennsylvania State University* | University Libraries | James G. Neal |
| University of Michigan* | Engineering-Transportation Library | Maurita Peterson Holland |
| University of Houston* | | Scott Chafin (University Counsel) |
| University of Cincinnati* | | Dorothy Byers |
| University of Wisconsin at Madison* | | Alexander Rolich |
| State University of New York at Buffalo* | This is a documented visit, but OIF considers it different in that a specific request was made in relation to a specific individual, and the FBI subsequently followed up with a subpoena for the information. | |
| University of Utah* | Government Documents Library | Roger K. Hanson |
| *Public Institutions* | | |
| Broward County (FL) Public Library System | | Selma Algaze |
| Brooklyn Public Library | | Ellen Rudley |
| New York Public Library | | Paul Fasana |
| *Other* | | |
| Information Industry Association* | | Ken Allen |

*Visits by FBI agents to these libraries have been confirmed and documented. It has not been verified, however, that they are part of the Bureau's acknowledged "Library Awareness Program."

*Source:* U.S. Congress, House Committee on the Judiciary, *FBI Counterintelligence Visits to Libraries*, 100th Congress, 2nd Session, July 13, 1988 (Washington, DC: GPO, 1989), pp. 39–40.

my staff that no information on library patrons should be given to anyone without a proper subpoena, I began my own investigation into library surveillance. I worked with the Washington-based National Security Archive to acquire previously secret FBI memos through the Freedom of Information Act. Though heavily redacted, those memos revealed a program begun in the 1970s, whose mission was to prevent foreign nationals from accessing "open" scientific literature at America's public and university libraries and to enlist librarians in identifying foreign agents who sought to read America's unclassified scientific and technical literature.

The FBI claimed that it was unable to search its files for all possible visits to libraries, but the American Library Association's Office for Intellectual Freedom documented its own list, including the nature of the FBI inquiry. That list, as of May 10, 1988, appears in Table 1.1.

# FURTHER READINGS

"Effort to Limit Access to Unclassified Data Bases Draws Criticism," *Chronicle of Higher Education* (March 4, 1987), p. 12.

"FBI Asks Libraries to Help It Find Spies on Campuses," *College Press Service* (January 18, 1988), p. 3.

"FBI Wanted Her to Catch Spies in Columbia Stacks," *New York Daily News* (May 1, 1988), p. 25.

Federal Bureau of Investigation, Headquarters, Intelligence Division. *The KGB and the Library Target, 1962–Present* (February 1988).

"Librarians as Counterspies," *New York Times* (September 28, 1987), p. A24.

Phillips, David Atlee. "FBI's Timing Is Questionable, Not Its Morals," *Newsday* (October 16, 1987), p. 83.

## IN HISTORY

### History of Library Surveillance

In 1970, Senator John McClellan's Subcommittee on Investigations asked the Alcohol, Tobacco and Firearms (ATF) Division of the IRS to initiate a program to investigate suspected users of explosives. The ATF decided to examine library borrower records to see who was reading material that might be related to explosives. Once the investigation was begun, it became so broad as to reveal the names of high school students working on term papers. The American Library Association and the National Education Association denounced the investigations, calling on all librarians to defend library confidentiality and academic freedom.

On July 29, 1970, David Kennedy, Secretary of the Treasury, announced that ATF agents would no longer be allowed to make general searches of libraries, but would still be allowed to request library records concerning specific suspects. Senator Sam Irvin (D-NC) then sent a letter to Kennedy expressing his concern and concluding: "Throughout history, official surveillance of the reading habits of citizens has been a litmus test of tyranny."

In response, the Secretary of the Treasury announced that the ATF investigation of libraries had been terminated, adding ominously that "it is our judgment that checking such records in certain limited circumstances is an appropriate investigative technique." Within a few years, the FBI had begun its secret Library Awareness Program.

*SOURCE*: Herbert N. Foerstel, *Surveillance in the Stacks: The FBI's Library Awareness Program* (Westport, CT: Greenwood Press, 1991), p. 6.

# FBI Assistant Director James H. Geer Describes Library Awareness Program

- *Document:* Opening statement of James H. Geer, Assistant Director, Federal Bureau of Investigation, before the House Subcommittee on Civil and Constitutional Rights, Committee on the Judiciary
- *Date:* July 13, 1988
- *Where:* Washington, DC
- *Significance:* Assistant Director Geer's formal statement before the House Subcommittee on Civil and Constitutional Rights contained the FBI's most detailed public description and defense of the Library Awareness Program.

---

## DOCUMENT

### Congressional Testimony of FBI Assistant Director James H. Geer

FBI investigations since the early 1960s have thoroughly documented SIS [Soviet Intelligence Services] contacts with librarians in specialized science and technology libraries....In response to this SIS effort, the New York Office (NYO) initiated an awareness program which has come to be known as the Library Awareness Program. Interviews of library personnel under this program are patterned after the FBI's "Development of Counterintelligence Awareness" (DECA) program, which seeks to heighten the awareness of corporate executives and their employees to the hostile intelligence services threat. Our library contacts seek to inform selected librarians that they and their libraries are, and have historically been, significant SIS targets for intelligence activities and recruitment....

The proactive approach of this program, which alerts librarians generally of the SIS threat, should not be confused with occasional interviews of librarians in other areas of the United States which are in response to specific investigative leads involving Soviet or other Soviet-bloc nationals. The FBI, within the purview of its Foreign Counterintelligence (FCI) responsibilities, frequently finds it necessary to investigate contacts between Soviet intelligence officers, and other known or suspected hostile intelligence officers and their agents and American citizens. These may include contacts with libraries or librarians. The least intrusive technique available to the FBI to resolve such contacts is direct interview of the person(s) contacted....

The FBI has visited libraries because of the demonstrated need to alert them of the policies and practices of hostile intelligence services and to seek their cooperation.... The program is a very measured response to a well planned and organized effort by the SIS and other hostile intelligence services to exploit our specialized scientific and technical libraries and recruit our citizens.

SOURCE: U.S. Congress, House Committee on the Judiciary, *FBI Counterintelligence Visits to Libraries*, 100th Congress, 2d Session, July 13, 1988 (Washington, DC: GPO, 1989), pp. 110–20.

---

# ANALYSIS

The July 1988 testimony by Assistant Director James Geer revealed a formal FBI program designed to discourage SIS from using America's public and university libraries and to discover the scientific needs and interests of the Soviet Union and Soviet-Bloc countries. By the time of Geer's testimony, numerous specific acts of surveillance had been documented by libraries, but the nature and scope of the program remained hidden. The testimony before Congress, along with the release of previously secret FBI memos in response to the Freedom of Information Act (FOIA) requests, clarified the nature of the Library Awareness Program.

The Library Awareness Program was begun in New York City during the 1970s. Its creation is documented in three heavily-redacted FBI memos from the New York Office (NYO) to FBI headquarters. Acquired through the FOIA, the first memo, its date and major contents blacked out, concludes:

"In view of the above intense interest of the KGB in developing sources among librarians, the NYO is opening a control case, bearing this caption, to more closely follow this activity by the KGB.... The NYO will furnish additional recommendations to the Bureau as to what action can be initiated to counter the KGB efforts to develop sources and contacts among librarians" (U.S. Congress, House Committee on the Judiciary, *FBI Counterintelligence Visits to Libraries*, 100th Congress, 2d Session, July 13, 1988 (Washington, DC: GPO, 1989), p. 283).

FBI Headquarters responded to the NYO as follows:

> Prior to authorizing implementation of the program set forth in referenced airtel, the Bureau desires that your office submit an estimate as to the approximate number of librarians who may be interviewed and the amount of manpower that might be expended.
>
> While it appears that your suggested approach to this problem is logical, the Bureau desires that such an interview program be most selective in nature and that an unwieldy and unnecessary caseload is not created.
>
> Upon receipt of your comments in this regard, the Bureau will give further consideration to your proposal. (ibid., 285)

The next heavily redacted memo from the NYO shows its continued enthusiasm for the program:

> In view of the emphasis being placed on the development of librarians in the greater New York area as sources for the KGB, the NYO is proposing the following investigative action in an attempt to counter this KGB activity.
>
> ▮▮▮▮▮▮▮▮▮▮▮▮▮▮▮▮▮▮▮▮▮▮▮▮▮▮▮▮▮▮▮▮▮▮▮▮▮▮▮▮▮▮
>
> As an adjunct to the above procedure, consideration will be given to an interview of the chief librarian at a particular company or installation where the library staff is large. This individual would be interviewed as outlined above, but in addition he would be requested to alert members of his staff to our interest in this regard.

It is felt such an approach would be effective and would reduce the necessity of interviewing each librarian.

████████████████████████████████████████████████████████."

(ibid., 286)

In a follow-up memo, NYO said:

Regarding manpower to be expended, it is difficult to estimate. However, ███████████████████████████████████████████████████████it is not believed the manpower expended per case would be excessive. It is further strongly believed that the manpower expended would certainly be justified in view of the Soviet activity in this area and the necessity for the Bureau to fulfill its responsibilities in attempting to effectively counter this activity....If this program is authorized, investigation conducted therein should enable the NYO to determine whether additional efforts should be considered.

████████████████████████████████████████████████████

Additional recommendations and observations in this regard can be submitted when further analysis is made. The NYO recommends strongly the Bureau authorize implementation of this Program without delay. (ibid., 291)

Despite the strong recommendation, FBI HQ rejected the NYO proposal, except in very narrow circumstances:

The Bureau has carefully reviewed the program proposed in your referenced airtel to interview a number of librarians employed in technical libraries of interest to the Soviet intelligence services (SIS).

While it is recognized that such a program could be of some value in alerting those librarians to contacts by SIS personnel, could encourage their prompt reporting of such contacts to your office and might even uncover some individuals who have already been contacted, the Bureau does not feel that in light of other investigative priorities the results which might be obtained warrant a substantial expenditure of manpower at this time. Librarians at technical facilities having control over classified material should have been alerted to prompt reporting of contacts with communist-bloc officials by the military intelligence components responsible for their establishments. At those libraries where there is no classified material but where there is material which is of interest to SIS, it is recognized that SIS may indeed acquire such data. In an open society, however, it is impractical to attempt to prevent all Soviet acquisition of such readily available material and we must recognize realistic limitations in this regard.

████████████████████████████████████████████████████

Of course, where there is specific information developed concerning SIS interest in a given library, then such selective interviews of personnel of that facility would be fully warranted and will be considered on the merits of the specific case....

With the ever increasing number of Soviets assigned to this country in an official capacity and the present limitations of available manpower to counter their activities, it is simply not practical to enter into such a program as is proposed by NYO at this time. It is recognized that some value would be derived from the program proposed by NYO but it is not believed that the results achieved would offset the losses in other investigative areas which would be necessitated by this use of our manpower resource. (ibid., 292–93)

Despite headquarters' (HQ) rejection of its broader proposal, NYO apparently continued its library activities as a "control case," as indicated in the next FBI HQ memo:

As will be recalled, this investigation was initiated by your office as a control case to follow the activities of the KGB New York Residency in its efforts to develop sources among librarians in the New York City area. ▆▆▆▆▆▆▆▆▆▆▆▆▆▆▆▆▆▆▆▆▆▆▆▆▆▆▆▆▆▆ you recommended a program which called for interviewing a select number of librarians employed in technical libraries of interest to the Soviet intelligence services (SIS). FBIHQ reviewed your proposals at that time and decided that in view of other investigative priorities, the anticipated results did not warrant the expenditure of manpower.

A current review of this matter at FBIHQ reflects that you have opened a number of cases and it is requested that you review the results of investigation conducted in these cases with purpose of evaluating the SIS's progress in its development of technical librarians.

Submit your analysis and observations under the ▆▆▆▆ caption. (ibid., 294)

Finally, a memo from NYO indicated its continuing interest in libraries and its hope of expanding the program to match its original proposal.

Through this judicious initiation of cases and subsequent interviews, contact of librarians by a HIS [hostile intelligence service] can be definitely determined and those who have not been contacted will be alerted to the possibility of contact by a HIS, either alternative will serve to effectively counter attempts by the HIS to fulfill its responsibilities in recruiting sources of intelligence. ▆▆▆▆▆▆▆▆▆▆▆▆▆▆▆▆▆▆▆▆▆▆▆▆▆▆▆▆▆▆▆▆▆▆ is recommended this program be reinstituted. (ibid., 306)

No further memos in this series between FBIHQ and NYO were acquired through the FOIA, but one can only assume that NYO's final request that the Library Awareness Program be "reinstated" was granted. The result was what came to be known as the Library Awareness Program, confined to libraries in the New York City area. This would explain the highly publicized FBI visits to Columbia University, New York University, the New York Public Library, and other local institutions. But what of the numerous FBI visits to university libraries around the country? Subsequent congressional hearings would attempt to explain the apparent national scope of the Library Awareness Program.

# FURTHER READINGS

Ahlerich, Milt. "Soviets Are Exploiting USA's Libraries," *USA Today* (May 28, 1988), p. 10A.

Buchwald, Art. "I Was a Bookworm for the FBI," *Washington Post* (April 28, 1988), p. C1.

"The FBI Library Awareness Program." *American Federation of Teachers Convention Report*, 1988.

FBI Presentation to U.S. National Commission on Libraries and Information Science by Thomas DuHadway, San Antonio, Texas, January 14, 1988.

"Informer Please." *Common Cause Magazine* (November/December 1987), p. 10.

Kranich, Nancy. "The KGB, the FBI, and Libraries," *Our Right to Know* (Summer 1988) p. 5.

Schlafly, Phyllis. "It's Librarians' Duty to Help Catch Spies," *USA Today* (May 24, 1988), p. 10A.

"Spying in the Stacks." *Time* (May 30, 1988), p. 23.

"Why the FBI Is Interested in Talking to Librarians." *Washington Times* (February 15, 1988), p. F5.

# Congress Condemns Library Awareness Program as the FBI Defends It

- *Document:* Representative Don Edwards (D-CA), chairman of the House Subcommittee on Civil and Constitutional Rights, criticizing the Library Awareness Program
- *Date:* July 13, 1988, Representative Edwards speaking before his investigative subcommittee
- *Where:* Washington, DC
- *Significance:* The congressional hearings chaired by Representative Edwards found the FBI's Library Awareness Program to be an infringement of the First Amendment and privacy rights of library users.

---

## DOCUMENT

### Subcommittee Chairman Representative Don Edwards Deplores Library Awareness Program

This morning the subcommittee resumes its oversight hearings on the FBI's so-called "Library Awareness Program" and other FBI attempts to collect counterintelligence information on library use and users.

What disturbs some of us about this program is the FBI's apparent failure to recognize the special status of libraries in our society. The FBI apparently believes that libraries are no different from defense contractors and is applying to libraries a program originally designed for developing counterintelligence awareness in the defense industry.

The FBI should recognize that libraries and books and reading are special. In our nation, libraries are sacred institutions which should be protected and nurtured. Going into libraries and asking librarians to report on suspicious users has ominous implication for freedom of speech and privacy. Everybody in this country has a right to use libraries, and they have a right to do so with confidentiality....

I would hope that the FBI would reconsider this program, admit that it is over-broad, and get on to more productive work.

SOURCE: U.S. Congress, House Committee on the Judiciary, *FBI Counterintelligence Visits to Libraries*, 100th Cong., 2d Session, June 20 and July 13, 1988 (Washington, DC: GPO, 1989), pp. 105–106.

# ANALYSIS

The congressional hearings on the Library Awareness Program, chaired by Rep. Don Edwards' House Subcommittee on Civil and Constitutional Rights during June and July 1988, provided critics of the Bureau's program a high profile forum, but it also gave the FBI an opportunity to explain and justify its activities. James H. Geer, Assistant Director of the FBI's Intelligence Division, used his testimony to defend the Library Awareness Program and clarify some of the confusion about the difference between the New York program and the national program.

According to Geer, all of the FBI contacts with libraries outside the New York City area, including the visit to my libraries at the University of Maryland, were following up on specific leads and were not part of the narrowly defined Library Awareness Program. Despite Geer's explanation, the confusion persisted because the incidents reported by librarians around the country sounded almost identical to the descriptions given by New York City librarians. All of the visits seemed to focus on unclassified scientific and technical libraries, whether in New York or elsewhere. In any case, critics questioned the appropriateness of either kind of surveillance, concluding: Get a subpoena if the information sought is important, but stop the fishing expeditions in libraries.

Subcommittee Chairman Edwards, a former FBI agent, gave ample time to witnesses critical of the Library Awareness Program. Prominent among them were librarians, including: Duane Webster, Executive Director, Association of Research Libraries (ARL); C. James Schmidt, Executive Vice President, Research Libraries Group; David Bender, Executive Director, Special Libraries Association (SLA); Paula Kaufman, University Librarian, Columbia University; and me, Head of the Engineering and Physical Sciences Library, University of Maryland.

My own testimony focused primarily on the FBI's visits to the University of Maryland, while the other witnesses spoke more generally. Duane Webster declared:

"There are a number of reasons ARL opposes FBI, or any other government agency actions to cajole or intimidate library staff to cooperate in monitoring library use or users.

- There is a conflict between such requests and state law (in 38 states and the District of Columbia) and individual library policies that protect the confidentiality of library use.
- The privilege of confidentiality between library user and librarians is founded on the same principles of personal privacy that exist between doctor and patient or lawyer and client....
- Monitoring and reporting on library users is the antithesis of a librarian's professional code of ethics that protects each user's right to privacy with respect to information sought or received, and materials consulted, borrowed, or acquired.
- Even the suggestion of library cooperation with such government requests will have a frightening effect on library users who begin to question how public their use of a library may become.
- The FBI's assumption that foreign access to unclassified U.S. information services and products is damaging to the U.S. has not been adequately demonstrated.

- Any restrictions or inhibition on the exchange of unclassified scientific data, and the results of scientific research, have a detrimental impact on scientific and technological accomplishments and are counterproductive to the best interest of the country." (U.S. Congress, House Committee on the Judiciary, *FBI Counterintelligence Visits to Libraries*, 100th Cong., 2d Session, July 13, 1988 (Washington, DC: GPO, 1989), pp. 8–9)

C. James Schmidt gave similar reasons for opposing the FBI's intrusions on libraries, and he concluded, "The Library Awareness Program is a threat to the fundamental freedom of this nation. If continued, it will seriously and unnecessarily invade the intellectual life of citizens" (ibid., 24).

David Bender, representing the Special Libraries Association, was the most restrained of the critics testifying before the subcommittee. The libraries represented by his organization are, for the most part, government and industry libraries, many of them associated with the Defense Department, the Justice Department, or the military. Indeed, the FBI's own library is a member of SLA. Seen in that context, it was surprising that Bender, speaking for SLA, declared, "The Association opposes the activities of the FBI Library Awareness Program" (ibid., 47).

Paula Kaufman, whose public criticism of the Library Awareness Program first brought the issue to the national press, recounted the Bureau's visit to Columbia University in 1987, and concluded:

> The right to privacy is a fundamental part of the First Amendment right to information.... I support the American Library Association in calling upon the FBI to end the Library Awareness Program and to desist from recruiting librarians and the library staff to monitor patrons' use of libraries. I urge this Committee to consider enacting legislation to ensure this. (ibid., 83)

## FURTHER READINGS

Hentoff, Nat. "The FBI in the Library," *Washington Post* (July 22, 1988), p. A23.
"Librarians Tell Congress FBI Is Spying on Readers," *News Media and the Law* (Summer 1988), p. 38.
People for the American Way. *The FBI's Library Awareness Program Background Report.* Washington, DC: People for the American Way, 1988.
Robins, Natalie. "The FBI's Invasion of Libraries," *Nation* (April 9, 1988), p. 498.
Robins, Natalie. "Library Follow-up," *Nation* (June 25, 1988), p. 885.

# Critics of Library Awareness Program Go Public but Suffer Consequences

- *Documents:* Secret memo to FBI Director from ADIC, New York concerning "indices checks" on critics of Library Awareness Program; Letter from Morton H. Halperin, Director, American Civil Liberties Union, to Representative Don Edwards (D-CA), chairman of the House Subcommittee on Civil and Constitutional Rights, complaining about indices checks
- *Date:* FBI memo addressing a New York teletype dated 1/25/88; Halperin letter dated November 20, 1989
- *Where:* FBI memo: New York City to Washington, DC; Halperin letter: ACLU Washington Office to Justice Department, Washington, DC
- *Significance:* In his letter to Representative Don Edwards, ACLU Director Morton Halperin describes the FBI's practice of investigating critics of the Library Awareness Program and attaches a copy of his letter to FBI Director William Sessions.

---

## DOCUMENTS

### 1. FBI Memo Concerning "Indices Checks"

UNITED STATES DEPARTMENT OF JUSTICE
FEDERAL BUREAU OF INVESTIGATION

<u>AIRTEL</u>

TO: DIRECTOR, FBI ███████████

FROM: ADIC, NEW YORK ███████████

SUBJECT: ███████████
███████████

00: NEW YORK

This communication is classified "Secret in its entirety."

Re New York teletype to FBIHQ dated 1/25/88

After a review of 266 New York indices checks conducted on the names of individuals which were connected in any way with this investigation since 10/87 in an attempt to determine whether a Soviet active measures campaign had been initiated to discredit the LIBRARY AWARENESS PROGRAM (LAP), only the following eight references were noted. All other indices checks were either negative or of no significance to this study.

SOURCE: Memo from ADIC, New York, to Director, FBI, February 6, 1989. Released pursuant to a FOIA request by the National Security Archive, George Washington University, October 30, 1989.

## 2. Letter from ACLU to Representative Don Edwards

AMERICAN CIVIL LIBERTIES UNION
WASHINGTON OFFICE

November 20, 1989

The Honorable Don Edwards, Chairman
Subcommittee on Civil and Constitutional Rights
House Judiciary Committee
806 House Annex 1
Washington, DC 20515

Dear Mr. Chairman:

Enclosed is a copy of a letter that I sent to FBI Director William Sessions expressing the American Civil Liberties Union's grave concern about the recently disclosed FBI practice of conducting background checks on persons who write or criticize the Bureau.

Director Sessions acknowledged that it is routine procedure for the FBI to do such checks on anyone who writes a letter to the Director or other high level Bureau officials. FOIA documents show that the FBI did at least 266 such checks on persons who opposed the Bureau's Library Awareness Program.

In our view, such practice is illegal and unconstitutional. The FBI should not be engaging in any kind of investigative activity towards persons who engage solely in First Amendment activities, such as letter writing or criticism of Bureau policy. We believe that the FBI should stop this practice: it should completely segregate the maintenance and referencing of its correspondence files from its investigative files and it should refrain from keeping files or doing checks on Bureau critics.

We hope that you share our concerns and urge you to work to ensure that this practice is stopped.

Sincerely,
Morton H. Halperin

SOURCE: U.S. Congress, House Committee on the Judiciary, *FBI Counterintelligence Visits to Libraries*, 100th Cong., 2d Sess., June 20 and July 13, 1988 (Washington, DC: GPO, 1989), pp. 326–27.

# ANALYSIS

From the moment that the Library Awareness Program was exposed, libraries and academic institutions responded with outrage. On September 18, 1987, the same day that the

*New York Times* revealed the FBI's visit to Columbia University, Joseph S. Murphy, Chancellor of the City University of New York, issued the following press release:

> All those who value academic freedom are dismayed to learn that the F.B.I. has asked certain librarians in New York City to participate in a national counter-intelligence effort known as the Library Awareness Program....I share the outrage of the city's librarians, who regard it as inconceivable that they should be asked to serve as informants for the F.B.I. as part of their professional duties....A professional librarian's responsibility is to provide, without discrimination, the fullest possible access to learning. To deny that access is to deny access to knowledge. Such restrictive measures infringe upon the right to privacy and the right to free access to information of those who use the library; they also hinder the academic freedom and compromise the professionalism of those librarians who may be asked to exercise surveillance over library users.
>
> The City University of New York must and will continue to provide this vital access to knowledge for all those who use its libraries. It is a fundamental principle of the University that it not cooperate with any efforts to restrict the freedom of those who use our libraries. I ask all those who value freedom of learning to join with me in urging the committees on intelligence of the United States Senate and the House of Representatives to conduct a thorough investigation of this apparent violation of academic freedom by the F.B.I. ("Statement by Chancellor Joseph S. Murphy, The City University of New York," September 18, 1987. Reprinted in: U.S. Congress, House Committee on the Judiciary, *FBI Counterintelligence Visits to Libraries*, 100th Cong., 2d Session, June 20 and July 13, 1988 (Washington, DC: GPO, 1989))

The vocal critics of the Library Awareness Program attracted the attention of the press and public, but the FBI took notice as well. The Bureau badly misread the motivation of its critics. Because the Bureau assumed that their critics were being directed or manipulated by foreign agents, an investigation of these troublemakers seemed appropriate. When the FBI memo describing 366 "indices checks" on critics of LAP was acquired through the FOIA, many feared a McCarthy-like witch hunt. The ACLU complained to FBI Director Sessions, and the ALA issued the following resolution:

## RESOLUTION ON FBI LIBRARY AWARENESS PROGRAM

| | |
|---|---|
| Whereas, | The American Library Association has previously condemned the FBI Library Awareness Program and similar programs because of their infringement on the exercise of First Amendment rights; and |
| Whereas, | The American Library Association has expressed its strong support for H.R. 50, "a bill to regulate the conduct of the Federal Bureau of Investigation in certain matters relating to the exercise of rights protected by the first article of amendment of the Federal Constitution;" and |
| Whereas, | Documents recently released by the FBI under the Freedom of Information Act reveal that 266 checks were conducted on names of individuals connected in any way with the Library Awareness Program since October 1987 "to determine whether a Soviet active measures campaign had been initiated to discredit the Library Awareness Program;" and |
| Whereas, | The FBI has continued to visit libraries and seek out librarians, including a documented visit as recently as December 20, 1989, now therefore be it |
| Resolved, | That the American Library Association request that the FBI provide the 266 individuals and subsequent others for whom indices checks were made with copies of their own files at no cost; and be it further |

Resolved,   That the American Library Association request that the FBI, after providing the information to the individuals involved, expunge such records from FBI files; and be it further

Resolved,   That the American Library Association express its outrage at the continuation of the Library Awareness Program and all similar attempts to intimidate the library community and to interfere with the privacy rights of users; and be it further

Resolved,   That copies of this resolution be forwarded to the President of the United States, the Senate Judiciary Subcommittee on Technology and the Law, the House Judiciary Subcommittee on Civil and Constitutional Rights and to the Director of the Federal Bureau of Investigation.

(Adopted by the Council of the American Library Association, January 10, 1990, in Chicago, Illinois)

John Berry, editor-in-chief of the prestigious *Library Journal*, summed up the library profession's response to the index checks on critics of the Library Awareness Program:

It hurt when the FBI director impugned the patriotism of librarians who wouldn't enlist in the Bureau's Library Awareness Program. It angered us to find out that the FBI was investigating the nearly 250 librarians who refused to take part in the program.... The FBI nearly always sees something subversive in any opposition to its effort to protect the "secrets" of our government or to limit access to our libraries.... We the people plant the seeds of subversion. They are there in our Bill of Rights, our elections, our free press, and, of course, in our libraries. (John N. Berry, "Little Shops of Subversion," *Library Journal*, December 1989, p. 6)

# FURTHER READINGS

American Civil Liberties Union. Washington Office, *Privacy* (December 1988), p. 1.

"Documents Disclose F.B.I. Investigations of Some Librarians." *New York Times* (November 17, 1989), p. A1.

"FBI Chief Defends Acts on Librarians." *New York Times* (November 8, 1989), p. A21.

Memo on Library Awareness Program and related matters from C. James Schmidt, Chair, Intellectual Freedom Committee, to ALA Executive Board/Council, January 8, 1989.

"New Theory on FBI Program." *American Libraries* (February 1989), p. 104.

"Reports That FBI Checked on Librarians Prompt Call for Congressional Hearings." *Chronicle of Higher Education* (November 15, 1989), p. A3.

# State Confidentiality Laws as Bulwark against Library Surveillance

- **Documents:** Maryland State Confidentiality Statute, as amended on May 2, 1988; letter from Morton H. Halperin, Director, American Civil Liberties Union, to Representative Don Edwards (D-CA), chairman of the House Subcommittee on Civil and Constitutional Rights
- **Date:** New statute amended May 2, 1988; Morton Halperin's letter to Representative Don Edwards dated June 20, 1988
- **Where:** Washington, DC
- **Significance:** The Maryland statute on library confidentiality was broadened significantly as an immediate reaction to the Library Awareness Program. ACLU Director Morton Halperin's letter to Representative Don Edwards, chairman of the House Subcommittee on Civil and Constitutional Rights, strongly urged congressional hearings on the Library Awareness Program to ensure that the FBI complied with state confidentiality laws.

---

## DOCUMENTS

### 1. Maryland State Confidentiality Statute

STATE OF MARYLAND HOUSE OF DELEGATES
HOUSE BILL No. 1239

Article—Education
223-107
A FREE ASSOCIATION, SCHOOL, COLLEGE OR UNIVERSITY LIBRARY IN THIS STATE SHALL DENY INSPECTION OF A <u>ANY</u> CIRCULATION RECORD <u>OR OTHER ITEM, COLLECTION, OR GROUPING OF INFORMATION ABOUT AN INDIVIDUAL THAT;</u>
<u>(1) IS MAINTAINED BY A LIBRARY;</u>
<u>(2) CONTAINS AN INDIVIDUAL'S NAME OR THE IDENTIFYING NUMBER, SYMBOL, OR OTHER IDENTIFYING PARTICULAR ASSIGNED TO THE INDIVIDUAL, AND</u>

(3) IDENTIFIES THE USE A PATRON MAKES OF THAT LIBRARY'S MATERIALS, SERVICES, OR FACILITIES, ~~THAT IDENTIFIES THE TRANSACTION OF A BORROWER~~.

Article—State Government 10-616

(a) Unless otherwise provided by law, a custodian shall deny inspection of a circulation record, as provided in this section

(b) A custodian shall deny inspection of a circulation record of a public library that identifies the transaction of a borrower.

OR OTHER ITEM, COLLECTION, OR GROUPING OF INFORMATION ABOUT AN INDIVIDUAL THAT

(1) IS MAINTAINED BY A LIBRARY;

(2) CONTAINS AN INDIVIDUAL'S NAME OR THE IDENTIFYING NUMBER, SYMBOL, OR OTHER IDENTIFYING PARTICULAR ASSIGNED TO THE INDIVIDUAL, AND;

(3) IDENTIFIES THE USE A PATRON MAKES OF THAT LIBRARY'S MATERIALS, SERVICES, OR FACILITIES.

SECTION 2. AND BE IT FURTHER ENACTED, That this Act shall take effect July 1, 1988.

EXPLANATION: CAPITALS INDICATE MATTER ADDED TO EXISTING LAW. [Brackets] indicate matter deleted from existing law. Underlining indicates amendments to the bill. ~~Strike out~~ indicates matter stricken from the bill by amendment or deleted from the law by amendment.

SOURCE: As passed on May 2, 1998, this amendment now resides in: Annotated Code of Maryland, State Government Article, Section 10-616, Subsection E, and Education Article, Section 23-107.

---

## 2. Letter from ACLU to Representative Don Edwards

AMERICAN CIVIL LIBERTIES UNION
WASHINGTON OFFICE

June 20, 1988

The Honorable Don Edwards, Chairman
Subcommittee on Civil and Constitutional Rights
House Judiciary Committee
2307 Rayburn House Office Building
Washington, DC 20515

Dear Congressman Edwards:

On behalf of the ACLU, we write to you today to express our concern about the FBI's counterintelligence activities in the library community, known as the "Library Awareness Program."

The ACLU believes that the FBI should be prohibited from engaging in an ill-conceived, broad-based counterintelligence campaign in our nation's libraries....

We are opposed to the FBI asking library personnel to violate state confidentiality laws by divulging patrons' records related to use of unclassified, publicly available materials. Thirty-seven states, including the District of Columbia, require a court order be presented before library records may be released. In addition, library personnel are being asked to act in contravention of their own policies by divulging records and informing the FBI of suspicious, out of the ordinary behavior by library users.

Contrary to the implication of recent testimony by FBI Director William Sessions, the FBI's broad-based library activities are not limited to New York libraries. Investigative activities, virtually identical to the Library Awareness Program, have been reported at more than twenty libraries nationwide. The FBI has asked library personnel in academic and public libraries to divulge records related to library use and to report on "anomalous" library use....

We suggest the Subcommittee request that the FBI produce guidelines and procedures on the Library Awareness Program and related activities. More importantly, we urge the Subcommittee: (1) to require the FBI to abide by state law and to honor the professional and ethical codes of the library community; and (2) to narrowly circumscribe the scope of FBI intelligence gathering activities in institutions, such as libraries, that play a crucial role in preserving the freedom of citizens to receive and exchange ideas....

Sincerely,
Morton H. Halperin
Director

SOURCE: U.S. Congress, House Committee on the Judiciary, *FBI Counterintelligence Visits to Libraries*, 100th Cong., 2d Session, June 20 and July 13, 1988 (Washington, DC: GPO, 1989), pp. 326–27.

---

# ANALYSIS

Despite strong opposition from Congress, the press, and the public during 1988 and 1989, the FBI continued to pursue its Library Awareness Program, causing librarians in many states to pursue a local solution. Many states already had some form of statutory protection for library confidentiality, but the wording was often inadequate to deal with the subtleties of the Library Awareness Program. As a result, librarians in states without confidentiality statutes worked to create them, and in states with weak statutes, librarians attempted to strengthen them. A good example of the latter was Maryland, where I had the privilege of working with Delegate Sandy Rosenberg to craft the amended statute shown above.

During my testimony before the Maryland House of Delegates on behalf of the Rosenberg-Kopp bill, I described the FBI's visits to the University of Maryland and judgment of the university's legal officer that current Maryland law neither required nor prohibited the divulging of personal borrower or user information at the university. I then declared, "However, as a result of these unwarranted FBI intrusions on academic freedom, the University of Maryland Libraries have clarified and formalized a policy protecting confidentiality of library records. Still, I would feel much more secure knowing that the weight of law was behind our internal policy, and that it could not be rescinded or compromised arbitrarily or frivolously" (Herbert N. Foerstel, testimony before the Maryland House of Delegates, April 27, 1988).

The Rosenberg-Kopp bill passed the Maryland House of Delegates by an amazing vote of 133 to 0, and was sent on to the Senate for final passage. The FBI immediately sent out a memo to Assistant Director James Geer under the heading: "This communication is classified 'secret' in its entirety." The memo stated:

PURPOSE:
To advise of legislation passed by the Maryland House of Delegates which would prohibit the FBI from reviewing, without a subpoena, the records of Maryland's academic library patrons. (A copy of an article appearing in the "Sun" dated March 19, 1988, is attached).

<u>RECOMMENDATIONS:</u>

1. That the Maryland State Senate be provided with an unclassified version of the library study, accompanied by a letter clarifying misrepresentations by the press in the attached article. This matter will be coordinated with the Office of Congressional and Public Affairs.
2. That a copy of the study and a corresponding letter be sent to the Governor of Maryland. This matter will be coordinated with the Office of Congressional and Public Affairs.

## IN HISTORY

### Executive Authority versus State Law

Almost twenty years after the Library Awareness Program, President George W. Bush justified two secret, seemingly illegal, domestic surveillance programs, National Security Administration (NSA) phone taps and broad banking surveillance, on the sole basis of executive authority. Could the Reagan and Carter administrations have done the same during the Library Awareness Program?

On November 7, 1988, Senator Daniel Patrick Moynihan (D-NY) wrote to Nancy Kranich at New York University:

The FBI claims that they have the right to investigate library files based on an Executive Order, 12333.1.14, adopted on December 4, 1981. This EO gives the executive branch the authority to override state law when conducting counterintelligence operations within the United States. The remaining question is whether the information found in library records is really essential to those intelligence operations—so essential that the basic right to privacy can be violated. I am doubtful this is the case.

On December 19, 1988, Moynihan wrote to FBI Director Sessions saying, "When first learning of the [Library Awareness] program, I was led to believe that Executive Order 12333 gave the executive branch the authority to override state law when conducting counterintelligence operations within the United States. I now question that understanding....I would hope that the FBI has recognized and operated in accordance with this law."

At this point, newly elected President Jimmy Carter would have had to assert Executive authority in that regard. When he did not, the conflict between state law and Presidential authority disappeared. (U.S. Congress, House Committee on the Judiciary, *FBI Counterintelligence Visits to Libraries*, 100th Cong., Second Session, June 20 and July 13, 1988 [Washington, DC: GPO, 1989], pp. 326–27)

(Memo from D.E. Stukey, FBI New York, to J. H. Geer, FBI Assistant Director, May 6, 1988. FOIA release available at National Security Archive, George Washington University)

Despite the FBI's aggressive lobbying, the Maryland Senate overwhelmingly passed the library confidentiality bill, and it was soon signed into law. At this time, there were already similar laws in thirty-eight states and the District of Columbia. Following is the list of those statutes:

| | |
|---|---|
| Alabama | Missouri |
| Alaska | Montana |
| Arizona | Nebraska |
| California | Nevada |
| Colorado | New Jersey |
| Connecticut | New York |
| Delaware | North Carolina |
| District of Columbia | North Dakota |
| Florida | Oklahoma |
| Georgia | Oregon |
| Illinois | Pennsylvania |
| Indiana | Rhode Island |
| Iowa | South Carolina |
| Kansas | South Dakota |
| Louisiana | Tennessee |
| Maine | Virginia |
| Maryland | Washington |
| Michigan | Wisconsin |
| Massachusetts | Wyoming |
| Minnesota | |

New or revised confidentiality statutes were soon offered in other states, many of them in specific response to the FBI's Library Awareness Program, and civil rights organizations added their voices to the clamor for state protection against federal surveillance. Just a week after the ACLU's Morton Halperin wrote the letter shown at the beginning of this section, John H. Buchanan, Jr. and Arthur J. Kropp of People for the American Way (PAW) wrote a similar letter to Representative Don Edwards, chairman of the House Subcommittee on Civil and Constitutional Rights, Their letter began:

I am writing to you on behalf of the 270,000 members of the People for the American Way

Action Fund, a nonpartisan constitutional rights organization.... We believe that the FBI's counterintelligence activities in our nation's libraries raise serious constitutional and policy questions. The FBI has the dual responsibility to conduct itself within the framework of the Constitution and law, and to be accountable to Congress and the American people. We believe that the FBI has failed in this regard....

Thirty-eight states in the nation have laws protecting the confidentiality of library circulation records. Yet, the evidence suggests that the FBI is circumventing those laws by requesting information regarding the reading habits of individuals. Not only is the FBI's policy of training librarians to become spycatchers an invasion of citizen's privacy rights, but the program also forces librarians to violate their own professional and ethical standards. Moreover, the FBI's "counterintelligence" effort restricts citizens' access to unclassified information that should be available to all Americans....

The letter concluded: "From all available evidence, the FBI's "Library Awareness Program and its related activities are infringing on the rights of Americans. The FBI cannot justify programs which undercut fundamental democratic values in the name of promoting and protecting democracy" (U.S. Congress, House Committee on the Judiciary, *FBI Counterintelligence Visits to Libraries*, 100th Congress, 2d Session, July 13, 1988 (Washington, DC: GPO, 1989), pp. 328–29).

By this time, the FBI's Library Awareness Program was on the defensive and essentially moribund. Faced with congressional opposition, public disapproval, ridicule in the press, and state laws rendering it impotent, the surveillance program quietly withdrew. Nonetheless, the FBI continued to maintain the right to conduct such surveillance if circumstances required it.

Today, forty-eight states plus the District of Columbia have confidentiality statutes covering libraries. Hawaii and Kentucky are the only states without statutes specifically protecting library records, but even they have Attorney General opinions providing the same protection. As we will see in the following chapters, *all* of these state statutes and guidelines have been rendered irrelevant by the USA PATRIOT Act.

# FURTHER READINGS

Anderson, Jack. "FBI Still Checking Out Libraries," *Washington Post* (December 15, 1988), p. Md17.

Birch, Doug. "Md. Bill to Curb Library Probes Pushed," *Baltimore Sun* (March 19, 1988), p. 1A.

Conyers, John. "When the FBI Is Looking through the Keyhole," *Christian Science Monitor* (March 31, 1988), p. 13.

Edwards, Don. "Government Information Controls Threaten Academic Freedom," *Thought and Action: The NEA Higher Education Journal* (Spring 1989), p. 87.

Kennedy, Bruce M. "Confidentiality of Library Records: A Survey of Problems, Policies, and Laws," *Law Library Journal* (Fall 1989), p. 733.

Lee, Janis. "Confidentiality: From the Stacks to the Witness Stand," *American Libraries* (June 1988), p. 444.

"New Law Protects Confidentiality of Users' Records/NYLA Adopts Supporting Policy." *Metro* (July/August 1988), p. 6.

Rosenberg, Samuel I. "Library Snoops," Letter to *Baltimore Evening Sun* (August 24, 1988), p. A15.

# CHAPTER 2

# The Legislative Response to 9/11: Conceived under Seige, Passed in Haste

Figure 3. The Pentagon in the aftermath of the 9/11 attack. Air Force Link: Official Website of the United States Air Force.

# After 9/11, President Bush Addresses the Nation and Congress Pledges Solidarity

- *Documents:* Shortly after the 9/11 attacks, President George Bush's address to the nation; Senate Majority leader Tom Daschle saying that Congress and the White House "will speak with one voice"
- *Date:* September 11, 2001
- *Where:* Washington, DC
- *Significance:* President Bush reassures the nation and the world that "the functions of our government" will continue without interruption and asks all Americans to unite in the war on terrorism. Majority Leader Daschle says Congress will stand united behind the president.

---

## DOCUMENTS

### 1. President Bush's Address to the Nation after Terrorist Attacks on Washington and New York

Today, our fellow citizens, our way of life, our very freedom came under attack in a series of deliberate and deadly terrorist attacks.

The victims were in airplanes or in their offices – secretaries, businessmen and women, military and federal workers. Moms and dads. Friends and neighbors.

Thousands of lives were suddenly ended by evil, despicable acts of terror. The pictures of airplanes flying into buildings, fires burning, huge structures collapsing, have filled us with disbelief, terrible sadness, and a quiet, unyielding anger. These acts of mass murder were intended to frighten our nation into chaos and retreat. But they have failed. Our country is strong. A great people has been moved to defend a great nation.

Terrorist attacks can shake the foundations of our biggest buildings, but they cannot touch the foundations of America. These acts shatter steel, but they cannot dent the steel of American resolve.

America was targeted for attack because we're the brightest beacon for freedom and opportunity in the world. And no one will keep that light from shining.

Today, our nation saw evil, the very worst of human nature, and we responded with the best of America, with the daring of our rescue workers, with caring for strangers and neighbors who came to give blood and help in any way they could.

Immediately following the first attack, I implemented our government's emergency response plans. Our military is powerful, and it's prepared. Our emergency teams are working in New York City and Washington, DC, to help with local rescue efforts.

Our first priority is to get help to those who have been injured and to take every precaution to protect our citizens at home and around the world from further attacks.

The functions of our government continue without interruption. Federal agencies in Washington which had to be evacuated today are reopening for essential personnel tonight and will be open for business tomorrow.

Our financial institutions remain strong, and the American economy will be open for business as well.

The search is underway for those who are behind these evil acts. I've directed the full resources for our intelligence and law enforcement communities to find those responsible and bring them to justice. We will make no distinction between the terrorists who committed these acts and those who harbor them.

I appreciate so very much the members of Congress who have joined me in strongly condemning these attacks. And on behalf of the American people, I thank the many world leaders who have called to offer their condolences and assistance. America and our friends and allies join with all those who want peace and security in the world and we stand together to win the war against terrorism....

This is a day when all Americans from every walk of life unite in our resolve for justice and peace. America has stood down enemies before, and we will do so this time.

None of us will ever forget this day, yet we go forward to defend freedom and all that is good and just in our world.

Thank you. Good night and God bless America.

SOURCE: White House, September 11, 2001. www.whitehouse.gov/news/releases/2001/09/20010911-16

---

## 2. Majority Leader Tom Daschle's Statement on September 11, 2001

Today's despicable acts were an assault on our people and on our freedom. As the representatives of the people, we are here to declare that our resolve has not been weakened by these horrific and cowardly acts.

Congress will convene tomorrow. And we will speak with one voice to condemn these attacks, to comfort the victims and their families, to commit our full support to the effort to bring those responsible to justice.

We, Republicans and Democrats, House and Senate, stand strongly united behind the president, and we'll work together to ensure that the full resources of the government are brought to bear in these efforts.

Our heartfelt thought and our fervent prayers are with the injured and the families of those who have been lost.

SOURCE: "September 11, 2001: Special Coverage of the Attacks in NY, DC," PBS, Online NewsHour, September 11, 2001. www.pbs.org/newshour/bb/military/terroristattack/sept11/

# ANALYSIS

On the morning of September 11, 2001, President George W. Bush was in Sarasota, Florida for a publicly announced visit to the Emma E. Broker Elementary School. He awoke at about 6 a.m. and by 6:30 began a 4-mile jog with a reporter friend and the Secret Service crew. After his jog he showered and sat down for an 8 a.m. intelligence briefing. During that briefing, the first commercial aircraft that would be hijacked by terrorists, American Airlines Flight 11, took off from the Boston airport at 7:59 a.m. It was followed by the other targeted flights: United Airlines Flight 175, American Airlines Flight 77, and United Airlines Flight 93.

At about 8:13 a.m., Flight 11 failed to obey an order from traffic controllers and shut off its transponder. At that point, the traffic control manager considered Flight 11 to be a possible hijacking. The hijackers had stabbed and killed at least one passenger and two flight attendants, and at about 8:46 the plane crashed into New York's World Trade Center North Tower. The first media reports of the crash began around 8:48 a.m.

Meanwhile, President Bush arrived at the Emma E. Booker Elementary School shortly before 9 a.m., apparently unaware of the hijacking. He may have been informed of the first plane crash, but still thought it was an accident. The second airliner, Flight 175, had turned off its transponder at about 8:42 a.m., and NORAD was notified that the plane had been hijacked. At about 8:46 a.m., Flight 77 went severely off course, heading toward Washington. Its last radio contact occurred at 8:50 a.m. Flight 93 wasn't hijacked until about 9:16 a.m.

Flight 175 crashed into the South Tower of the World Trade Center at 9:03 a.m. President Bush was in the elementary school classroom when Andrew Card, his Chief of Staff, told him about the second plane crash. The children were just about to read from a story called *The Pet Goat*. Bush picked up the book and began to read with the children, continuing the process for about ten minutes. The president left the elementary school at about 9:12 a.m. At 9:16 a.m., NORAD was notified that Flight 93 had been hijacked and was heading toward Washington. The president, now on his way to the Sarasota airport where Air Force One awaited, was notified. Bush was hustled aboard Air Force One, which departed for Washington at about 9:55 a.m. Once airborne, Bush talked to Vice President Cheney, who recommended that the president order U.S. fighter planes to shoot down the hijacked airliners.

Fearing an attack on Air Force One, the plane turned away from Washington and headed for Barksdale Air Force Base near Shreveport, Louisiana, landing there at about 11:45 a.m. Air Force One departed once more at 1:30 p.m., heading toward Offutt Air Force Base in Nebraska, where it landed shortly before 3 p.m. Bush passed through security to the U.S. Strategic Command Underground Command Center and was taken into an underground bunker designed to withstand a nuclear blast. There he held a conference call with Vice President Cheney, National Security Adviser Rice, Defense Secretary Rumsfeld, Deputy Secretary of State Richard Armitage, CIA Director Tenet, Transportation Secretary Norman Mineta, and others. During the meeting, Tenet told Bush, "Sir, I believe it's al-Qaeda. We're doing the assessment, but it looks like, it feels like, it smells like al-Qaeda" (CBS News, September 11, 2002, reprinted in "An Interesting Day: President Bush's Movements and Actions on 9/11," *Cooperative Research*, May 9, 2003).

## IN HISTORY

### Why Did President Bush Remain in the Classroom after the Terrorist Attacks Were Underway?

Much has been made of the president's extended stay at the Sarasota elementary school well after the first airliner crashed into the World Trade Center. By the time President Bush arrived at the school, a number of people there had already heard news reports of the attacks. The Bush entourage carried all manner of phones, electronic equipment, and e-mail devices. As Bush approached the school he was told to take an important call from National Security Adviser Rice, who updated the president on the situation. Still, Bush proceeded to the children's classroom where he participated in reading aloud from "The Pet Goat" for about ten minutes. Why did he linger there when he knew the nation was under attack? Andrew Card would later explain, "Without all the facts at hand, George Bush had no intention of upsetting the school children" (MSNBC, October 29, 2002, as reprinted in "An Interesting Day: President Bush's Movements and Actions on 9/11," *Cooperative Research*, May 9, 2003. www.cooperative research.net).

Bush decided to return to Washington the next day to address the nation, but before going to sleep at about 11:30 p.m. he wrote in his diary: "The Pearl Harbor of the 21st century took place today....We think it's Osama bin Laden" ("10 Days in September: Inside the War Cabinet," *Washington Post*, January 27, 2002, p. A13).

# FURTHER READINGS

Ahmed, Nafeez Mosaddeq. *The War on Freedom: How and Why America Was Attacked September 11, 2001.* Joshua Tree, CA: Tree of Life Publications, 2002.

Bergen, Peter L. *Holy War, Inc.: Inside the Secret World of Osama bin Laden.* New York: Simon & Schuster, 2002.

Brill, Stephen. *After: How American Confronted the September 12 Era.* New York: Simon & Schuster, 2003.

Fouda, Yosri, and Fielding, Nick. *Masterminds of Terror: The Truth behind the Most Devastating Terrorist Attack the World Has Seen.* New York: Arcade Publishing, 2003.

Griffin, David Ray. *The New Pearl Harbor: Disturbing Questions about the Bush Administration and 9/11.* Northampton, MA: Olive Branch Press, 2004.

Sammon, Bill. *Fighting Back: The War on Terrorism—From Inside the Bush White House.* Washington, DC: Regnery Publishing, 2003.

Thompson, Paul. *The Terror Timeline: A Comprehensive Chronicle of the Road to 9/11—and America's Response.* New York: Harper Collins, 2004.

Williams, Mary E., ed. *The Terrorist Attack on America.* San Diego, CA: Greenhaven Press, 2003.

# Removing Restraints from FISA and Other Surveillance Statutes

- **Documents:** President Jimmy Carter's Signing Statement on Foreign Intelligence Surveillance Act of 1978 (FISA); Senator John Edwards (D-SC) describing changes to FISA proposed in USA PATRIOT Act
- **Date:** President Carter's statement issued on October 25, 1978; Senator Edwards's statement made on October 11, 2001
- **Where:** Washington, DC
- **Significance:** In an attempt to prevent domestic abuse of foreign intelligence surveillance, Congress passed the Foreign Intelligence Surveillance Act of 1978 (FISA), defining broad surveillance authority, but specifying clear limits on such powers. The authors of the USA PATRIOT Act regarded such restraints as an unnecessary impediment to the effective conduct of the war on terrorism and made amendment to FISA the focus of the new legislation. Senator John Edwards, a civil liberties advocate, accepted the need for some change in FISA, but warned that the Bush Administration's proposals would pose constitutional problems.

---

## DOCUMENTS

### 1. President Carter's Signing Statement on Foreign Intelligence Surveillance Act of 1978

I am pleased to sign into law today the Foreign Intelligence Surveillance Act of 1978. As I said a year and a half ago at the beginning of the process that produced this bill, "one of the most difficult tasks in a free society like our own is the correlation between adequate intelligence to guarantee our Nation's security on the one hand, and the preservation of basic human rights on the other."

This is a difficult balance to strike, but the act I am signing today strikes it. It sacrifices neither our security nor our civil liberties. And it assures that those who serve this country in intelligence positions will have the affirmation of Congress that their activities are lawful.

In working on this bill, the Congress dealt skillfully with sensitive issues. The result shows our country benefits when the legislative and executive branches of Government work together toward a common goal.

The bill requires, for the first time, a prior judicial warrant for all electronic surveillance for foreign intelligence or counterintelligence purposes in the United States in which communications of U.S. persons might be intercepted. It clarifies the Executive's authority to gather foreign intelligence by electronic surveillance in the United States. It will remove any doubt about the legality of those surveillances which are conducted to protect our country against espionage and international terrorism. It will assure FBI field agents and others involved in intelligence collection that their acts are authorized by statute and, if a U.S. person's communications are concerned, by a court order. And it will protect the privacy of the American people.

In short, the act helps to solidify the relationship of trust between the American people and their Government. It provides a basis for the trust of the American people in the fact that the activities of their intelligence agencies are both effective and lawful. It provides enough secrecy to ensure that intelligence relating to national security can be securely acquired, while permitting review by the courts and Congress to safeguard the rights of Americans and others.

This legislation is the first long step toward the goal of establishing statutory charters for our intelligence agencies. I am committed to that goal, and my administration will work with the Congress to achieve it. Many people played important roles in securing passage of this bill.

I am convinced that the bill would not have passed without the leadership of Attorney General Bell; the personal commitment of the Director of Central Intelligence, Admiral Turner; and the work of Admiral Inman of the National Security Agency and Directors Webster and Kelley of the FBI. I extend my personal appreciation to these men and their staffs.

My administration's bill was based on some fine work during the Ford administration under the leadership of Attorney General Levi. His contribution to this legislation was substantial, illustrating the bipartisan nature of this process.

There was strong, effective, and bipartisan leadership in the Congress as well. I particularly want to commend Senators Kennedy, Bayh, and Garn for helping to guide this bill to overwhelming approval in the Senate. Chairman Boland and Congressman Morgan Murphy of the House Intelligence Committee and Chairman Rodino and Congressman Kastenmeier of the House Judiciary Committee undertook the hard work of moving the bill through the House. And, once again, I am indebted to the efforts of Speaker O'Neill and Majority Leader Wright.

I wish as well to express my appreciation to the Vice President, who long supported this foreign intelligence reform in the Senate and who assured the wholehearted commitment of the executive branch to this important legislation.

I have said so often, one of the central goals of my administration is to restore the confidence of the American people in their governmental institutions. This act takes us one more step down that road.

SOURCE: www.presidency.ucsb.edu/ws/index.php?pid=30048

---

## 2. Senator John Edwards Comments on Proposed Changes to FISA

When I met with FBI agents in North Carolina shortly after September 11, they told me their number one priority was to streamline the FISA process....Under current law, a FISA wiretap order may only enter if the primary purpose of the surveillance is foreign intelligence gathering. The administration initially proposed changing the "primary purpose" requirement to a requirement of "a purpose," any foreign intelligence purpose. At a recent Intelligence Committee hearing, I was one of several senators to raise constitutional questions about the Administration's initial proposal. The last thing we want is to see FISA investigations lost, and convictions overturned, because the surveillance is not constitutional.... As the

Department of Justice has stated in its letter regarding the proposed FISA change, the FISA court has "an obligation," whatever the statutory standard, "to reject FISA applications that do not truly qualify" as constitutional. I anticipate continued close congressional oversight and inquiry in this area.

SOURCE: *Congressional Record—Senate*, October 11, 2001, p. S10589.

---

# ANALYSIS

In the days following 9/11, the pressure on Congress to do something dramatic to protect the country from terrorist attacks was overpowering. The Bush Administration wanted to rewrite the entire body of law defining and limiting government surveillance, and congressional leaders, both Democratic and Republican, knew that any opposition would be seen as weakness by the American electorate. The USA PATRIOT Act, drafted by the Justice Department, seemed to be the right tool for the times. Tailored to protect against the unprecedented threats and tactics of the terrorists, it would expand the powers of law enforcement and intelligence agencies in ways appropriate to the post-9/11 world.

In reality, the Patriot Act was not a bold new anti-terrorism bill. It was a resurrected wish-list of executive powers that had accumulated in the Justice Department over many years, powers that, when conceived, had little or no relevance to terrorism and which Congress rejected as unnecessary infringements on civil liberties. Senator Orrin Hatch (R-Utah), an aggressive champion of the Patriot Act, told his Senate colleagues, "[A] lot of the provisions we have in this bill are not brand new; a lot of them have been requested for years....The fact is, that the bulk of these proposals have been requested by the Department of Justice for years, and have languished for years because we have been unable to muster the collective political will to enact them into law" (*Congressional Record—Senate*, October 11, 2001, p. S10560).

Now, with the war on terrorism as its inspiration, Congress had the political will to approve the Justice Department's entire wish-list. But creating new powers was not as simple a matter as it seemed. First, one had to remove existing legal restraints on executive power. At issue were laws like the Foreign Intelligence Surveillance Act (FISA) of 1978 that regulated domestic surveillance; Title III of the Omnibus Crime Control and Safe Streets Act of 1968 that governed electronic eavesdropping; and a broad set of laws on "pen register, trap and trace" rules, including the Electronic Communications Privacy Act (ECPA).

FISA gave the government broad counterintelligence authority to monitor agents of foreign countries, but its primary purpose was to protect individuals and groups from past abuses by agencies like the CIA and FBI. FISA required the government to demonstrate to a supersecret FISA court that the "principal purpose" for their surveillance was foreign intelligence, thus restricting the use of the new surveillance powers in domestic criminal investigations. In the wake of 9/11, the Justice Department argued that restricting FISA's powers to investigations whose "principle purpose" was foreign intelligence placed unnecessary barriers between criminal and intelligence investigators. They sought to replace the restrictive phrase "principle purpose" with the more permissive "a purpose."

The Justice Department had similar concerns about the Omnibus Crime Control and Safe Streets Act of 1968. Like FISA, this statute granted broad surveillance powers to the government, but with restraints on their use. In particular, Title III required a judge to certify that there was "probable cause" that the individual being investigated was committing a specified crime and that the facilities under surveillance were being used in connection with the offense.

The morning after the 9/11 attacks, Assistant Attorney General Viet Dinh convened a meeting of Justice Department policy advisers and lawyers where they addressed the legacy of statutory restraints on government surveillance authorities. Attorney General Ashcroft, along with other senior government officials, was in seclusion for security reasons, so Dinh's group addressed the ambiguities of current law with respect to tracking e-mail communications. Could they be tracked in the same way that phone calls were? Did warrants for telephone records cover voice mail? How much information could intelligence agents and criminal investigators share?

As Dinh and his allies constructed their legislative strategy, civil libertarians sensed a disaster in the making. Morton Halperin, a senior fellow at the council for Foreign Relations and former head of the American Civil Liberties Washington Office, organized his own strategy team, including Marc Rotenberg from the Electronic Privacy Information Center, and Jim Dempsey from the Office for Democracy and Technology. Together, they prepared a manifesto called "In Defense of Freedom at a Time of Crisis." The document was soon signed by representatives of more than 150 groups, including religious organizations, gun owners, police, and conservative activists. They held a press conference that was sparsely attended. In the post-9/11 hysteria, the manifesto was ignored. White House and Justice Department officials would later say they had never heard of the document.

Soon, Attorney General Ashcroft was back on the public stage. He held a press conference calling on Congress to approve the Justice Department package within one week. Senator Patrick Leahy, who chaired the Senate Judiciary Committee, remarked that the implication was that "we were going to have another attack if we did not agree to this immediately" (Robert O'Harrow Jr., "Six Weeks in Autumn," *Washington Post Magazine*, October 27, 2002, p. 17). It was in this highly charged political atmosphere that Congress began its deliberations on the USA PATRIOT Act.

## FURTHER READINGS

Birkenstock, Gregory E. "The Foreign Intelligence Surveillance Act and Standards of Probable Cause: and Alternative Analysis." *Georgetown Law Journal* 80 (February 1992), 843–71.

Brown, Cynthia, ed. *Lost Liberties: Ashcroft and the Assault of Personal Freedom.* New York: New Press, 2003.

Cinquegrana, Americo R. "The Walls (and Wires) Have Ears: The Background and First Ten Years of the Foreign Intelligence Surveillance Act of 1978." *University of Pennsylvania Law Review* 137 (January 1989), 793–828.

Leone, Richard C. *The War on Our Freedoms: Civil Liberties in an Age of Terrorism.* New York: Perseus Publishing, 2003.

Schulhofer, Stephen J. *The Enemy Within: Intelligence Gathering, Law Enforcement and Civil Liberties in the Wake of September 11.* New York: Twentieth Century Foundation, 2002.

## IN HISTORY

### Were Wiretapping Laws prior to the Patriot Act Too Restrictive of Government Eavesdropping?

Among the existing statutes targeted by the Bush administration after 9/11 as being too restrictive of government surveillance were Title III of the Omnibus Crime Control and Safe Streets Act of 1968, which dealt with wiretapping and eavesdropping. The Bush Justice Department felt that Title III's requirement that a court certify "probable cause" before approving surveillance would unduly restrict the ability to intercept terrorists. Did President Lyndon Johnson share this concern at the time he signed Title III into law? On the contrary, in his signing statement he declared,

My views on this subject are clear. In a special message to Congress in 1967 and again this year, I called … for an end to the bugging and snooping that invade the privacy of citizens. I urge that the Congress outlaw all wiretapping and electronic eavesdropping, public and private, wherever and whenever it occurs. The only exceptions would be those instances where the security of the Nation itself was at stake—and then only under the strictest safeguards. …

But the Congress, in my judgment, has taken an unwise and potentially dangerous step by sanctioning eavesdropping and wiretapping by Federal, State, and local law officials in an almost unlimited variety of situations. If we are not very careful and cautious in our planning, these legislative provisions could result in producing a nation of snoopers bending through the keyholes of the homes and offices in America, spying on our neighbors. No conversation in the sanctity of the bedroom or relayed over a copper telephone wire would be free of eavesdropping by those who say they want to ferret out crime. Thus, I believe this action goes far beyond the effective and legitimate needs of law enforcement. … I call upon the Congress immediately to reconsider the unwise provisions of Title III and take steps to repeal them. … We need not surrender our privacy to win the war on crime. (The American Presidency Project, http://www.presidency.ucsb.edu/ws/?pid=28939)

# Congressional Bill Hijacked by the Justice Department

- **Document:** Transcript of interview with Representative John Conyers (D-MI), co-sponsor of the original Patriot Act
- **Date:** August 21, 2002
- **Where:** Baltimore, MD
- **Significance:** Representative Conyers candidly describes how the original Patriot Act bill, passed unanimously out of the House Judiciary Committee, was rewritten that night by the Justice Department.

---

## DOCUMENT

### Interview with Representative John Conyers

What you need to know is the Patriot Act that I sponsored is not the Patriot Act that was passed. After chairman of the Judiciary Committee and I had worked to get a unanimous Committee vote in favor of the original version of the Act, it went before the leadership on the way to the Rules Committee. At that point, the bill was scrapped and replaced by a bill written by the staff of the Attorney General's office. So it was a bill that was foreign to all of us on the Committee. It was quite different, and it was a bill that I voted against.

First of all, I voted against the procedure. For Attorney General Ashcroft, a former United States Senator, to throw out the unanimous work product of a congressional committee and substitute his own bill, that alone would have prevented me from voting for it. We had very carefully crafted a bill that did not ignore constitutional questions in the way the present Patriot Act did. How, in a time or urgency and crisis, could the Attorney General decide to become a legislative member and replace all 43 members of the House Judiciary Committee? It was so arrogant, so uncalled for. We were not consulted. We came the next morning to go to the Rules Committee, and there was a different document in front of us. Nobody had read it, nobody knew about it, but we had to vote out the administration's bill. It was a usurpation of the congressional prerogative.

*SOURCE: Marc Steiner Show, WYPR, Baltimore, Maryland, August 21, 2002.*

---

# ANALYSIS

The process by which the final bill called the USA PATRIOT Act was created was highly unusual. Normally, bills are drafted and approved in the appropriate Senate and House committees, usually the Judiciary Committees, and then reported out for debate, amendments, and a full vote. But the Patriot Act was created at breakneck speed. It relied heavily on "unofficial" drafts supplied by the White House or Justice Department, leading the Senate and House into separate and parallel negotiations with administration officials.

On September 19th, representatives of the White House, Department of Justice, and both houses of Congress met in the Capitol to exchange legislative proposals. Representing the White House were Attorney General John Ashcroft, Assistant Attorney General Viet Dinh, White House counsel Alberto Gonzales, and the Justice Department entourage. Among the senators present were Orrin Hatch (R-UT), Richard Shelby (R-AL), and Patrick Leahy (D-VT). House Majority Leader Richard Armey (R-TX) and John Conyers (D-MI) were among the representatives from the House.

Viet Dinh opened the meeting by handing out copies of the Justice Department's draft of a Patriot Act bill that represented the administration's desire for increased anti-terrorism authority. The draft was severe, calling for such things as indefinite detention of any noncitizen who may "further or facilitate acts of terrorism." It also authorized unchecked sharing of grand jury and eavesdropping data throughout the government, permitted Internet service providers to allow the FBI to tap e-mail, and lowered the FISA standard for surveillance authority.

Discussions on a compromise draft quickly emerged and continued for several days. On September 30, Leahy reached a deal with White House Deputy Counsel Timothy Flanigan, who was representing Attorney General Ashcroft. The deal included an agreement that the government could not use illegally obtained evidence against U.S. citizens and that a court must review information before it was shared among intelligence and law enforcement agencies. But when Ashcroft himself came to Leahy's office to sign off on the agreement, he told Leahy that the deal was off. Leahy felt betrayed. He later recalled his disappointment over Ashcroft's behavior. "I said, 'John, when I make an agreement, I make an agreement. I can't believe you're going back on your commitment'" (Robert O'Harrow Jr., "Six Weeks in Autumn," *The Washington Post Magazine*, October 27, 2002, p. 20).

Ashcroft was adamant. He knew that no bill could pass the full Senate without his consent, and Leahy was forced to accept a bill he didn't like.

The bill that reached the Senate was virtually the same as the draft that Viet Dinh had passed out at the September 19th meeting in the Capitol. It had been sent directly to the Senate floor without a committee vote. On the Senate floor, Leahy told his colleagues, "I wish the administration had kept to the agreement they made September 30. We would have a more balanced bill. I still am not sure why the administration backed away from their agreement. I am the old style Vermonter: When you make an agreement, you stick with it" (*Congressional Record—Senate*, October 11, 2001, p. S10604).

Meanwhile, the House Judiciary Committee seemed to be developing a more balanced Patriot Act bill, providing new national security authorities without sacrificing fundamental civil liberties. Late on October 3, the Judiciary Committee passed its bill, H.R. 2975, *unanimously*. On October 11, the Senate passed a much tougher version of the bill, written by the Justice Department. That night, without warning, the House substituted the Senate language for the original House language. (See interview with Rep. John Conyers in document above.) The House Judiciary Committee was unaware that its unanimously approved bill had been replaced, and when that bill reached the House floor, few members had even read it, and there was no opportunity for amendments. The bill was passed late in the afternoon of Friday, October 12 by a vote of 337 to 79.

# FURTHER READINGS

Foerstel, Herbert. *Refuge of a Scoundrel: The Patriot Act in Libraries*. Westport: Libraries Unlimited, 2004.

Hentoff, Nat. "The 'PATRIOT' Game," *Editor and Publisher* (August 25, 2003), p. 26.

Michell, Malkin. "Be Grateful for the PATRIOT Act," *Human Events* (July 14, 2003), p. 10.

Sarasohn, David. "Patriots vs. the PATRIOT Act," *Nation* (September 22, 2003), p. 23.

Torr, James T., ed. *Civil Liberties*. San Diego, CA: Greenhaven Press, 2003.

# Limited Debate Threatens Constitutionality of Patriot Act

- *Documents:* Letter from Senator Arlen Specter (R-PA) to Senator Patrick Leahy (D-VT) warning that the lack of meaningful deliberation on the USA PATRIOT Act may jeopardize its ultimate constitutionality; a transcript of an interview with Senator Russ Feingold (D-WI), the only senator to vote against the Patriot Act
- *Date:* Senator Specter's letter dated October 3, 2001; Senator Feingold's interview in May 2002 describing the Senate debate on October 11, 2001
- *Where:* Washington, DC
- *Significance:* Senator Specter, a Republican leader, constitutional expert, and supporter of the PATRIOT Act, warns that undue restrictions on debate could ultimately jeopardize the constitutionality of the bill. Senator Feingold expresses surprise and disappointment at the complicity of his own party leadership in preventing amendments to the PATRIOT Act.

---

## DOCUMENTS

### 1. Letter from Senator Specter to Senator Leahy

U.S. SENATE

Washington, D.C.
October 3, 2001

Hon. Patrick J. Leahy
Chairman, Senate Judiciary Committee
Washington, D.C.

DEAR SENATOR LEAHY:

I am very much concerned about the delay in acting on the anti-terrorism legislation and also about the absence of hearings to establish a record for the legislative package.

In recent decisions, the Supreme Court of the United States has declared acts of Congress unconstitutional when there has been an insufficient record or deliberative process to justify the legislation.

On the anti-terrorism legislation, perhaps more than any other, the Court engages in balancing the needs of law enforcement with the civil rights issues so that it is necessary to have the specification of the problems to warrant broadening police power.

In my judgment, there is no substitute for the hearings, perhaps in closed session, to deal with these issues.

As you know, I have been pressing for hearings. I am now informed that Senator Hatch has convened a meeting of all Republican senators to, in effect, tell us what is in a proposed bill where Judiciary Committee members have had no input.

We could still have meaningful hearings this week and get this bill ready for prompt floor action.

Sincerely,
Arlen Specter

SOURCE: *Congressional Record—Senate*, October 11, 2001, p. S10568.

---

## 2. Interview with Senator Russ Feingold

When the original Ashcroft anti-terrorism bill came in, they wanted us to pass it two days later. I thought this thing was going to be greatly improved.... But then something happened in the Senate, and I think the Democratic leadership was complicit in this. Suddenly the bottom fell out. I was told that a unanimous consent agreement was being offered with no amendments and no debate. They asked me to give unanimous consent. I refused. The majority leader [Sen. Tom Daschle (D-Mich.)] came to the floor and spoke very sternly to me, in front of his staff and my staff, saying, you can't do this, the whole thing will fall apart. I said, what do you mean it'll fall apart, they want to pass this too. I said, I refuse to consent. He was on the belligerent side for Tom Daschle....

What happened in the Senate was that even though the Attorney General was going to allow these changes to make it moderately better, the Administration insisted, and Daschle went along with pushing this through. I finally got to offer the amendments late at night, and I got up there and I made my arguments. And a lot of senators came around to me, who, of course, voted for the bill, and said, you know, I think you're right. Then Daschle comes out and says, I want you to vote against this amendment and all other Feingold amendments; don't even consider the merits. This was one of the most fundamental pieces of legislation relating to the Bill of Rights in the history of our country! It was a low point for me in terms of being a Democrat and somebody who believes in civil liberties.

SOURCE: Matthew Rothschild, "Russ Feingold," *The Progressive*, May 2002, p. 32. Reprinted by permission from *The Progressive*, 409 E. Main St., Madison, WI, 53703. www.progressive.org

---

# ANALYSIS

Senator Specter's October 3, 2001 letter to Judiciary Committee chairman Leahy revealed his early concern about the haste and superficiality of congressional debate on the Patriot Act. In response to Specter's letter, Leahy wrote:

On October 3, 2001, you wrote that you were concerned about the lack of hearings. I share that concern.... As you know, the Attorney General consented to appear at our September 25, 2001 hearing for only about an hour and we had to prevail upon him to stay a few extra minutes so that Senator Feinstein and you could have a brief opportunity to ask the Attorney General a single question. I invited him to rejoin us the following Tuesday to complete the hearing…, but he has not accepted any of my follow up invitations. In addition, although Members of the Committee submitted questions to the Attorney General…, they have yet to be answered. I agree with you that these are important matters that justify a more thorough record than we have been able to establish.

During the brief Senate debate that followed on October 11, Senator Specter introduced his correspondence with Leahy into the record and took the time to describe a few of the cases where the Supreme Court of the United States had invalidated acts of Congress. He warned his colleagues, "The act of Congress in expanding law enforcement has to be very carefully calibrated to permit civil liberties and be in accordance with the Constitution," and then recounted his meeting with Attorney General Ashcroft just 8 days after the terrorist attacks, at which Ashcroft demanded that legislation be enacted in just two or three days. "My response at that time was I thought it could not be done in that time frame, but I thought we could hold hearings in the remainder of that week," testified Specter. "The Judiciary Committee then held a hearing on September 25 where the Attorney General testified for about an hour and 20 minutes. At that time,… only a few senators were able to ask questions. In fact,… most of the Judiciary Committee did not have a chance to raise questions…. On this state of the record, which I hope can yet be perfected, I am concerned about our meeting the standards of the Supreme Court of the United States for a sufficient deliberative process."

Specter concluded, "I am concerned about the procedures on establishing a record which will withstand constitutional scrutiny. I shall not repeat the citations from decisions of the Supreme Court of the United States which I cited earlier, except to say that the Supreme Court has invalidated acts of Congress where there is not a considered judgment" (*Congressional Record—Senate*, October 11, 2001, pp. S10568–69, S10578).

Surprisingly, Specter, a Republican ally of the White House, found little support from the Democrats, who still held a majority in the Senate. In particular, majority leader Tom Daschle (D-MI) pushed for a "unanimous consent agreement" which would require acceptance of the bill without amendments.

Senator Russ Feingold (D-WI) was the only member of the Senate who refused to comply with the "unanimous consent agreement," and he sought to introduce three amendments to improve protection for civil liberties. A significant number of Feingold's colleagues agreed that the bill lacked adequate civil liberties protections, but they feared that an even worse bill would emerge if amendments were allowed. Many other senators feared that allowing amendments would prevent any bill from being passed, something no one wanted. During the October 11th floor debate, Feingold expressed his concerns:

There is no doubt that if we lived in a police state, it would be easier to catch terrorists. If we lived in a country where police were allowed to search your home at any time for any reason; if we lived in a country where the government was allowed to open your mail, eavesdrop on your telephone conversations, or intercept your e-mail communications; if we lived in a country where people could be held in jail indefinitely based on what they write or think, or based on mere suspicion that they were up to no good, the government would probably discover and arrest more terrorists, or would-be terrorists, just as it would find more law-breakers generally. But that would not be a country in which we would want to live, and it would not be a country for which we could, in good conscience, ask our young people to fight and die. In short, that country would not be America….That is why this exercise of considering the administration's proposed legislation and fine-tuning it to minimize the infringement of civil liberties is so necessary and important.

Feingold then attempted to introduce his amendments: "There are quite a number of things in this bill that I am concerned about, but my amendments focus on a small discreet number of items. At this point I would like to turn to one of the amendments" (*Congressional Record—Senate*, October 11, 2001, p. S10570).

Majority leader Daschle quickly interrupted Feingold, explaining:

> My difficulty tonight is not substantive as much as it is procedural. There is no question, all 100 of us could go through this bill with a fine-tooth comb and pinpoint those things which we could improve....I have looked at this bill, and there are a lot of things, were I to write it alone, upon which I could improve....What we did was to say: Let's take this product and work with it; let's review it; if we have to make some changes, let's consider them; but let's recognize that if we were to take this bill open-ended, there would be no end to the amendments—that is the result that would most likely occur in such a circumstance....Given those circumstances, my argument is not substantive. It is procedural. We have a job to do. The clock is ticking. The work needs to get done. We have to make our best judgment about what is possible, and that progress goes on.
>
> I hope my colleagues will join me tonight in tabling this amendment and tabling every other amendment that is offered, should he choose to offer them tonight. Let's move on and finish the bill....Then let's let law enforcement do its job, and let's use our power of oversight to ensure that civil liberties are protected.
>
> I make a motion to table. (*Congressional Record—Senate*, October 11, 2001, p. S10574)

Republican committee chairman Specter was clearly bothered by Daschle's willingness to squelch amendments without even considering their substance. He noted:

> [W]hen the majority leader says he is concerned about procedure and not about substance, we are regrettably establishing a record where we have not only not shown the deliberative process to uphold constitutionality but we are putting on the record a disregard for constitutionality and elevating procedure over substance, which is not the way you legislate in a constitutional area where the Supreme Court of the United States balances law enforcement's needs with the incursion on privacy. (ibid., S10578)

But Democratic Senator Patrick Leahy, perhaps the strongest champion of civil rights in the Senate, rose to support Daschle's motion to table, explaining, "I can tell you right now, if we start unraveling this bill, we are going to lose all the parts we won and we will be back to a proposal that was blatantly unconstitutional in many parts. So I join, with no reluctance whatsoever, in the leader's motion" (ibid., S10575).

Feingold attempted to explain the danger involved in suppressing genuine deliberation on matters of such monumental significance:

> [O]n this bill, there was not a single moment of markup or vote in the Judiciary Committee. I accepted that because of the crisis our nation faces. This is the first substantive amendment in the Senate on this entire issue, one of the most important civil liberties bills of our time, and the majority leader has asked Senators to not vote on the merits of the issue. I understand the difficult task he has, but I must object to the idea that not one single amendment on this issue will be voted on the merits on the floor of the Senate. What have we come to when we don't have either committee or Senate deliberation on amendments on an issue of this importance?

Feingold's plea was unavailing. The Senate voted 83 to 13 to table his amendment.

Feingold rose once more to offer his second amendment, which addressed Section 206 of the Patriot Act. He explained, "The amendment simply provides that before conducting surveillance, the person implementing the order must ascertain that the target of the surveillance is actually in the house that has been bugged, or using the phone that has been tapped."

Daschle quickly rose to oppose the amendment, stating, "As I said before, I am sympathetic to many of these ideas, but I am much more sympathetic to arriving at a product that will bring us to a point where we can pass something into law. The record reflects…the very delicate balance that we have achieved. It is too late to open up the amendment process in a way that might destroy that delicate balance. For that reason, I move to table this amendment" (*Congressional Record—Senate*, October 11, 2001, pp. S10575–78).

Once more, the motion to table was passed overwhelmingly, 90 to 7.

Feingold rose wearily to offer his final amendment, addressing the controversial Section 215, which allows the government to seize "any tangible thing" from any business, library, hospital, or other establishment, overriding any and all state laws against such actions. "The amendment makes it clear that existing Federal and state statutory protections for the privacy of certain information are not diminished or superseded by Section 215," he declared.

Once more, Senator Daschle rose: "Mr. President, I move to table the amendment and ask for the yeas and nays" (*Congressional Record—Senate*, October 11, 2001, pp. S10584–10586).

There were eighty-nine yeas and eight nays. The final amendment was tabled. Nothing remained in the path of the steamroller known as the USA PATRIOT Act.

# FURTHER READINGS

Brzezinski, Matthew. *Fortress America: On the Front Lines of Home Security—An Inside Look at the Coming Surveillance State.* New York: Bantam Books, 2004.

Chang, Nancy. *Silencing Political Dissent: How September 11 Anti-terrorism Measures Threaten Our Civil Liberties.* New York: Seven Stories Press, 2002.

Daschle, Tom. *Like No Other Time: The Two Years That Changed America.* New York: Three Rivers Press, 2003.

Goldberg, Danny, ed. *It's a Free Country: Personal Freedom in America after September 11.* New York: RDV Books, 2002.

Hamud, Randall. "We're Fighting Terror, But Killing Freedom," *Newsweek* (September 2003), p. 11.

# After the Votes Are Cast, the Battle Lines Are Drawn

- **Document:** *Insatiable Appetite: The Government's Demand for New Unnecessary Powers after September 11*, an ACLU report
- **Date:** April 2002
- **Where:** The American Civil Liberties Union, Washington National Office, Washington, DC
- **Significance:** The USA PATRIOT Act was passed in a climate of exigency and a spirit of solidarity. Its doubters and critics had been ignored in the rush to action, but immediately after its passage, they became a new force for reform. Led by organizations like the American Civil Liberties Union, the Patriot Act was soon viewed in a new light, warts and all.

---

## DOCUMENT

### The Government's Demand for New Powers

Public Law 107-56 bears an extravagant title: The Uniting and Strengthening America by Providing Appropriate Tools Required to Intercept and Obstruct Terrorism Act. Its acronym—the USA PATRIOT Act—seems calculated to intimidate....Congress passed the far-reaching law after abbreviated debate, handing [Attorney General] Ashcroft virtually all the investigative tools he sought and several he had not even asked for. Yet the Government's hunger for new powers was not satisfied. Soon after passage of the USA PATRIOT Act, Justice Department spokeswoman Mindy Tucker declared: "This is just the first step. There will be additional items to come."

When challenged, government officials insist their actions represent a natural reordering of the balance between liberty and security. But while the loss of liberty is apparent, there is surprisingly little evidence that the new powers will actually enhance security. The losses of liberty accrued with these new measures have taken a variety of forms, but can be distilled into three basic overarching themes:

- An unprecedented and alarming new penchant for government secrecy and abandonment of the core American principle that a government for the people and by the people must be transparent to the people.

- A disdain and outright removal of the checks and balances that have been a cornerstone of American democracy for more than 225 years. Specifically, the administration and Congress have sought and obtained legislative and administrative measures that weaken judicial check on government excess.

- A refusal to protect the American value of equality under the law. The government's continued questioning, arrest and detention of persons based solely on their country of origin, race, religion or ethnicity poses serious threats to the civil liberties of citizens and non-citizens alike.

SOURCE: Ronald Welch, *Insatiable Appetite: The Government's Demand for New and Unnecessary Powers after September 11*, American Civil Liberties Union, April 2002.

---

# ANALYSIS

The passage of the USA PATRIOT Act was a truly bipartisan response to 9/11, but that political unity quickly evaporated. President Bush and Republican congressional candidates soon realized that identifying with the Patriot Act and the war on terrorism was good politics, but accusing Democrats of being soft on terrorism was even better.

Lee Hamilton, the former Democratic congressman from Indiana and co-chairman of the 9/11 Commission, said, "You would not expect the massive unity you saw in the immediate aftermath of the attacks to continue indefinitely. But you would also not expect it to dissipate as quickly as it did. The president could have consulted more with Congress...and generally been more inclusive, rather than expand executive power as much as he did" ("How Common Ground of 9/11 Gave Way to Partisan Split," *Washington Post*, July 16, 2006, p. A11).

The intelligence agencies gained the most from this expanded executive power. On the very day that President Bush signed the USA PATRIOT Act, October 26, 2001, the FBI's Office of the General Counsel sent a memo to all its divisions enthusiastically describing its new legal authorities. The memo began, "In the wake of the September 11, 2001 attacks, the Administration proposed to Congress a variety of proposals to increase the efficiency and effectiveness of FCI/IT operations." The memo then itemized the major provisions of the Patriot Act and urged all agents to take advantage of the new authorities.

For example, in describing Section 215, the provision authorizing the seizure of "any tangible thing," the memo stated:

In the past, the FBI has encountered situations in which the holders of relevant records refused to produce them absent a subpoena or other compelling authority. When those records did not fit within the defined categories for National Security Letters or the four categories then defined in the FISA business records section, the FBI had no means of compelling production. With the new language the FBI can seek a FISA court order for any such materials....The field may continue to request business records orders through FBIHQ in the established manner. However, such requests may now seek production of any relevant information, and need only contain information establishing such relevance.

The memo also gave a candid interpretation of the Patriot Act's lone reference to constitutional rights, the requirement that no counterintelligence investigation be conducted on a U.S. person "solely on the basis of activities protected by the first amendment of the Constitution." Perhaps it should have been obvious that this was flimsy protection at best, but the FBI made that brutally clear:

> Congress inserted this to indicate that the technique will not be used against U.S. persons who are merely exercising constitutionally protected rights. However, it is highly unlikely, if not entirely impossible, for an investigation to be authorized... that is "solely" based on protected activities. In other words, all investigations of U.S. persons will likely involve some allegation or possibility of illegal activity... which is not protected by the First Amendment. ("New Legislation: Revisions to the FCI/IT Legal Authorities," FBI memo to all divisions from the Office of the General Counsel, October 26, 2001, pp. 5–6)

But as the Bush Administration exulted over the Patriot Act, critics began to speak out, perhaps realizing that they had lost a historic battle on civil liberties. The library community was particularly aggressive in its early criticism. Writing for the American Library Association, columnist Karen Schneider pulled no punches in her appraisal of the newly passed legislation:

> The USA Patriot Act is treason pure and simple, and you need to know how and why, because it presents particularly pernicious issues for the users who rely on your Internet services.
> The Patriot Act is not anti-terrorism legislation; it's anti-speech legislation, and is no more a direct response to the September 11 attacks than the Children's Internet Protection Act is a direct result of sincere concern by members of Congress about the safety of minors. The cold, cynical reality is that the Patriot Act is a bloated hodge-podge of speech-chilling laws that lurked in congressional corridors not only before September 11, but in large part before the Bush administration. It was hustled into reality in the post-9/11 environment so quickly, secretively, and undemocratically that our Bill of Rights had been clocked with a one-two punch well before any of us realized it was under attack. (Karen G. Schneider, "The Patriot Act: Last Refuge of a Scoundrel," *American Libraries*, March 2002. www.ala.org/alonline/netlib/i1302.html)

On January 23, 2002, the American Library Association passed its "Resolution Reaffirming the Principles of Intellectual Freedom in the Aftermath of Terrorists Attacks." The resolution, which was sent to the President of the United States and the Attorney General, began with the famous quote from Benjamin Franklin: "They that can give up liberty to obtain a little temporary safety deserve neither liberty nor safety." It then reaffirmed the need for unfettered and unmonitored access to information, opposition to government censorship, the protection of privacy and confidentiality, and tolerance for dissent.

The Freedom to Read Committee of the Association of American Publishers followed with a June 2002 statement declaring that the Patriot Act "contains provisions that threaten the First Amendment-protected activities of book publishers, book sellers, librarians and readers." Attached to the statement was a form letter that supporters could send to Senator Patrick Leahy or Representative James Sensenbrenner urging them to hold hearings on the Patriot Act. The letter concluded with the warning, "If people come to believe that the government can readily obtain access to their library and bookstore records, they will no longer feel free to request the books and other materials they want and need out of a fear that they might become a target of government surveillance" ("The Patriot Act and the First Amendment," A Statement from the Freedom to Read Committee of the Association of American Publishers, June 10, 2002).

James Dempsey, one of the authors of the 2001 manifesto "In Defense of Freedom at a Time of Crisis," which civil liberties advocates had hoped to serve as a balanced template for the Patriot Act, now expressed his disappointment in the bill. "The tragedy of the response to September 11 is not that the government has been given new powers—it is that those new powers have been granted without standards or checks and balances," he wrote in the journal *Human Rights*. "In the name of fighting terrorism, changes have been adopted that…weaken the role of the judiciary. They relieve the government of the responsibility to focus its investigations on specific suspects. They permit government agencies to cast their nets far wider than ever before" (James X. Dempsey, "Civil Liberties in a Time of Crisis," *Human Rights* (Winter 2002), pp. 9–10).

Understandably, a Congress that voted overwhelmingly for the Patriot Act was slow to join the critics of their legislation, but as public concern grew over some of the more extreme provisions of the Patriot Act, even members of Congress began to express misgivings.

# FURTHER READINGS

Cassel, Elaine. *The War on Civil Liberties: How Bush and Ashcroft Have Dismantled the Bill of Rights*. Chicago: Lawrence Hill Books, 2004.

Cole, David. *Terrorism and the Constitution: Sacrificing Civil Liberties in the Name of National Security*. 2nd ed. New York: New Press, 2002.

Hentoff, Nat. *The War on the Bill of Rights and the Gathering Resistance*. New York: Seven Stories Press, 2003.

Korb, Lawrence J. *A New National Security Strategy in an Age of Terrorists, Tyrants, and Weapons of Mass Destruction*. New York: Council on Foreign Relations, 2003.

Michaels, William C. *No Greater Threat: America after September 11 and the Rise of a National Security State*. New York: Algora Publications, 2002.

# CHAPTER 3

# The USA PATRIOT Act: The Bill That Defined America's Domestic War on Terrorism

Figure 4. Signing ceremony for the USA PATRIOT Act. AP Images © 2001.

# The USA PATRIOT Act

- **Documents:** Remarks by President George W. Bush at Signing of USA PATRIOT Act; Table of Contents and List of Sections of the USA PATRIOT Act of 2001
- **Date:** Signed October 26, 2001
- **Where:** Washington, DC
- **Significance:** The USA PATRIOT Act was one of the longest, most complex, and most controversial bills ever passed by Congress. It was the legislative marker that defined the beginning of the post-9/11 world.

---

# DOCUMENTS

### 1. President Bush's Comments at Signing Ceremony

Good morning and welcome to the White House. Today, we take an essential step in defeating terrorism, while protecting the constitutional rights of all Americans. With my signature, this law will give intelligence and law enforcement officials important new tools to fight a present danger....

The changes, effective today, will help counter a threat like no other our nation has ever faced. We've seen the enemy, and the murder of thousands of innocent, unsuspecting people. They recognize no barrier of morality. They have no conscience. The terrorists cannot be reasoned with....

These terrorists must be pursued, they must be defeated, and they must be brought to justice. And that is the purpose of this legislation. Since the 11th of September, the men and women of our intelligence and law enforcement agencies have been relentless in their response to new and sudden challenges.

We have seen the horrors terrorists can inflict. We may never know what horrors our country was spared by the diligent and determined work of our police forces, the FBI, ATF agents, federal marshals, custom officers, Secret Service, intelligence professionals and local law enforcement officials, under the most trying conditions. They are serving this country with excellence, and often with bravery.

They deserve our full support and every means of help that we can provide. We're dealing with terrorists who operate by highly sophisticated methods and technologies, some of which were not even available when existing laws were written. The bill before me takes account of the new realities and dangers posed by modern terrorists. It will help law enforcement to identify, to dismantle, to disrupt, and to punish terrorists before they strike.

For example, this legislation gives law enforcement officials better tools to put an end to financial counterfeiting, smuggling, and money-laundering. Secondly, it gives intelligence operations and criminal operations the chance to operate not on separate tracks, but to share vital information so necessary to disrupt a terrorist attack before it occurs.

As of today, we're changing the laws governing information-sharing. And as importantly, we're changing the culture of our various agencies that fight terrorism. Countering and investigating terrorist activity is the number one priority for both law enforcement and intelligence agencies.

Surveillance of communications is another essential tool to pursue and stop terrorists. The existing law was written in the era of rotary telephones. This new law that I sign today will allow surveillance of all communications used by terrorists, including e-mails, the Internet, and cell phones.

As of today, we'll be able to better meet the technological challenges posed by this proliferation of communications technology. Investigations are often slowed by limits on the reach of federal search warrants.

Law enforcement agencies have to get a new warrant for each new district they investigate, even when they're after the same suspect. Under this new law, warrants are valid across all districts and across all states. And, finally the new legislation greatly enhances the penalties that will fall on terrorists or anyone who helps them....

We are enacting new and harsh penalties for possession of biological weapons. We're making it easier to seize the assets of groups and individuals involved in terrorism. The government will have wider latitude in deporting known terrorists and their supporters. The statute of limitations on terrorist acts will be lengthened, as will prison sentences for terrorists....

This legislation is essential not only to pursuing and punishing terrorists, but also preventing more atrocities in the hands of the evil ones. This government will enforce this law with all the urgency of a nation at war. The elected branches of our government, and both political parties, are united in our resolve to fight and stop and punish those who would do harm to the American people.

It is now my honor to sign into law the USA PATRIOT Act of 2001.

*SOURCE*: The White House. www.whitehouse.gov/news/releases/2001/10/20011026-5.html

## 2. USA PATRIOT Act: Table of Contents and List of Sections

An Act
To deter and punish terrorist acts in the United States and around the world, to enhance law enforcement investigative tools, and for other purposes.
*Be it enacted by the Senate and House of Representatives of the United States of America in Congress assembled,*

**Section 1. Short Title and Table of Contents.**

(a) SHORT TITLE—This Act may be cited as the "Uniting and Strengthening America by Providing Appropriate Tools Required to Intercept and Obstruct Terrorism (USA PATRIOT ACT) Act of 2001."

(b) TABLE OF CONTENTS—The table of contents for this Act is as follows:
Section 1. Short Title and Table of Contents.
Section 2. Construction; severability.

---

### IN HISTORY

#### Who Authored the Patriot Act?

As the legislative branch of our government, the U.S. Congress has the responsibility to prepare, debate, and pass the bills that become our laws. But the USA PATRIOT Act was written by the Department of Justice, not by members of Congress. Attorney General John Ashcroft is the official most closely associated with the Patriot Act, but he did not author it. In fact, on the morning after 9/11 when Justice Department officials met to draft a legislative response, Ashcroft and other top government officials were in seclusion for security reasons. It was Assistant District Attorney Viet Dinh who convened the meeting and oversaw the drafting of the bill.

---

*Title I—Enhancing Domestic Security Against Terrorism*

Section 101. Counterterrorism fund

Section 102. Sense of Congress condemning discrimination against Arab and Muslim Americans.

Section 103. Increased funding for the technical support center at the Federal Bureau of Investigation.

Section 104. Requests for military assistance to enforce prohibition in certain emergencies.

Section 105. Expansion of National Electronic Crime Task Force Initiative.

Section 106. Presidential authority.

*Title II—Enhanced Surveillance Procedures*

Section 201. Authority to intercept wire, oral, and electronic communications relating to terrorism.

Section 202. Authority to intercept wire, oral, and electronic communications relating to computer fraud and abuse offenses.

Section 203. Authority to share criminal investigative information.

Section 204. Clarification of intelligence exceptions from limitations on interception and disclosure of wire, oral, and electronic communications.

Section 205. Employment of translators by the Federal Bureau of Investigation.

Section 206. Roving surveillance authority under the Foreign Intelligence Surveillance Act of 1978.

Section 207. Duration of FISA surveillance of non-United States persons who are agents of a foreign power.

Section 208. Designation of judges.

Section 209. Seizure of voice-mail messages pursuant to warrants.

Section 210. Scope of subpoenas for records of electronic communications.

Section 211. Clarification of scope.

Section 212. Emergency disclosure of electronic communications to protect life and limb.

Section 213. Authority for delaying notice of the execution of a warrant.

Section 214. Pen register and trap and trace authority under FISA.

Section 215. Access to records and other items under the Foreign Intelligence Surveillance Act.

Section 216. Modification of authorities relating to use of pen registers and trap and trace devices.

Section 217. Interception of computer trespasser communications.

Section 218. Foreign intelligence information.

Section 219. Single-jurisdiction search warrants for terrorism.

Section 220. Nationwide service of search warrants for electronic evidence.

Section 221. Trade sanctions.

Section 222. Assistance to law enforcement agencies.

Section 223. Civil liability for certain unauthorized disclosures.

Section 224. Sunset.

Section 225. Immunity for compliance with FISA wiretap.

*Title III—International Money Laundering Abatement and Anti-Terrorist Financing Act of 2001*

Section 301. Short title.

Section 302. Findings and purposes.

Section 303. 4-year congressional review; expedited consideration.

*Subtitle A—International Counter Money Laundering and Related Matters*
Section 311. Special measures for jurisdictions, financial institutions, or international transactions of primary money laundering concern.
Section 312. Special due diligence for correspondent accounts and private banking accounts.
Section 313. Prohibition on United States correspondent accounts with foreign shell banks.
Section 314. Cooperative efforts to deter money laundering.
Section 315. Inclusion of foreign corruption offenses as money laundering crimes.
Section 316. Anti-terrorist forfeiture protection.
Section 317. Long-arm jurisdiction over foreign money launderers.
Section 318. Laundering money through a foreign bank.
Section 319. Forfeiture of funds in United States interbank accounts.
Section 320. Proceeds of foreign crimes.
Section 321. Financial institutions specified in subchapter II of chapter 53 of title 31, United States Code.
Section 322. Corporation represented by a fugitive.
Section 323. Enforcement of foreign judgments.
Section 324. Report and recommendation.
Section 325. Concentration accounts at financial institutions.
Section 326. Verification of identification.
Section 327. Consideration of anti-money laundering record.
Section 328. International cooperation on identification of originators of wire transfers.
Section 329. Criminal penalties.
Section 330. International cooperation in investigations of money laundering, financial crimes, and the finances of terrorist groups.

*Subtitle B—Bank Secrecy Act Amendments and Related Improvements*
Section 351. Amendments relating to reporting of suspicious activities.
Section 352. Anti-money laundering programs.
Section 353. Penalties for violations of geographic targeting orders and certain record-keeping requirements, and lengthening effective period of geographic targeting orders.
Section 354. Anti-money laundering strategy.
Section 355. Authorization to include suspicions of illegal activity in written employment references.
Section 356. Reporting of suspicious activities by securities brokers and dealers; investment company study.
Section 357. Special report on administration of bank secrecy provisions.
Section 358. Bank secrecy provisions.
Section 359. Reporting of suspicious activities by underground banking systems.
Section 360. Use of authority of United States Executive Directors.
Section 361. Financial crimes enforcement network.
Section 362. Establishment of highly secure network.
Section 363. Increase in civil and criminal penalties for money laundering.
Section 364. Uniform protection authority for Federal Reserve facilities.
Section 365. Reports relating to coins and currency received in nonfinancial trade or business.
Section 366. Efficient use of currency transaction report system.

*Subtitle C—Currency Crimes and Protection*
Section 371. Bulk cash smuggling into or out of the United States.
Section 372. Forfeiture in currency reporting cases.
Section 373. Illegal money transmitting businesses.
Section 374. Counterfeiting domestic currency and obligations.

*Title VII—Increased Information Sharing for Critical Infrastructure Protection*

Section 711. Expansion of regional information sharing system to facilitate Federal-State-local law enforcement response related to terrorist attacks.

*Title VIII—Strengthening the Criminal Laws Against Terrorism*

Section 801. Terrorist attacks and other acts of violence against mass transportation systems.

Section 802. Definition of domestic terrorism.

Section 803. Prohibition against harboring terrorists.

Section 804. Jurisdiction over crimes committed at U.S. facilities abroad.

Section 805. Material support for terrorism.

Section 806. Assets of terrorist organizations.

Section 807. Technical clarification relating to provision of material support to terrorism.

Section 808. Definition of Federal crime of terrorism.

Section 809. No statute of limitation for certain terrorism offenses.

Section 810. Alternate maximum penalties for terrorism offenses.

Section 811. Penalties for terrorist conspiracies.

Section 812. Post-release supervision of terrorists.

Section 813. Inclusion of acts of terrorism as racketeering activity.

Section 814. Deterrence and prevention of cyberterrorism.

Section 815. Additional defense to civil actions relating to preserving records in response to Government requests.

Section 816. Development and support of cybersecurity forensic capabilities.

Section 817. Expansion of the biological weapons statute.

*Title IX—Improved Intelligence*

Section 901. Responsibilities of Director of Central Intelligence regarding foreign intelligence collected under Foreign Intelligence Surveillance Act of 1978.

Section 902. Inclusion of international terrorist activities within scope of foreign intelligence under National Security Act of 1947.

Section 903. Sense of Congress on the establishment and maintenance of intelligence relationships to acquire information on terrorists and terrorist organizations.

Section 904. Temporary authority to defer submittal to Congress of reports on intelligence and intelligence-related matters.

Section 905. Disclosure to Director of Central Intelligence of foreign intelligence-related information with respect to criminal investigations.

Section 906. Foreign terrorist asset tracking center.

Section 907. National Virtual Translation Center.

Section 908. Training of government officials regarding identification and use of foreign intelligence.

*Title X—Miscellaneous*

Section 1001. Review of the Department of Justice.

Section 1002. Sense of Congress.

Section 1003. Definition of "electronic surveillance."

Section 1004. Venue in money laundering cases.

Section 1005. First Responders Assistance Act.

Section 1006. Inadmissibility of aliens engaged in money laundering.

Section 1007. Authorization of funds for DEA police training in South and Central Asia.

Section 1008. Feasibility study on use of biometric identifier scanning system with access to the FBI integrated automated fingerprint identification system at overseas consular posts and points of entry to the United States.

Section 1009. Study of access.

Section 1010. Temporary authority to contract with local and State governments for performance of security functions at United States military installations.

Section 1011. Crimes against charitable Americans.

Section 1012. Limitation on issuance of hazmat licenses.

Section 1013. Expressing the sense of the Senate concerning the provision of funding for bioterrorism preparedness and response.

Section 1014. Grant program for State and local domestic preparedness support.

Section 1015. Expansion and reauthorization of the Crime Identification Technology Act for antiterrorism grants in States and localities.

Section 1016. Critical infrastructures protection.

SOURCE: http://frwebgate.access.gpo.gov/cgi-in/getdoc.cgi?dbname=107_cong_public_laws&docid=f:pub1056.107

---

# ANALYSIS

A full analysis of the massive USA PATRIOT Act would take volumes, but a brief description of its major provisions can provide an adequate understanding of its power and scope.

Section 101: Establishes a new counterterrorism fund without fiscal year limitation and of unnamed amount, to be administered by the Justice Department.

Section 103: Re-invigorates the Justice Department's Technical Support Center and gives it $200 million for the years 2002 through 2004.

Section 105: Establishes a "national network of electronic crimes task forces" to be set up by the Secret Service throughout the country to prevent, detect, and investigate various electronic crimes.

Section 203: Mandates the sharing of "foreign intelligence" information between numerous federal agencies. The broad definition of foreign intelligence includes virtually anything related to national defense, national security, or foreign affairs. All such information in the possession of any federal investigative or law enforcement officer may be shared with any other federal "law enforcement, intelligence, protective, immigration, national defense, or national security officer." No court order is necessary and the information is not limited to the person being investigated.

Section 206: Provides "roving wire tap" authority to FISA.

Section 207 and 208: Increases the duration of FISA warrants and the number of FISA court judges.

Section 209 and 212: Enacts numerous technical changes and enhancements to standard surveillance techniques, including the authorization of the government's controversial "Carnivore" electronic surveillance programs.

Section 213: Allows delayed notification of "non-physical search warrants" known as "sneak and peek" warrants.

Section 214: Allows pen/trap orders concerning foreign intelligence information. The target of such an order may be a U.S. person, provided that the investigation is not conducted *solely* on the basis of First Amendment-protected activities.

Section 215: Allows federal investigators to seize "any tangible thing" in FISA type investigations by showing only that the items sought are "relevant" to an ongoing investigation related to terrorism or intelligence activities. The court *must* grant the warrant to the requesting agency, even if the judge believes the request is without merit.

Section 216: Explicitly places access to Internet information, including e-mail and Web browsing information, within the reach of pen/trap orders, without need to show probable cause. Again, law enforcement need only certify that what they seek is "relevant" to an ongoing terrorism investigation.

Section 217: Allows any government employee to conduct electronic content surveillance of U.S. persons.

Section 218: Lowers the standard for obtaining FISA warrants.

Section 219 and 220: Establish single jurisdiction search warrants and nationwide service of warrants.

Section 311, 312, 316, and 319: Allow federal investigators to impose "special measure" on any domestic bank or financial institution and impose new due diligence requirements on such institutions as a way of revealing terrorist financing. Set a 120-hour deadline for financial institutions to respond to information requests by federal investigators. Create new forfeiture provisions for those charged or convicted of certain terrorist crimes. Permit access by federal investigators to records of certain "correspondent accounts" in foreign banks.

Section 326: Establishes new or expanded requirements to track identities of persons opening new bank accounts and authorizes a study to track aliens or foreign nationals by a numerical system similar to social security numbers.

Section 358: Allows government investigators access to consumer records without a court order.

Section 403: Mandates a new information system to allow State Department access to certain criminal files kept by the FBI and requires a new technology standard to be applied to all visas and all border checkpoints.

Section 411: Creates a new definition of terrorism, establishing three types of "terrorist organizations," with wide latitude for federal investigators to identify such groups.

Section 412: Provides for mandatory detention of suspected aliens, allowing a person to be held for seven days without charge and possible indefinite detention for aliens deemed not removable. Requires a biannual report to Congress on aliens detained, but the report need not contain fundamental information like names, when seized, where detained, or nature of charges.

Section 414–417: Establish new standards for entry and exit systems and data systems for border entry points. Expand the foreign student monitoring program.

Section 503: Greatly expands the DNA information bank on criminals.

Section 504: Links the investigation of any crime with the search for foreign intelligence, including information sharing.

Section 505: Amends three statutes to facilitate the FBI's use of "National Security Letters," a form of administrative subpoena that allows the FBI to seek information from libraries and other institutions without the need for a court order.

Section 507 and 508: Allow government investigators access to educational records without a court order.

Section 701: Establishes a major initiative for a "secure information sharing system" to investigate and prosecute multijurisdictional terrorist activities.

Section 802: Creates a new crime called "domestic terrorism," defined as "activity that involves acts dangerous to human life that violate the laws of the United States or any state and appear to be intended: (i) to intimidate or coerce a civilian population; (ii) to influence the policy of a government by intimidation or coercion; or (iii) to affect the conduct of a government by mass destruction, assassination or kidnapping."

Section 803: Expands the crimes of harboring, concealing, or providing material support for terrorists.

Section 808: Expands the list of "federal crime of terrorism."

Section 809–812: Allow increased penalties for certain terrorist crimes, with no statute of limitations.

Section 901 and 905: Mandate information sharing by the CIA with the Justice Department and by the Justice Department with the CIA.

Section 903: Deputizes all "officers and employees" of the "intelligence community" and authorizes them to investigate terrorism.

Section 908: Establishes a cross-agency training program for law enforcement officials and agencies, including state and local, so they can better handle "foreign intelligence" investigations.

Section 1005: Provides grants for state and local fire and emergency service departments.

Section 1016: Establishes new programs for critical infrastructure protection.

# FURTHER READINGS

Bradley, Lynne E. "The USA Patriot Act," *College and Research Libraries News* (December 2001), p. 1123.

Breinholt, Jeff. "How about a Little Perspective: The USA PATRIOT Act and the Uses and Abuses of History," *Texas Review of Law and Politics*, 9, no. 1 (2004), p. 17.

Dowley, Michael F. "Government Surveillance Powers under the USA PATRIOT Act: Is It Possible to Protect National Security and Privacy at the Same Time? A Constitutional Tug-of-War," *Suffolk University Law Review*, 36 (2002), p. 165.

Gross, Emanuel. "The Struggle of a Democracy Against Terrorism—Protection of Human Rights: The Right to Privacy Versus the National Interest—The Proper Balance," *Cornell International Law Journal*, 37 (2003–2004), p. 27.

Hockeimer, Jr., Henry E. "USA Patriot Act Is Broader Than You Might Imagine," *New Jersey Law Journal* (April 14, 2002), p. 29.

Rackow, Sharon. "How the USA PATRIOT Act Will Permit Governmental Infringement upon the Privacy of Americans in the Name of 'Intelligence' Investigations," *University of Pennsylvania Law Review*, 150, no. 5 (May 2002), p. 1651.

"The USA Patriot Act: A Legal Analysis," A Report for Congress by the Congressional Research Service, April 15, 2002. http://www.fas.org/irp/crs/RI.31377.pdf

Whitehead, John W. "Forfeiting 'Enduring Freedom' for 'Homeland Security': A Constitutional Analysis of the USA PATRIOT Act and the Justice Department's Anti-Terrorism Initiatives," *American University Law Review*, 51, no. 6 (2002), p. 1081.

# Sharing Investigative Information

- *Document:* Section 203 of the USA PATRIOT Act of 2001
- *Date:* Signed October 26, 2001
- *Where:* Washington, DC
- *Significance:* Section 203 removes virtually all barriers to information-sharing within the federal government, authorizing federal agencies to share grand jury information, intercepted information, and foreign intelligence information.

---

## DOCUMENT

### Section 203, USA PATRIOT Act

### Section 203. Authority to Share Criminal Investigative Information

(a) AUTHORITY TO SHARE GRAND JURY INFORMATION....

(C)(i) Disclosure otherwise prohibited by this rule of matters occurring before the grand jury may also be made—

.... (V) when the matters involve foreign intelligence or counterintelligence (as defined in section 3 of the National Security Act of 1947 (50 U.S.C. 401a)), or foreign intelligence information (as defined in clause (iv) of this subparagraph), to any Federal law enforcement, intelligence, protective, immigration, national defense, or national security official in order to assist the official receiving that information in the performance of his official duties....

(c) AUTHORITY TO SHARE ELECTRONIC, WIRE, AND ORAL INTERCEPTION INFORMATION—....

(6) Any investigative or law enforcement officer, or attorney for the Government, who by any means authorized by this chapter, has obtained knowledge of the contents of any wire, oral, or electronic communication, or evidence derived therefrom, may disclose such contents to any other Federal law enforcement, intelligence, protective, immigration, national defense, or national security official to the extent that such

contents include foreign intelligence or counterintelligence (as defined in section 3 of the National Security Act of 1947 (50 U.S.C. 401a)), or foreign intelligence information (as defined in subsection 19 of section 2510 of this title), to assist the official who is to receive that information in the performance of his official duties....

(d) FOREIGN INTELLIGENCE INFORMATION—

(1) IN GENERAL—Notwithstanding any other provision of the law, it shall be lawful for foreign intelligence or counterintelligence ... or foreign intelligence information obtained as part of a criminal investigation to be disclosed to any Federal law enforcement, intelligence, protective, immigration, national defense, or national security official in order to assist the official receiving that information in the performance of his official duties....

SOURCE: http://frwebgate.access.gpo.gov/cgi-in/getdoc.cgi?dbname=107_cong_public_laws &docid=f:pub1056.107

---

# ANALYSIS

Section 203 of the USA PATRIOT Act amended the Federal Rules of Criminal procedure to permit disclosure of "matters occurring before the grand jury" to "any federal, law enforcement, intelligence, protective, immigration, national defense, or national security official," when the matters involve foreign intelligence or counterintelligence. Section 203 also amended 18 U.S.C. 2517, which governs the disclosure and use of intercepted communications. Under the Patriot Act, intercepted information relating to foreign intelligence and counterintelligence may be shared broadly within the executive branch in the same way allowed for grand jury information. In addition to Section 203, Sections 218, 403, 504, and 905 increase the authority of intelligence and law enforcement agencies to share investigative information.

Supporters of the Patriot Act insist that sharing such information is essential to the success of international terrorism investigations, and they note that Section 203 permits sharing only of "foreign intelligence information." But critics say that provision is insufficient to limit disclosure to investigations of terrorist activities, making American citizens subject to the loose standards for intelligence investigations, even when the case itself falls under criminal law.

After the passage of the Patriot Act, congressional supporters joined the Department of Justice chorus in extolling the removal of the firewall separating foreign intelligence investigations from criminal investigations, allowing the sharing of surveillance data among federal agencies. During congressional debate, Senator Orrin Hatch (R-UT) said,

> I believe most of our citizens would be shocked to learn that, even if certain government agents had prior knowledge of the September 11 attacks, under many circumstances they would have been prohibited by law from sharing that information with the appropriate intelligence or national security authorities. This legislation makes sure that, in the future, this information flows freely within the Federal government, so that it will be received by those responsible for protecting against terrorist attacks.... In this new war, terrorists are a hybrid between domestic criminals and intelligence agents. We must lower the barriers that discourage our law enforcement and intelligence agencies from working together to stop these terrorists. (*Congressional Record—Senate*, October 11, 2001, p. S10560)

Senator Patrick Leahy (D-VT) agreed with the goal of greater interdepartmental sharing of investigative information, but said the Patriot Act addressed that goal in a clumsy and potentially dangerous way.

For those of us who have been concerned about the leaks from the FBI that can irreparably damage reputations of innocent people and frustrate investigations by alerting suspects to flee or destroy material evidence, the Administration's insistence on the broadest authority to disseminate such information, without any judicial check, is disturbing.... If there are specific laws that the Administration believes impeded the necessary sharing of information on terrorism and foreign intelligence within the executive branch, we should address those problems through legislation that is narrowly targeted to those statutes. Tacking on a blunderbuss provision whose scope we do not fully understand can only lead to consequences that we cannot foresee. Further, I am concerned that such legislation, broadly authorizing the secret sharing of intelligence throughout the executive branch will fuel the unwarranted fears and dark conspiracy theories of Americans who do not trust their government. (*Congressional Record—Senate*, October 11, 2001, pp. S10555–56)

In 2003, the Justice Department responded to questions by the House Judiciary Committee concerning the effect of removing barriers between law enforcement and intelligence:

The USA PATRIOT Act has enabled the U.S. government to more effectively process and analyze law enforcement and intelligence information. Prior to the Act, intelligence and law enforcement agencies and personnel were discouraged from sharing certain types of information. This restriction represented a serious impediment to effective antiterrorism efforts and risked unproductive approaches to the apprehension and prosecution of terrorists and criminals. Provisions of the Act, such as sections 203, 218, 403, 504, and 905, have enabled the intelligence arm and the law enforcement arm of the U.S. government to coordinate their efforts by breaking down the "wall.".... Such exchanges of information have occurred between the law enforcement and intelligence agencies on numerous occasions. Sections 218 and 504 were essential to the success of the Sami al Arian investigation in Tampa, Florida.... Information exchange under sections 203 and 905 has occurred via FBI JTTFs. The number of Joint Terrorism Task Forces has nearly doubled since September 11th, and the staff has greatly increased. These task forces have been integral to the dissemination of information between agencies, which has resulted in actual convictions. The information-sharing proscribed by section 403 has also yielded significant results. (Hearing before the Committee on the Judiciary, House of Representatives, 108th Congress, 1st Session, June 5, 2003, pp. 117–18)

# FURTHER READINGS

Collins, Jennifer. "And the Walls Came Tumbling Down: Sharing Grand Jury Information with the Intelligence Community under the USA PATRIOT Act," *American Criminal Law Review* 1261 (2002).

"Implementation of the USA PATRIOT Act: Effect of Sections 203 (B) and (D) on Information Sharing," *Subcommittee on Crime, Terrorism, and Homeland Security, Committee on the Judiciary, U.S. House of Representatives*, April 2005, Report Number: 109–15.

"Moving from 'Need to Know' to 'Need to Share': A Review of the 9/11 Commission's Recommendations," *Committee on Government Reform, U.S. House of Representatives*, August 2004, Report Number: Serial Number 108–217.

"9/11 Commission Report: Reorganization, Transformation and Information Sharing," *Government Accountability Office*, August 2004, Report Number: GAO-04-1033T.

Vartanian, Thomas P. "Information Sharing under the USA PATRIOT Act," *The Banking Law Journal*, 119, no. 7 (July/August 2002), p. 600.

# Sneak and Peek: Secret Search Warrants

- *Document:* Section 213 of the USA PATRIOT Act of 2001
- *Date:* Signed October 26, 2001
- *Where:* Washington, DC
- *Significance:* By allowing delay of notice for an undefined "reasonable period," Section 213 opens the possibility of indefinite secrecy warrants.

---

## DOCUMENT

### Section 213, USA PATRIOT Act

### Section 213. Authority for Delaying Notice of the Execution of a Warrant

Section 3103a of Title 18, United States Code, is amended—....

1. DELAY—With respect to the issuance of any warrant or court order under this section, or any other rule of law, to search for and seize any property or material that constitutes evidence of a criminal offense in violation of the laws of the United States, any notice required, or that may be required, to be given may be delayed if—

   (1) the court finds reasonable cause to believe that providing immediate notification of the execution of the warrant may have an adverse result (as defined in section 2705);
   (2) the warrant prohibits the seizure of any tangible property, any wire or electronic communication (as defined in section 2510), or, except as expressly provided in chapter 121, any stored wire or electronic information, except where the court finds reasonable necessity for the seizure; and
   (3) the warrant provides for the giving of such notice within a reasonable period of its execution, which period may thereafter be extended by the court for good cause shown.

*SOURCE:* USA PATRIOT Act (H.R.3162). www.epic.org/privacy/terrorism/hr3162.html

---

# ANALYSIS

Normally, when law enforcement officers execute a search warrant, they must leave a copy of the warrant and a receipt for all property seized at the premises searched. Thus, even if the search is conducted when the owner of the premises is not present, the owners will receive notice that the premises have been searched pursuant to a warrant rather than, for example, burglarized. Section 213 of the Patriot Act eliminates the previous requirement that law enforcement provide a subject to a search warrant with contemporaneous notice of the search. The new "secret search" provision may be used wherever the court "finds reasonable cause to believe that providing immediate notification of the execution of the warrant may have an adverse effect." The new law requires only that notice be given within a "reasonable period," which can be extended by the court for "good cause." Because of the ambiguity of terms like "reasonable period," the Justice Department's own guidelines on the new authorities in the Patriot Act advise that Section 213 should be regarded as a "flexible standard."

The 1986 Electronics Communications Privacy Act had already granted the government the authority to delay notification for search of some forms of electronic communications that are in the custody of a third party. Section 213 of the Patriot Act statutorily extends the ability of law enforcement to delay the notice to any physical or electronic search with a showing that giving notice would create an "adverse result." This provision is an effort to improve the government's ability to investigate suspected terrorists by granting law enforcement greater leeway to operate clandestinely. This significant change in the law applies to all government searches for material that "constitutes evidence of a criminal offense in violation of the laws of the United States" and is not limited to investigations of terrorist activity. Prior law authorized delay of notification of a search only under a very small number of circumstances. The expansion of this extraordinary authority to all searches constitutes a radical departure from Fourth Amendment standards and could result in routine surreptitious entries by law enforcement agents.

Understandably, the Justice Department has been effusive in its praise of its new "sneak and peek" authority. In 2003, the Department told Congress, "Section 213 has been essential in increasing the safety of government officials and witnesses as well as the effectiveness of terrorist investigations. Advanced notification to terrorist suspects of searches or surveillance could result in destroyed evidence, notification of co-conspirators, attacks on agents and potential witnesses, or even a terrorist plot.... Section 213 has enabled investigators to obtain decisive evidence for the prosecution of serious offenders" (Hearing before the Committee on the Judiciary, House of Representatives, 108th Congress, 1st Session, June 5, 2003, p. 118).

On June 5, 2003, when asked about his use of "sneak and peek" warrants, Attorney General John Ashcroft told the House Judiciary Committee,

> In addition to delayed notice of searches, we can give delayed notice of seizure.... We have asked for that 15 times. In 14 cases the Court said, yes, you can do that. In the 15th case the Court said why don't you just take a picture of it and leave it?...The most common period of delays has been 7 days.... The Department sometimes has to seek an extension in the period of delayed notice, and we've made a number of those requests. No court has ever rejected a request for an extension by the Justice Department. (ibid., 37)

James X. Dempsey, an early critic of the Patriot Act and co-author of the manifesto, "In Defense of Freedom at a Time of Crisis," says Section 213 of the Patriot Act allows the FBI to

> secretly enter your apartment or house while you are asleep or away, take, alter or copy things, and not tell you they were there for days, weeks, or even months later.... Instead of limiting the so-called "sneak and peek" authority to aliens

## IN HISTORY

### Legal Precedent for Sneak and Peek Searches

Two circuit courts of appeal, the Second and Ninth Circuits, have recognized a limited exception to the need for contemporaneous notice. When specifically authorized by the issuing judge, the officers may delay providing notice of the search to avoid compromising an ongoing investigation. The Second and Ninth Circuit decisions dealt only with cases where the officers searched premises without seizing any tangible property. As the Second Circuit explained, such searches are "less intrusive than a conventional search with physical seizure because the latter deprives the owner not only of privacy but also of the use of his property" (*United States v. Villegas*, 899 F.2d 1324 (2d Cir. 1990)).

These cases have required that the officers seeking the warrant show good reason for the delay and that the delay be no more than seven days. The reasons for these limitations were spelled out by Judge Sneed of the Ninth Circuit:

The mere thought of strangers walking through and examining the center of our privacy interest, our home, arouses our passion for freedom, as does nothing else. That passion, the true source of the Fourth Amendment, demands that surreptitious entries be closely circumscribed. (*United States v. Freitas*, 800 F.2d 1451 (9th Circ. 1986))

The Supreme Court has also held that contemporaneous notice is normally required by the Fourth Amendment and could be dispensed with only under extraordinary circumstances (*Wilson v. Arkansas*, 514 U.S. 927 (1995) and *Richards v. Wisconsin*, 520 U.S. 385 (1997)).

The Patriot Act has discarded this interpretation of the Fourth Amendment.

suspected of terrorism, Congress applied it to the homes of citizens also. Moreover, what is most remarkable about this provision is that it is not limited to terrorism cases: it applies to drug cases, tax fraud, providing false information on student loan applications, or any other federal crime. (James X. Dempsey, *Human Rights* (Winter 2002), p. 9)

## FURTHER READINGS

Association of Research Libraries. Draft Memo from Wiley Rein & Fielding, "The Search & Seizure of Electronic Information: The Law Before and After the USA Patriot Act." http:www.arl.org/info/frn/other/matrix.pdf

Breglio, Nola K. "Leaving FISA Behind: The Need to Return to Warrantless Foreign Intelligence Surveillance," *Yale Law Journal*, 113, no. 1(2003), p. 179.

"The Fourth Amendment and New Technologies: Constitutional Myths and the Case for Caution." *Michigan Law Review*, 102, no. 801 (2004).

Kollar, Justin F. "USA PATRIOT Act, The Fourth Amendment, and Paranoia: Can They Read This While I'm Typing It?" *Journal of High Technology Law*, 3, no. 1 (2004), p. 67.

Mell, Patricia. "Big Brother at the Door: Balancing National Security with Privacy under the USA PATRIOT Act," *Denver University Law Review*, 80, no. 2 (2002), p. 375.

Osher, Steven A. "Privacy, Computers and the PATRIOT Act: The Fourth Amendment Isn't Dead, but No One Will Insure It," *Florida Law Review*, 54, no. 3 (July 2002), p. 521.

"Searches and Seizures in a Digital World." *Harvard Law Review*, 119, no. 531 (2005).

# Seizing "Any Tangible Things": Section 215 of the Patriot Act

- *Document:* Section 215 of the USA PATRIOT Act of 2001
- *Date:* Signed October 26, 2001
- *Where:* Washington, DC
- *Significance:* Section 215 allows federal investigators involved in terrorism or national security investigations to seize "any tangible things" from businesses and other entities.

---

## DOCUMENT

### Section 215, USA PATRIOT Act

#### Section 215. Access to Records and Other Items under the Foreign Intelligence Surveillance Act

Title V of the Foreign Intelligence Surveillance Act of 1978 (50 U.S.C. 1861 et seq.) is amended by striking sections 501 through 503 and inserting the following:

#### Section 501. Access to Certain Business Records for Foreign Intelligence and International Terrorism Investigations

(a) (1) The Director of the Federal Bureau of Investigation or a designee of the Director (whose rank shall be no lower than Assistant Special Agent in Charge) may make an application for an order requiring the production of any tangible things (including books, records, papers, documents, and other items) for an investigation to protect against international terrorism or clandestine intelligence activities, provided that such investigation of a United States person is not conducted solely upon the basis of activities protected by the first amendment to the Constitution....

(b) Each application under this section—

  (1) shall be made to—

    (A) a judge of the court established by section 103 (a); ...

(c) (1) Upon an application made pursuant to this section, the judge shall enter an ex parte order as requested, or as modified, approving the release of records if the judge finds that the application meets the requirements of this section.

(2) An order under this subsection shall not disclose that it is issued for purposes of an investigation described in subsection (a).

(d) No person shall disclose to any other person (other than those persons necessary to produce the tangible things under this section) that the Federal Bureau of Investigation has sought or obtained tangible things under this section....

SOURCE: USA PATRIOT Act (H.R.3162). www.epic.org/privacy/terrorism/hr3162.html

---

# ANALYSIS

Section 215 of the Patriot Act allows an FBI agent to obtain a search warrant for "any tangible thing" without demonstrating "probable cause" of an illegal act. Agents need only claim that the desired materials *may* be related to any ongoing investigation related to terrorism or intelligence activities. During the October 2001 Senate debate on the Patriot Act, Senator Russ Feingold stated:

> [U]nder Section 215 of this bill, all business records can be compelled to be produced, including those containing sensitive personal information such as medical records from hospitals or doctors, or educational records, or records of what books someone has taken out of the library. This is an enormous expansion of authority, compounded by the elimination of the requirement that the records have to pertain to an agent of a foreign power. Under this provision, the Government can apparently go on a fishing expedition and collect information on anyone—perhaps someone who has worked with, or lived next door to, or has been seen in the company of, or went to school with, or whose phone number was called by the target of an investigation.... All the FBI has to do is to allege... that the information is sought for an investigation of international terrorism or clandestine intelligence gathering.... This is truly a breathtaking expansion of the police power, one that I do not think is warranted. (*Congressional Record—Senate*, October 11, 2001, pp. S10583–84)

Section 215 is popularly described as the Patriot Act's "library provision" because the library profession has anticipated its use to seize library records and has publicly warned of the abuse of such power. The fact that the first two examples given in Section 215 of materials subject to seizure are "books" and "records" makes librarians' concerns understandable.

Nonetheless, Section 215 is far too broad to be associated with any particular kind of materials. An indication of that breadth was seen in Attorney General Ashcroft's answers to questions from Representative Tammy Baldwin (D-WI) during congressional hearings in 2003.

> **Baldwin:** Prior to the enactment of the USA PATRIOT Act, a FISA order for business records related only to common carriers, accommodation and storage facilities, and vehicle rentals, is that correct?
>
> **Ashcroft:** Yes it is.
>
> **Baldwin:** And what was the evidentiary standard for obtaining that court order?

*Ashcroft:* [Long pause] I don't think the evidentiary standard has changed. [Whispers from Ashcroft's legal staff cause him to turn around.] OK, maybe it has. It used to be that the target is an agent of a foreign power.

*Baldwin:* Right. It was relevance and specific arguable facts giving reason to believe that a person to whom the records related was an agent of a foreign power. Is that your understanding?

*Ashcroft:* I think that sounds good to me.

*Baldwin:* And as evidentiary standards go, that's a pretty low standard, or maybe I should say, it's one of the lower thresholds that's possible, correct?

*Ashcroft:* Well, yeah,…in criminal matters, certainly, they don't have high standards.

*Baldwin:* It's lower than reasonable suspicion or probable cause, is it not?

*Ashcroft:* I think it may be said to be lower than probable cause.

*Baldwin:* Now, under Section 215 the government can obtain any relevant tangible items, is that correct?

*Ashcroft:* I think they are authorized to ask for relevant tangible items.

*Baldwin:* And that would include things like book purchase records?

*Ashcroft:* I think it's possible that, in the narrow arena in which they are authorized to ask, yes.

*Baldwin:* Library book or computer records?

*Ashcroft:* I think it could include library book or computer records.

*Baldwin:* Medical records?

*Ashcroft:* I don't know. Do you guys know? [Turns around to his staff] Some of them are nodding, and some of them are nodding in the other direction.

*Baldwin:* Education records?

*Ashcroft:* I think that there are some education records that would be susceptible to demand under the court's supervision of FISA, yes.

*Baldwin:* Genetic information?

*Ashcroft:* I don't know about that. It might be that DNA in the possession of someone who had committed a crime had taken a drink of water and left a little DNA on the glass. We might be able to get that. (House Judiciary Committee, Hearings on the USA PATRIOT Act, June 5, 2003. Televised on C-SPAN)

### IN HISTORY

#### Does the Patriot Act Override State Confidentiality Statutes?

Although Section 215 of the Patriot Act does not specifically address the question of state statutes, other provisions make the primacy of the Patriot Act clear. Indeed, fears about the loss of state protections were expressed during the October 11, 2001 Senate debate on the Patriot Act when Senator Russ Feingold tried to introduce an amendment that would protect state confidentiality laws:

[M]y fear is that what section 215 does is effectively trump any and all of these State and Federal privacy protections. I think that is a result that most of our citizens and their State representatives would not countenance…. [W]hile the amendment maintains the expansion of the FISA authority to all business records, it also requires the FBI to comply with State and Federal laws that contain a higher standard for the disclosure of certain private information. The amendment makes clear that existing Federal and State statutory protections for the privacy of certain information are not diminished or superseded by section 215. (*Congressional Record—Senate*, October 11, 2001, p. S10584)

Feingold's amendment, like all other attempted amendments to the Patriot Act, was tabled and never reached a full vote.

## FURTHER READINGS

Drake, Miriam A. "Safeguarding Patrons' Privacy: Report from the Field; Teleconference Participants Discuss Patrons' Privacy Amid Passage of USA PATRIOT Act," *Information Today*, 20, no. 35 (February 1, 2003).

Flanders, Laura. "Librarians under Siege," *The Nation* (August 5–12, 2002), pp. 43–44.

Martin, Kathryn. "The USA Patriot Act's Application to Library Patron Records," *Journal of Legislation*, 29, no. 283 (2003).

Minow, Mary. "The USA PATRIOT Act—Three Librarians Explore the Controversial Patriot Act and How You Can Protect Patron Privacy Legally," *Library Journal*, 127, no. 6 (2002), p. 52.

O'Donnell, Michael J. "Reading for Terrorism: Section 215 of the USA PATRIOT Act and the Right to Information Privacy," *Journal of Legislation*, 31, no. 45 (2004).

Strickland, Lee S. "Patriot in the Library: Management Approaches When Demands for Information Are Received from Law Enforcement and Intelligence Agencies," *Journal of College and University Law*, 30, no. 2 (2004), p. 363.

# Detention of Suspected Terrorists

- *Document:* Section 412 of the USA PATRIOT Act of 2001
- *Date:* Signed October 26, 2001
- *Where:* Washington, DC
- *Significance:* Section 412 allows suspected aliens to be detained for 7 days without charge or held indefinitely if determined not to be "removable."

---

## DOCUMENT

### Section 412, USA PATRIOT Act

### *Section 412. Mandatory Detention of Suspected Terrorists; Habeas Corpus; Judicial Review*

(a) IN GENERAL—The Immigration and Nationality Act (8 U.S.C. 1101 et seq.) is amended by inserting after section 236 the following:....

(1) CUSTODY—The Attorney General shall take into custody any alien who is certified under paragraph (3).

(2) RELEASE—Except as provided in paragraphs (5) and (6), the Attorney General shall maintain custody of such an alien until the alien is removed from the United States. Except as provided in paragraph (6), such custody shall be maintained irrespective of any relief from removal for which the alien may be eligible, or any relief from removal granted the alien, until the Attorney General determines that the alien is no longer an alien who may be certified under paragraph (3). If the alien is finally determined not to be removable, detention pursuant to this subsection shall terminate.

(3) CERTIFICATION—The Attorney General may certify an alien under this paragraph if the Attorney General has reasonable grounds to believe that the alien—

(A) is described in section 212(a)(3)(A)(iii), 212(a)(3)(b), 237 (a)(4)(A)(i), 237(a)(4)(A)(iii), or 237(a)(4)(B), or

(B) is engaged in any other activity that endanger the national security of the United States....

(5) COMMENCEMENT OF PROCEEDINGS—The Attorney General shall place an alien detained under paragraph (1) in removal proceedings, or shall charge the alien with a criminal offense, not later than 7 days after the commencement of such detention....

(6) LIMITATION ON INDEFINITE DETENTION—An alien detained solely under paragraph (1) who has not been removed under section 241(a)(1)(A), and whose removal is unlikely in the reasonably foreseeable future, may be detained for additional periods of up to six months only if the release of the alien will threaten the national security of the United States or the safety of the community or any person.

(7) REVIEW OF CERTIFICATION—The Attorney General shall review the certification made under paragraph (3) every 6 months. If the Attorney General determines, in the Attorney General's discretion, that the certification should be revoked, the alien may be released on such conditions as the Attorney General deems appropriate, unless such release is otherwise prohibited by law....

(b) HABEAS CORPUS AND JUDICIAL REVIEW—

(1) IN GENERAL—Judicial review of any action or decision relating to this section including judicial review of the merits of a determination made under subsection (a)(3) or (a)(6) is available exclusively in habeas corpus proceedings consistent with this subsection. Except as provided in the preceding sentence, no court shall have jurisdiction to review, by habeas corpus petition or otherwise, any such action or decision....

SOURCE: USA PATRIOT Act (H.R.3162). www.epic.org/privacy/terrorism/hr3162.html

---

# ANALYSIS

Section 412 and the other immigration provisions of the Patriot act go far beyond exclusion and deportation of aliens. During the Senate debate on the Patriot Act, Senator Jon Corzine (D-NJ) declared

> I am especially concerned about the provisions in this bill that require the detention of immigrants who are not terrorists, who are not criminals, but are merely suspected of future wrongdoing. In fact, these provisions go further than that. Lawful permanent residents who are charged with being deportable on terrorism grounds could be held indefinitely even if an immigration judge determines that the terrorism charges are false. I understand that we need to give the government sufficient authority to protect Americans from those who pose a real threat to public safety. But this provision goes too far. (*Congressional Record—Senate*, October 11, 2001, p. S10588)

As the Patriot Act sailed through Congress, Anita Ramasastry, professor of law at the University of Washington and Associate Director of the Shidler Center for Law, Commerce and Technology, wrote of her personal concern that her husband, an Irish immigrant holding a green card, could be detained indefinitely, locked up, or deported under the new law. She explains, "[I]f my husband were, for example, simply to write a letter to an Irish newspaper that supports the political party Sinn Fein, or give $51 to a friend found to have ties to the IRA, he might be detained indefinitely....Indefinite detention upon secret evidence—which the Patriot Act allows—sounds more like Taliban justice than ours" (Anita Ramasastry,

"Indefinite Detention Based on Suspicion," *FindLaw*, October 5, 2001, p. 1, http:writ/news/findlaw/com/commentary/20011005_ramasastry.html).

Ramasastry notes that the Patriot Act authorizes the deportation of aliens for contributing funds or material support to a terrorist organization or for contributing to *any* organization if the alien knows or reasonably should have known that the contributions would further terrorist activity. Under the Patriot Act, if the Attorney General certifies that an alien *may* facilitate acts of terrorism, the alien will be taken into custody, initially for seven days. During this period the Attorney General must initiate deportation proceedings or charge the person with a crime. As long as the Attorney General initiates removal proceedings within the seven-day period he can continue to detain the person. Indeed, even if an immigration judge concludes that the person is eligible for relief from removal, the Attorney General has explicit authority to continue detention. The individual can be detained indefinitely until either decertified by the Attorney General or released by the District Court. In fact, the Attorney General has the authority to indefinitely detain anyone believed to be engaged in any other activity that endangers the national security of the United States.

David Cole, professor at the Georgetown University Law Center, says the Patriot Act has sacrificed the rights of immigrants—especially Arab and Muslim immigrants—for the purported security of the rest of us.

> Congress has made immigrants deportable for their political associations and excludable for pure speech, and subject to indefinite detention on the basis of an executive official's certification....Before the advent of the Patriot Act, immigrants were deportable for engaging in or supporting *terrorist activity*. The Patriot Act makes them deportable for virtually any *associational activity* with a terrorist organization, irrespective of whether the alien's support has any connection to an act of violence, much less terrorism. (David Cole, "Terrorizing Immigrants in the Name of Fighting Terrorism," *Human Rights* (Winter 2002), p. 11)

The Patriot Act also resurrects ideological exclusion, the practice of denying entry to aliens for pure speech. It excludes aliens who "endorse or espouse terrorist activity" or who "persuade others to support terrorist activity or a terrorist organization." Cole concludes, "Excluding people for their ideas is flatly contrary to the spirit of freedom for which the United States stands" (ibid.).

# FURTHER READINGS

Davis, Derek. "The Dark Side to a Just War: The USA PATRIOT Act and Counterterrorism's Potential Threat to Religious Freedom," *Journal of Church and State*, 44, no. 1 (2002), p. 5.

Germain, Regina. "Rushing to Judgment: The Unintended Consequences of the USA PATRIOT Act for Bona Fide Refugees," *Georgetown Immigration Law Journal*, 16, Part 2 (2002), p. 505.

Ivey, Lisa M. "Ready, Aim, Fire: The President's Executive Order Authorizing Detention, Treatment, and Trial of Certain Non-Citizens in the War against Terrorism Is a Powerful Weapon, But Should It Be Upheld?" *Cumberland Law Review*, 33, no. 1(2002), p. 107.

McWhirter, Robert James. *The Criminal Lawyer's Guide to Immigration Law: Questions and Answers: 2002 Supplement—USA PATRIOT Act (2003)*. Chicago: American Bar Association, 2003.

"Symposium: Civil Liberties after September 11th: A Closer Look at Detention Powers," *Connecticut Law Review*, 34 no. 6 (2002), p.1081.

Weiss, Dana B. "Protecting America First: Deporting Aliens Associated with Designated Terrorist Organizations That Have Committed Terrorism in America in the Face of Actual Threats to National Security," *Cleveland State Law Review*, 50, no. 2 (2003), p. 307.

# A New Definition of Terrorism

- *Document:* Section 802 of the USA PATRIOT Act of 2001
- *Date:* Signed October 26, 2001
- *Where:* Washington, DC
- *Significance:* A new crime called "domestic terrorism" was introduced in Section 802 of the Patriot Act. The definition is broad enough to include constitutionally protected acts of disobedience by civil rights and environmental groups.

## DOCUMENT

### Section 802, USA PATRIOT Act

### *Section 802. Definition of Domestic Terrorism*

(A) domestic terrorism defined—section 2331 of title 18, United States Code, is amended—....

(B) (5) the term "domestic terrorism" means activities that—

(A) involve acts dangerous to human life that are a violation of the criminal laws of the United States or of any State;

'(B) appear to be intended—

(i) to intimidate or coerce a civilian population;

(ii) to influence the policy of a government by intimidation of coercion; or

(iii) to affect the conduct of a government by mass destruction, assassination, or kidnapping; and

(C) occur primarily within the territorial jurisdiction of the United States....

SOURCE: USA PATRIOT Act (H.R.3162). www.epic.org/privacy/terrorism/hr3162.html

# ANALYSIS

Section 802 of the Patriot Act provides a broad new definition of domestic terrorism and Sections 803 through 813 flush out the details:

Section 802: Definition of Domestic Terrorism
Section 803: Prohibition against Harboring Terrorists
Section 804: Jurisdiction over Crimes Committed at U.S. Facilities Abroad
Section 805: Material Support for Terrorism
Section 806: Assets of Terrorist Organizations
Section 807: Technical Clarification Relating to Provision of Material Support to Terrorism
Section 808: Definition of Federal Crime of Terrorism
Section 809: No Statute of Limitation for Certain Terrorism Offenses
Section 810: Alternative Maximum Penalties for Terrorism Offenses
Section 811: Penalties for Terrorist Conspiracies
Section 812: Post-Release Supervision of Terrorists
Section 813: Inclusion of Acts of Terrorism as Racketeering Activity

The Justice Department's original draft of these sections included a laundry list of more than forty federal crimes ranging from computer hacking to malicious mischief to the use of weapons of mass destruction, all of which were designated as "Federal terrorism offenses." Crimes on the list would carry no statute of limitations. Penalties would include life imprisonment, and those released earlier would be subject to a lifetime of supervised release.

Senator Patrick Leahy succeeded in negotiating some improvements to the original draft, reducing the list of crimes that could be considered as terrorism and introducing more measured increases in penalties, depending on the severity of the offense, but the scope of the new definitions and their application are still dramatic. Section 802 expands the type of conduct that the government can investigate when it is investigating "terrorism." The American Civil Liberties Union (ACLU) has pointed out that the new definition of domestic terrorism is broad enough to encompass the activities of prominent activist campaigns and organizations such as Greenpeace, Operation Rescue, the Environmental Liberation Front, and protesters at the World Trade Organization and Vieques Island. The latter, a protest against the U.S. Army's use of the Puerto Rican island for weapons testing, was analyzed by the ACLU as an example of the vulnerability of protesters under the Patriot Act.

In 2002, when many people, including several prominent Americans, participated in civil disobedience at the military installation on Vieques Island, the protesters illegally entered the military base and tried to obstruct the bombing exercises. This conduct would fall within the Patriot Act's definition of domestic terrorism because the acts broke federal law and were for the purpose of influencing a government policy by intimidation or coercion. The disruption of the bombing exercises arguably created a danger to human life—that of the protesters and of military personnel. Since the Vieques protests fell within the new definition of domestic terrorism, the ACLU noted some of the penalties faced by the protesters.

First, Section 806 could be invoked, resulting in the civil seizure of the protesters' assets without a prior hearing and without them ever being convicted of a crime. The language is broad enough to authorize the government to seize any assets of any individuals involved in the Vieques Island protests or of any organization supporting the protests or from any individuals who were supporting the protesters in any way. Possible supporters of the Vieques protesters could include student organizations that sponsored participation in the demonstration, the Rainbow/Push Coalition, the Rev. Al Sharpton's National Action Network, and religious or community organizations that provided housing or food to the protesters.

Section 507 could be invoked, allowing the government to obtain private educational records if the Attorney General or his designee certifies that the records are necessary for investigating domestic terrorism. No independent judicial finding is required to verify that the records are relevant. Student protesters at Vieques could thus have their private records seized, including their grades, medical information, counseling, organizations the student belonged to, or any other student information collected by the educational institution.

Section 508 allows the government to obtain educational records of the Vieques protesters collected pursuant to the National Education Statistics Act. This would include a vast amount of student information from academic performance to health information, family income, and race. Until now, this information has been held to strict confidentiality requirements. Now, all the government needs to certify is that the information is relevant to a terrorism investigation.

Section 219 could be invoked against the Vieques protesters, allowing the government to go to a single judge to get a warrant to search the property or person of the Vieques activists in New York, Chicago, or wherever the protesters are from.

The ACLU makes clear that it does not oppose criminal prosecution of people who violate the law, even if they are doing it for political purposes, but they do oppose the Patriot Act's broad definition of terrorism and the authority that flows from that definition. The ACLU concludes:

> One way to ensure that the conduct that falls within the definition of domestic terrorism is in fact terrorism is to limit the scope of the conduct that triggers the definition. Thus, domestic terrorism could include acts which "cause serious physical injury or death" rather than all acts that are "dangerous to human life." This more narrow definition will exclude the conduct of organizations and individuals that engage in minor acts of property damage or violence. ("How the USA PATRIOT Act Redefines Domestic Terrorism," American Civil Liberties Union, December 6, 2002. www.aclu.org/natsec/emergpowers/14444leg20021206.html)

# FURTHER READINGS

Boykoff, Jules. "'Terrorism' or Terrorism?: A Case of Selective Morality," *Common Dreams News Center* (August 9, 2006). www.commondreams.org/views06/0129-31html

Farrington, Jay P. *Domestic Terrorism*. New York: Barnes & Noble, 2001.

Hentoff, Nat. "A Senate Coalition of Conscience," *Jewish World Review* (February 19, 2004). www.NewsandOpinion.com

Levin, John. *Domestic Terrorism*, New York: Chelsea House Publications, 2006.

McDonnell, James F. *Constitutional Issues in Federal Management of Domestic Terrorism Incidents*, New York: University/Barnes & Noble, 2004.

Ross, Gretchen. "Defining Domestic Terrorism," *Newtopia Magazine* (July 23, 2005). www.newtopiamagazine.net/articles/60

# Domestic Surveillance under the Patriot Act

Figure 5. Cartoon of John Ashcroft. Cagle Cartoons, Inc., © 2003.

# Searches and Seizures under the Patriot Act

- **Documents:** Attorney General John Ashcroft's 2003 congressional testimony on the FBI's use of delayed notices ("sneak and peek") for searches and seizures; cover letter to April 28, 2006 Department of Justice report to Congress on Patriot Act surveillance during 2005, highlighting the use of National Security Letters
- **Date:** Congressional hearings on June 5, 2003; cover letter and report dated April 28, 2006
- **Where:** Washington, DC
- **Significance:** Attorney General Ashcroft's June 2003 congressional testimony was the first public disclosure of the use of "sneak and peek" searches and seizures; the April 2006 Justice Department report was its first release of data on the use of National Security Letters (NSLs), a form of administrative subpoena that had been heavily used since being facilitated by the Patriot Act. The Justice Department figure of 9,254 NSLs issued during 2005 was considerably smaller than reported earlier by the *Washington Post*, but was substantial nonetheless.

---

# DOCUMENTS

## 1. Attorney General Ashcroft's June 2003 Testimony on Delayed Searches and Seizures

Can we delay giving notice of the search being made? Now, we have requested delayed notice of search 47 times under this provision, and the Court has granted every one of the requests. In addition to the delayed notice of search, we can give delayed notice of seizure; in other words, evidence can be taken but not notice given of that evidence taken till the Court has said it should be given. We have asked for that 15 times. In 14 cases the Court said, yes, you can do that. In the 15th case the Court said why don't you just take a picture of it and leave it? And that'll be good enough. And obviously, that's what we did. The most common period of delays has been 7 days…and there has been a delay as long as 90 days. The Department sometimes has to seek an extension in the period of delayed notice, and we've made a number of those requests. No court has ever rejected a request for an extension by the Justice Department.

SOURCE: Hearing before the Committee on the Judiciary, House of Representatives, 108th Congress, 1st Session, June 5, 2003, p. 37. Washington, DC: U.S. Government Printing Office, 2003.

## 2. Cover Letter to April 28, 2006 Department of Justice Report to Congress

April 28, 2006

U.S. Department of Justice
Office of Legislative Affairs
Office of the Assistant Attorney General

The Honorable J. Dennis Hastert
Speaker
United States House of Representatives
Washington, DC 20515

Dear Mr. Speaker:
During calendar year 2005, the Government made requests for certain information concerning 3,501 different United States persons pursuant to National Security Letters (NSLs). During this time frame, the total number of NSL requests (excluding NSLs for subscriber information) for information concerning U.S. persons totaled 9,254. In other words, there were 3,501 different U.S. persons involved in the total of 9,254 NSLs that related to U.S. persons.…
A similar letter has been sent to the Minority Leader, the Honorable Nancy Pelosi.

Sincerely,
William E. Moschella
Assistant Attorney General

SOURCE: *Foreign Intelligence Surveillance Act 2005 Annual Report*, Department of Justice. www.fas.org/irp/agency/doj/fisa/2005rept.html

# ANALYSIS

The Patriot Act's broad authorization of delayed notice ("sneak and peek") searches and seizures was regarded as controversial when first proposed, but it has been strongly defended by the Justice Department. In response to critics of Section 213, Attorney General Ashcroft told Congress: "For us to begin to limit the ability to use this law enforcement tool I think would expose the American people to jeopardy because we would have less capacity to enforce the law and keep people safe.… So what the PATRIOT Act did was to make the law a national law, which had previously been sort of varying in different areas."

The Justice Department responded to questions from the House Judiciary Committee with the following statement:

> Section 213 has been essential in increasing the safety of government officials and witnesses as well as the effectiveness of terrorist investigations. Advanced notification to terrorist suspects of searches or surveillances could result in destroyed evidence, notification of co-conspirators, attacks on agents and potential witnesses, or even the immediate execution of a terrorist plot. Between October 26, 2001, and the spring of 2003, 47 delayed notice warrants had been issued. Those instances include cases which have since been charged, e.g., *United States v. Odeh*, a narco-terrorism case, and *United States v. Dhafir*, a money-laundering case, and others still pending. Section 213 has allowed investigators to obtain decisive evidence for the prosecution of serious offenders. (Hearing before the Committee on the Judiciary, House of Representatives, 108th Congress, 1st Session, June 5, 2003, pp. 37, 118. Washington, DC: U.S. Government Printing Office, 2003)

Because of the government's ability to delay notification of search warrants and to extend those delays by request, little is known about the specific individuals or businesses that have been subject to "sneak and peek" warrants. Somewhat more is known about two other Patriot Act provisions, Section 215 (the business records section allowing seizure of "any tangible thing") and Section 505 (facilitating the use of National Security records). Because these two provisions have been associated with the seizure of library records, the library profession has lobbied aggressively and publicly against their use. Although the gag orders associated with both Section 215 and National Security Letters have made it impossible to conclusively verify their use in libraries, anonymous surveys and testimony strongly suggest that both have been used. The Justice Department has categorically denied any use of Section 215, telling Congress in 2003: "On September 18, 2003, the Attorney General declassified the number of times to date the Department of Justice, including

**U.S Department of Justice**
**Federal Bureau of Investigation**

In reply, Please Refer to
File No. ███████

███████████████
███████████████
███████████████

Dear ████████

Under the authority of Executive Order 12333, dated December 4, 1981, and pursuant to Title 18, United States Code (U.S.C.), Section 2709 (as amended, October 26, 2001), you are hereby directed to provide to the Federal Bureau of Investigation (FBI) any and all subscriber information, billing information and access logs of any person or entity related to the following:

████████████████████████

In accordance with Title 18, U.S.C.. Section 2709(b), I certify that the information sought is relevant to an authorized investigation to protect against international terrorism or clandestine intelligence activities, and that such an investigation of a United States person is not conducted solely on the basis of activities protected by the first amendment to the Constitution of the United States.

You are further advised that Title 18, U.S.C., Section 2709(c), prohibits any officer, employee or agent of your from disclosing to any person that the FBI has sought or obtained access to information or records under these provisions.

You are requested to provide records responsive to this request <u>personally</u> to a representative ████████ of the FBI. ████████ of the records are requested, if available. Any questions you have regarding this request should be directed only to the ████████. Due to security considerations, you should neither send the records through the mail nor disclose the substance of this request in any telephone conversation or electronic communication.

Your cooperation in this matter is greatly appreciated.

Sincerely,

██████████████████

Figure 6. A redacted sample of a National Security Letter.

the Federal Bureau of Investigation (FBI), had utilized Section 215 of the USA PATRIOT Act relating to the production of business records. At that time, the number of times Section 215 was used was zero" (Hearing before the Committee on the Judiciary, House of Representatives, 108th Congress, 1st Session, June 5, 2003, p. 19).

No such disclaimer has been issued with respect to the use of National Security Letters. In fact, in a July 26, 2002 letter to the House Judiciary Committee Assistant Attorney General Daniel J. Bryant answered a question about the use of Section 215 to acquire library records as follows: "If the FBI were authorized to obtain the [library] information the more appropriate tool for requesting electronic communication transactional records would be a National Security Letter (NSL)" (Letter from Daniel J. Bryant, Assistant Attorney General, to F. James Sensenbrenner, Jr., Chairman, Committee on the Judiciary, U.S. House of Representatives, July 26, 2002, p. 4).

From the time of the passage of the Patriot Act in October 2001 until late 2005, no official count of the government's use of NSLs was available to the public. The library community, the most vocal critics of Patriot Act surveillance, was more concerned about the use of Section 215, which appeared to target the kinds of records maintained by libraries. But when the Justice Department revealed that they considered NSLs to be the most appropriate tool for seizing library records, everyone began asking about this hitherto overlooked surveillance order. What are NSLs, what are they used for, and how often has the government used them?

At the January 2004 American Library Association (ALA) conference in Toronto, Chuck Rosenberg, then counsel to FBI Director Robert Mueller, was asked to provide the ALA with sample copies of the kinds of surveillance orders libraries were likely to receive, particularly NSLs. Rosenberg responded, "I think that's fair.... Why don't you call me and I'll see if I can get you some of those. You realize, we would have to redact some information out of them" (Chuck Rosenberg, counsel to FBI Director Robert Mueller, Remarks at the American Library Association Annual Conference, June 21, 2003, Toronto, Canada).

The ALA pursued the request as suggested, but no sample copies of NSLs or any other surveillance orders were forthcoming. Many months later, several news organizations managed to acquire redacted copies of NSLs, and a sample is shown in Figure 6. Information redacted from the form includes:

1. the file number
2. the identity and address of the official authorizing the order and the individual or entity on whom the order is served
3. the individual(s) or group(s) whose subscriber information, billing information and access logs are sought
4. the FBI representative to whom the requested records should be provided
5. the format in which the requested records should be provided
6. the Justice Department representative or office to whom all questions should be addressed.

In the first paragraph, of the sample NSL, the parenthetic "as amended October 26, 2001" refers to the passage of the Patriot Act. The second paragraph reveals the lowered standard for authorizing NSLs, mere "relevance," as opposed to the earlier requirement to show "specific and articulable" reasons to believe that the records sought belong to a terrorist or spy. The second paragraph suggests some constitutional restraints on the use of NSLs, prohibiting their use in an investigation conducted "solely" on the basis of activities protected by the First Amendment.

This unfortunate wording, created by the Patriot Act, would allow the government to direct its investigations "primarily" or "overwhelmingly" or "almost completely" against constitutionally protected activities. Anything other than "solely." And, of course, for non-U.S. persons there are no restrictions of any kind.

The third paragraph contains the notorious gag order provision, which prohibits the recipient or any associate "from disclosing to *any person* [emphasis added] that the FBI has sought or obtained access to" the records in question.

Under what authority are NSLs issued, how often have they been used since the passage of the Patriot Act and for what purposes? NSLs can be issued by any FBI field supervisor without the need for authorization from a prosecutor, a grand jury, or a judge. After their issuance, they receive no review from the Justice Department or Congress. Little was known about the frequency of use of NSLs until a lengthy, detailed study of NSLs, published by the *Washington Post* on November 6, 2005, revealed that the FBI "now issues more than 30,000 national security letters a year, according to government sources" (Barton Gelman, "The FBI's Secret Scrutiny," *Washington Post*, November 6, 2005, p. A1).

Shortly after the *Washington Post* story, the Justice Department felt compelled to release their own official figures on NSL use. Those figures, shown in the document heading this section, indicate that 9,254 NSLs were issued during 2005 that related to U.S. persons, excluding NSLs for subscriber information. Since subscriber information is the first item requested in the sample NSL shown above, we can assume that adding such NSLs to the total would increase it substantially. In addition, since the Justice Department figure includes only those NSLs relating to U.S. persons, and since many, if not most, NSLs are directed at aliens, the figure would again grow considerably, perhaps reaching the 30,000 estimate given to the *Post* by government sources. NSLs are particularly useful in acquiring electronic communications, allowing investigators to sift through the private affairs of anyone venturing into cyberspace. It can reveal how and where a person earns a living; how he spends his money; how much he gambles, borrows or pawns; who telephones or e-mails him at home or at work; and a wide variety of other activities and communications.

# FURTHER READINGS

American Civil Liberties Union. "Unpatriotic Acts: The FBI's Power to Rifle through Your Records and Personal Belongings Without Telling You," www.aclu.org/SafeandFree/SafeandFree.cfm?ID=13246&c=

Jenner & Block, LLC. Memorandum on National Security Letters from Theresa Chmara to Freedom to Read Foundation Board, January 21, 2003, p. 7.

"Let the Sun Set on PATRIOT—Section 215," Electronic Frontier Foundation, 2006. www.eff.org/patriot/sunset/215.php.

Lithwick, Dahlia. "A Guide to the Patriot Act, Part 4: Section 505, aka 'National Insecurity—Complex Letters," *Slate*, September 11, 2003. wwwlslate.com/id/2088239

Trivedi, Neema. "Section 215 of the USA PATRIOT Act and National Security Letters: An Update," The Free Expression Policy Project, October 2005. www.fepproject.org/commentaries/patriotact.oct2005

"Why the ACLU Is Right to Challenge the FBI's Access to Library, Bookstore, and Business Records under the USA PATRIOT Act," August 6, 2003. http://writ.corporate.find law.com/ramasastry/20030806

# Gag Orders Impede Documentation of Patriot Act Surveillance

- **Document:** Commentary from Chuck Rosenberg, Personal Counsel to FBI Director William Mueller, during press conference at the 2003 American Library Association (ALA) Annual Conference in Toronto, Canada
- **Date:** June 21, 2003
- **Where:** Toronto, Canada
- **Significance:** Under the Patriot Act, enforced silence is imposed on anyone receiving a warrant or subpoena issued under Section 215 or through a National Security Letter. Ambiguity continues to surround the length of the period of these gag orders and the penalties to be imposed. Mr. Rosenberg's answers to questions from Herbert Foerstel suggest that the gag orders are of indefinite duration.

---

## DOCUMENT

### Chuck Rosenberg's Response to Questions from Herbert Foerstel at ALA Press Conference

*Rosenberg:* I'm convinced that the gag order was not aimed at libraries. It was intended in the same way that prohibitions on disclosure are used in other places in the Federal Code.

*Foerstel:* But when do they end?

*Rosenberg:* They don't necessarily end because the purpose behind them is to protect the integrity of any ongoing investigation.

*Foerstel:* So when the investigation ends, librarians should be able to speak freely of the visit?

*Rosenberg:* I don't think that's the case.

*Foerstel:* I don't either.

*Rosenberg:* Nor do I think it should be, and I'll tell you why. In the grand jury context, for instance, grand jury proceedings are secret, and the intent is that they remain secret in perpetuity.

*Foerstel:* That's what I was afraid of.

SOURCE: Chuck Rosenberg, counsel to FBI Director Robert Mueller, at American Library Association Annual Conference, June 21, 2003, Toronto, Canada.

---

# ANALYSIS

Several provisions of the Patriot Act impose a nondisclosure requirement or gag order on persons served with a surveillance, search, or seizure order. The wording in Section 215 is: "No person shall disclose to any other person (other than those persons necessary to produce the tangible things under this section) that the Federal Bureau of Investigation has sought or obtained tangible things under this section." Another frequently used seizure order, a National Security Letter, contains a similar gag order provision.

Author and First Amendment advocate Nat Hentoff warns, "Because of the chilling effect of this section of the U.S.A. Patriot Act, it's uncertain how many booksellers and librarians will even call a lawyer. And for those who do, it's difficult to predict how successful a court challenge will be in the present, and long-term, atmospheres of fear of shadowy terrorists among us" (Nat Hentoff, "The FBI among the Bookshelves," *Jewish World Review*, February 25, 2002. www.jewishworldreview.com/cols/hentoff022502.asp).

Judith Krug, director of the American Library Association's Office of Intellectual Freedom, advised librarians, "I have been told that…the FBI has made at least three visitations under Section 215. That's the only information I have. I don't know if the searches have been in libraries or bookstores, and I can't reveal my sources without putting them in danger of punishment for disobeying a court order" (Nat Hentoff, "Are You Reading the Wrong Books?" *Smirking Chimp.com*, March 24, 2002, p. 3. www.smirkingchimp.com/article. php?sid=5827).

The imposition of gag orders on those served with legal orders under the Patriot Act makes it difficult to document the extent of current surveillance. The American Booksellers Foundation for Free Expression (ABFFE) has sent a letter to booksellers across the country advising them of their legal rights and obligations under the Patriot Act. "You remain entitled to legal counsel," says the letter. "Therefore, you may call your attorney and/or (the Booksellers Foundation or, if a librarian, the American Library Association) and simply tell us that you need to contact our legal counsel. Because of the gag order, however, you should not tell us that you have received a court order" (Nat Hentoff, "The FBI among the Bookshelves," *Jewish World Review*, February 25, 2002. www.jewishworldreview. com/cols/hentoff022502.asp).

Under the Patriot Act, anyone violating a gag order faces felony charges with heavy criminal penalties.

## IN HISTORY

### Do Gag Orders Impose Secrecy on Legal Challenges to the Patriot Act?

Critics of the Patriot Act believe that provisions like Section 215 are unconstitutional and that a court challenge would be successful. But would the Patriot Act's gag orders prevent a public hearing on the constitutionality of its powerful search authorities? Author and civil libertarian Nat Hentoff asks,

What happens when there is an actual case contesting these searches—will those court proceedings themselves be subject to a gag order under the Patriot Act? Attorneys who work with the American Library Association and the ABFFE [American Booksellers Foundation for Free Expression] have suggested that the gag order may indeed prevent the press, and therefore the public, from knowing about subsequent court proceedings. (Nat Hentoff, "Are You Reading the Wrong Books," *SmirkingChimp. com*, March 24, 2002)

An answer to this hypothetical quandary came in 2006 when a group of Connecticut librarians brought suit against the Justice Department, challenging the Patriot Act's gag orders (see Chapter 7). The result was a mixture of secrecy and public debate. The plaintiffs were forced to file suit under the anonymous pseudonym "John Doe," but the case, *Doe v. Gonzalez*, produced a compromise that placed limits on Patriot Act gag orders.

When Maurice Freedman, past president of the American Library Association, was asked why more librarians have not challenged the gag orders on constitutional grounds, he answered, "Because it's a felony.... If they challenge the constitutionality of it they have to say that they have had this unconstitutional request made of them. As soon as they open their mouth about that, they have committed a felony. People use the word gag order, but gag order isn't as strong as felony, which is what is written into the Patriot Act" ("Ashcroft Declassifies Number of Records Sought under Patriot Act," *Democracy Now*, September 18, 2003, p. 4. www.democracynow.org/article.pl?sid=03/09/18/).

Some librarians have attempted an end run around the gag orders by using a negative to make a positive. For instance, Anne Turner, chief librarian in Santa Cruz, California, says she reports to her library board in a roundabout way: "At each board meeting I tell them we have not been served by any [Patriot Act search warrants]. In any months that I don't tell them that, they'll know" (Bob Egelko, "Librarians Try to Alter Patriot Act," *San Francisco Chronicle*, March 10, 2003, p. 2).

The Patriot Act's severe penalties for violating gag orders forced librarians to use imaginative devices such as the one employed by Anne Turner in California. It was almost five years before a small group of bold librarians stepped forward to directly challenge the constitutionality of Patriot Act gag orders. Even then, the threat of felony charges forced them to maintain their anonymity in initiating two landmark court challenges, *John Doe v. Ashcroft* and *John Doe v. Gonzales*. The results of those cases are discussed in detail in Chapter 7.

# FURTHER READINGS

Blumner, Robyn. "National Security Letters Put Privacy at Risk," *St. Petersburg Times Online*, November 13, 2005. www.sptimes.com/2005/11/13/Columns/National_security_let.shtml

Coyle, Karen. "Make Sure You Are Privacy Literate: Three Librarians Explore This Controversial Act and How You Can Protect Privacy without Breaking the Law," *Library Journal*, 127, no. 54 (October 1, 2002).

Piore, Adam. "Librarians Keep Quiet," *Newsweek* (October 28, 2002), p. 12.

"USA PATRIOT Act Use for Library Records," *Confessions of a Mad Librarian*, August 26, 2005. http://edwards.orcas.net/blog/archives/000303.html

"What We Know about Bookstore and Library Searches Since 9/11," Campaign for Reader Privacy, 2005. www.readerprivacy.org/info.jsp?id=4

# Library Surveys Reveal FBI Surveillance

- **Document:** University of Illinois Library Research Center (LRC) Survey
- **Date:** Mailed October 2002
- **Where:** Distributed to libraries nationally
- **Significance:** The library profession quickly learned that the most effective way to assemble data on FBI visits to libraries was through anonymous surveys of librarians receiving such orders. In this way, librarians could skirt the gag rules attached to Patriot Act surveillance provisions and avoid prosecution.

---

## DOCUMENT

### Public Libraries and Civil Liberties—Questionnaire—Public Libraries Response to the Events of 9/11/2001: One Year Later

(Library Research Center, Graduate School of Library and Information Science, University of Illinois)

1. In response to events of September 11, 2001, to the best of your knowledge, has your library changed any of its policies regarding patron use of the Internet?

    Yes................................................... 9.7%

    No.................................................... 90.3%....

5. Has your library adopted or changed any policies in response to the passage of the USA PATRIOT Act?

    Yes................................................... 7.2%

    No.................................................... 78.3%

    No, but in process of developing policies..... 14.5%....

7. Have you received any expression of concern from patrons about their privacy under the USA PATRIOT Act?

    Yes................................................... 7.1%

    No.................................................... 92.9%....

9. Have authorities (e.g., FBI, INS, police officers) requested information about any of your patrons since September 11, 2001?

        Yes.................................................... 10.7%

        No.................................................... 89.3%

10. About how many separate requests about your patrons have you received since September 11, 2001?

        Only 1............................................ 81.3%

        2–5............................................... 18.1%

        6–10.............................................. 0.6%

        More than 10.................................... 0.0%

11. Who requested information?

        FBI............................................... 32.6%

        INS............................................... 0.6%

        Police............................................ 68.2%

        Secret Service.................................. 0.6%

        Other............................................ 7.6%

12. What kinds of information were requested?

        Information about specific library materials....... 5.4%

        Information about a specific patron............... 76.0%

        Other............................................ 22.3%

13. a. What form(s) did the request take?

        Verbal request for voluntary cooperation......... 83.1%

        Written request for voluntary cooperation...... 8.9%

        Subpoena......................................... 22.3%

        Court order...................................... 17.4%

   b. Did you cooperate?

        Yes.............................................. 49.7%

        No.............................................. 50.3%

14. If one or more requests was a court order, did any of the orders prohibit you from telling patrons that the authorities had requested information about them?

        Yes.............................................. 3.1%

        No.............................................. 14.3%

        No court order received.......................... 82.6%

15.a. Did any of the court orders reference Section 215 of the Patriot Act or Title 50, Section 1862 of the United States Code?

        Yes.............................................. 10.3%

        No.............................................. 89.7%

   b. If Yes, How many orders did you receive?

        Only 1............................................ 33.3%

        2–5.............................................. 66.7%....

20. As noted above, the Patriot Act contains provisions that prohibit those served with requests from disclosing the specifics of those requests to anyone else. Do you feel this is an abridgment of First Amendment rights?

        Yes.............................................. 59.9%

        No.............................................. 37.2%

        No opinion....................................... 14.9%

        Depends, no clear answer......................... 1.1%

        Don't know....................................... 2.1%.

28. If law enforcement officials asked you for information about one of your patrons and ordered you not to disclose that they had asked for information, would you challenge their order by disclosing the request to anyone (e.g., the patron, the press, and/or a public interest organization such as the ACLU) other than your library's attorney?

| | |
|---|---|
| Definitely would | 5.5% |
| Probably would | 16.1% |
| Probably would not | 53.7% |
| Definitely would not | 21.4% |
| Depends, no clear answer | 1.0% |
| Refused to answer question | 1.0% |
| Don't know | 1.3% |

SOURCE: Public Libraries Response to the Events of 9/11/2001: One Year Later. Library Research Center, Graduate School of Library and Information Science, University of Illinois. (Published in *Refuge of a Scoundrel: The Patriot Act in Libraries*, by Herbert Foerstel, Westport, CT: Libraries Unlimited, 2004.)

---

# ANALYSIS

Surveys have always been useful in revealing patterns of behavior that serve the public interest. Voting counts, consumer preferences, and TV ratings are among the behavior patterns most commonly documented through surveys. But in many ways, the surveys conducted by librarians following the passage of the Patriot Act were among the most significant use of this tool. Why? Because the behavior patterns revealed were secret government activities, the dissemination of which would have been a felony if the names of any libraries or librarians had been included. Gag orders imposed on all libraries and librarians served with Patriot Act search orders made it impossible to document the use of the new surveillance authorities in libraries, *except* through anonymous surveys.

The national study shown in the document above asked directors of 1,505 public libraries to describe how they have adapted their library policies to the post-9/11 society and to the passage of the Patriot Act. Perhaps the most surprising revelations in the survey came in the answers to questions concerning the numbers and kinds of court orders served on libraries. Question 15 asked: "Did any of the court orders reference Section 215 of the Patriot Act or Title 50, Section 1862 of the United States Code?" Despite the fact that Attorney General Ashcroft has claimed that Section 215 has *never* been used in libraries, 10.3% of respondents to the survey answered "Yes." Given the large number of respondents, this represents a significant contradiction to official claim of zero use.

Some state library associations have attempted to survey local libraries on their response to the Patriot Act. The most prominent of these state surveys was conducted by the California Library Association (CLA). The CLA questionnaire was distributed to 344 public, academic, school, and special libraries during September 2002, and its results are summarized below.

1. What type library are you affiliated with?

| | |
|---|---|
| Public: | 260 (75%) |
| Academic: | 47 (14%) |
| School: | 11 (3%) |
| Special: | 10 (3%) |
| Library school: | 6 (2%) |
| Other: | 10 (3%) |
| | 344 (100%).... |

4. Has your library instituted any new policies as a result of the USA PATRIOT Act?

| | |
|---|---|
| Yes: | 140 (41%) |
| No: | 201 (59%).... |

13. Among your stakeholders, who has expressed concern about the potential impact of the Patriot Act on library confidentiality? Check all that apply.

| | |
|---|---|
| Library administrators: | 190 (57%) |
| Library staff: | 239 (71%) |
| Library board members: | 116 (35%) |
| Library users: | 141 (42%) |
| Library volunteers: | 45 (13%) |
| Local government officials: | 70 (21%) |
| Local reporters: | 85 (25%) |
| No one: | 42 (13%) |
| Other: | 18 (5%) |

14. Has your library had any informal contact from the FBI since September 11, 2001?

| | |
|---|---|
| Yes: | 16 (5%) |
| No: | 304 (95%) |

15. If your library had informal contact from the FBI after September 11, 2001, did your library comply with its requests?

| | |
|---|---|
| Yes: | 6 (3%) |
| No: | 31 (13%) |
| Not applicable: | 198 (84%) |

16. Has your library had any formal contact from the FBI since September 11, 2001?

| | |
|---|---|
| Yes: | 14 (4%) |
| No: | 298 (96%) |

17. If your library had formal contact from the FBI since September 11, 2001, did you comply with their requests?

| | |
|---|---|
| Yes: | 11 (5%) |
| No: | 15 (6%) |
| Not applicable: | 217 (89%) |

Karen Schneider, chair of the CLA Intellectual Freedom Committee, oversaw the California survey. She said she constructed the survey so that respondents provided no personally identifiable information, thus shielding them from felony prosecution for violating a gag order. The CLA survey used the term "formal contact" to mean an official government visit under a court order. Schneider explained,

On the "formal" visits we left it intentionally vague. We set up the survey so we would not receive personal information. This not only protects the respondents but protects us as well. The government is not going to be able to come after us and get personal information because we haven't gathered it. We also steered clear of FISA or Section 215 questions. To some extent, that was to build the confidence of respondents, but I wouldn't be surprised if some of those authorities were used within the "formal" visits documented. I didn't expect so many libraries to actually reveal they had experienced "formal" government visits. (Author interview with Karen Schneider, California Library Association, October 20, 2003)

# FURTHER READINGS

Estabrook, Leigh S. "Public Libraries and Civil Liberties: A Profession Divided," Library Research Center, University of Illinois at Urbana-Champaign, January 22, 2002.

———. "Public Libraries' Response to the Events of 9/11/2001: One Year Later," Library Research Center, University of Illinois at Urbana Champaign, October 2002, p. 1. www.lis.uiuc.edu/glis/research/finalresults.pdf

———. "Public Libraries' Responses to September 11, 2001. http://alexia.lis.uiuc.edu/-leighe/02PLA.ppt

———. "The Response of Public Libraries to the Events of September 11, 2002," *Illinois Libraries* (Winter 2002).

Schneider, Karen G. "The Patriot Act: Last Refuge of a Scoundrel," *American Libraries* (March 2002).

# Attorney General John Ashcroft Ridicules Charges of Library Surveillance

- **Documents:** Speech by Attorney General John Ashcroft at National Restaurant Association Conference
- **Date:** September 15, 2003
- **Where:** Washington, DC
- **Significance:** In response to complaints from library administrators about surveillance of libraries under the Patriot Act, Attorney General Ashcroft dismisses such concerns as groundless hysteria.

---

# DOCUMENT

## Speech by Attorney General John Ashcroft before the National Restaurant Association

Unfortunately, at this moment Washington is involved in a debate where hysteria threatens to obscure the most important issues.... According to these breathless reports and baseless hysteria, some have convinced the American Library Association that under the bipartisanly enacted PATRIOT Act, the FBI is not fighting terrorism; instead, agents are checking how far you've gotten in the latest Tom Clancy novel.

Now you may have thought with all of this hysteria and hyperbole something had to be wrong. Do we at the Justice Department really care what you are reading? No. The law enforcement community has no interest in your reading habits. Tracking reading habits would betray our high regard for the First Amendment, and even if someone in government wanted to do so, it would represent an impossible workload and a waste of law enforcement resources.... [W]ith only 11,000 FBI agents in the entire country, it's simply ridiculous to think that we would track what citizens are reading....

The hysteria is ridiculous. Our job of securing America is not.

SOURCE: "John Ashcroft Delivers Remarks at National Restaurant Association's Annual Public Affairs Conference," September 15, 2003, Federal Documents Clearing House. CQ Transcripts Wire, Sept. 15, 2003, © 2007, Congressional Quarterly, Inc. All rights reserved.

---

## IN HISTORY

### Is Patriot Act Surveillance Authority Unnecessary?

During Attorney General Ashcroft's national tour in 2003 he derided criticism of Patriot Act surveillance authorities as "hysteria," asserting that the most controversial provisions, such as Section 215, had never been used. This led some members of Congress to ask how the Bush Administration could regard the Patriot Act as essential in the war on terrorism if the most powerful provisions were not being used.

In December 2005, the press broke the story of President Bush's secret order to allow the wiretapping of U.S. citizens without any judicial review. Representative Chris Van Hollen (D-MD) was one of many in Congress who asked why our legislators should agonize over the Patriot Act's controversial surveillance provisions when the Executive Branch was assuming such powers with no statutory authority at all. Van Hollen wrote,

The president's newly claimed authority renders significant portions of the Patriot Act debate meaningless. What is the point of Congress drawing legal standards and developing procedures to protect our security and secure our civil liberties if the president secretly decides he has the authority to ignore much of what we do?

SOURCE: Chris Van Hollen, Letters to the Editor, *Washington Post*, December 21, 2005, p. A19.

## ANALYSIS

On June 5, 2003, Attorney General John Ashcroft told the House Judiciary Committee:

Despite the terrorist threats to America, there are some, both in Congress and across the country, who suggest that we should not have a USA PATRIOT Act. Others who supported the act 20 months ago now express doubts about the necessity of some of the act's components. Let me state my view as clearly as possible. Our ability to prevent another catastrophic attack on American soil would be more difficult, if not impossible, without the PATRIOT Act. It has been the key weapon used across America in successful counterterrorist operations to protect innocent Americans from the deadly plans of terrorists. (Hearing before the Committee on the Judiciary, House of Representatives, 108th Congress, 1st Session, June 5, 2003, p. 8)

Despite Ashcroft's spirited defense of the Patriot Act, the library profession continued to criticize the FBI for snooping on readers. To support its characterization of library "hysteria" the Justice Department issued the following statement: "On September18, 2003, the Attorney General declassified the number of times the Department of Justice, including the Federal Bureau of Investigation (FBI), had utilized the USA PATRIOT Act relating to the production of business Records. At that time, the number of times Section 215 was used was zero" (ibid., p. 112).

The Justice Department (DOJ) was thus claiming that Section 215 had *never* been used to acquire *any* records, not just library records. This dramatic claim, if true, would support the charge that librarians were overreacting to the threat of surveillance in the stacks, but some contradictions remained. For one, anonymous library surveys had documented the use of Section 215 to acquire library records. Also, librarians were concerned about library surveillance generally, not about any particular provision of the Patriot Act. Indeed, the DOJ had acknowledged that NSLs, facilitated by the Patriot Act, were the preferred tool for acquiring library records and that they had been frequently used.

And finally, the DOJ had admitted that other authorities had been used to acquire library records. On May 20, 2003, Assistant Attorney General Viet Dinh answered a question from Rep. Steve Chabot (R-OH):

**Chabot:** Can you tell us how many times, if at all, library records have been accessed under the new FISA standards in the USA PATRIOT Act?...

**Dinh:** We have made, in light of the recent public information concerning visits to the library, we have conducted an informal survey of the field offices, relating to its visits to libraries. And I think the results from this informal survey is that libraries have been contacted approximately 50 times, based on articulatable suspicion or voluntary calls from libraries regarding suspicious activities. Most, if not all of these

contacts that we have identified were made in the context of a criminal investigation and pursuant to voluntary disclosure or a grand jury subpoena, in that context.
(Transcript, House Subcommittee on the Constitution, May 20, 2003. Department of Justice, www.usdoj.gov/opa/pr/2003/June/03_opa_323.html)

Barbara Comstock, Director of Public Affairs for DOJ, subsequently attempted to clarify Dinh's testimony, suggesting that he was speaking of ordinary criminal cases rather than national security cases, and that the latter could only be provided to Congress in a classified format. But ambiguity remained about the fifty visits to libraries. In light of all available evidence, the library profession continues to express concern about library surveillance, and librarians do not believe such concern is hysterical.

# FURTHER READINGS

"Ashcroft Hints PATRIOT Act Used." *American Libraries*, 36, no. 10 (March 2005).
Coolidge, Katherine K. "'Baseless Hysteria': The Controversy between the Department of Justice and the American Library Association over the USA PATRIOT Act," *Law Library Journal*, 97, no. 7 (2005).
"FBI Begins Visiting Libraries." *Newsletter on Intellectual Freedom* (September 2002), p. 239.
Ishizuka, Kathy. "Warning: Uncle Sam Watching?" *School Library Journal* (April 1, 2003), www.schoollibraryjournal.com/article/CA287124.html
Mendoza, Santa. "Librarians Should Shush Over Ashcroft Concerns," *Connecticut Law Tribune*, 29, no. 28 (February 17, 2003).

# Preparing for FBI Visits to Libraries

- **Documents:** American Library Association (ALA) Guidelines for the Library and Its Staff, issued after passage of the USA PATRIOT Act; statement by Chuck Rosenberg, counsel to FBI Director Robert Mueller, describing the nature of FBI visits and how librarians should deal with them
- **Dates:** ALA guidelines: January 23, 2002; Mr. Rosenberg's comments: June 21, 2003
- **Where:** ALA Council, Chicago, IL; Chuck Rosenberg's remarks, Toronto, Canada
- **Significance:** Anticipating Patriot Act surveillance, the American Library Association issued detailed guidelines on how to deal appropriately with law enforcement requests for library records. At the same time, the ALA contacted the FBI for advice on how to respond to agents and the particular court orders they may present.

---

## DOCUMENTS

### 1. Introduction to American Library Association Statement on Confidentiality and Coping with Law Enforcement Inquiries

Increased visits to libraries by law enforcement agents, including FBI agents and officers of state, county, and municipal police departments, are raising considerable concern among the public and the library community. These visits are not only a result of the increased surveillance and investigation prompted by the events of September 11, 2001 and the subsequent passage of the Patriot Act, but also as a result of law enforcement officers investigating computer crimes, including e-mail threats and possible violations of the laws addressing online obscenity and child pornography....

Librarians' professional ethics require that personally identifiable information about library users be kept confidential. This principle is reflected in Article III of the *Code of Ethics*, which states that "[librarians] protect each library user's right to privacy and confidentiality with respect to information sought or received, and resources consulted, borrowed, acquired, or transmitted."

SOURCE: "Confidentiality and Coping with Law Enforcement Inquiries: Guidelines for the Library and Its Staff," American Library Association, January 23, 2002. www.ala.org/alaorg/oif/guidelineslibrary

## 2. Remarks of Chuck Rosenberg, Counsel to FBI Director Robert Mueller

Any legitimate agent, FBI, state or local, absolutely should afford you the time and courtesy to check them out and give you a number at which to do it.... When an agent comes to your library, they should be dressed as I am dressed [coat and tie], they should identify themselves, they should show you their badge and their credentials, hopefully privately and discreetly. And you have every right to ask them for proof that they are who they say they are. If they have a search warrant, they should hand you a piece of paper that should look official and is signed by a clerk of the federal district court out of which it was issued.... A state search warrant could look very different. A grand jury subpoena would look yet again different.

SOURCE: Chuck Rosenberg, counsel to FBI Director Robert Mueller, at American Library Association Annual Conference, June 21, 2003, Toronto, Canada.

# ANALYSIS

With the passage of the Patriot Act, the library profession braced itself for an increase in visits from FBI agents carrying search and seizure orders. Most librarians were unfamiliar with the legal orders they were likely to be served, e.g., subpoenas, search warrants, FISA orders under the Patriot Act, etc. To prepare themselves, librarians turned to an unlikely source for help: the FBI. Who could better advise them on how to prepare for and appropriately respond to the new surveillance orders?

In June 2003, Chuck Rosenberg, counsel to FBI Director Robert Mueller, agreed to speak with a group of librarians at the American Library Association Annual Conference in Toronto, Canada. When one librarian complained to Rosenberg that, in the past, FBI agents visiting libraries had been vague in describing the court order, if any, under which they requested records, he responded,

> I cannot tell you why a particular agent may not know the parameters of the court order that he is handing you. They may not be sure themselves. Many of our agents are lawyers, but most are not. They all receive training, excellent training, but this is a very confusing area of the law.... So it's probably best to seek guidance from counsel, or if you're a county librarian, from your county attorney, or if in a university, from the university general counsel.

After passage of the Patriot Act, the American Library Association created new guidelines on "Confidentiality and Coping with Law Enforcement Inquiries." Among the new procedures are:

- Avoid creating unnecessary records.
- Avoid retaining records that are not needed for efficient operation of the library.

- Designate the person or persons who will be responsible for handling law enforcement requests.
- Train all library staff, including volunteers, on the library's procedure for handling law enforcement requests.
- Review the library's confidentiality policy and state confidentiality law with library counsel.
- Staff should immediately ask for identification if they are approached by an agent or officer, and then immediately refer the agent or officer to the library director or other designated officer of the institution.
- The director or officer should meet with the agent with library counsel or another colleague in attendance.
- If the agent or officer does not have a court order compelling the production of records, the director or officer should explain the library's confidentiality policy and the state's confidentiality law, and inform the agent or officer that users' records are not available except when a proper court order in good form has been presented to the library.
- Without a court order, neither the FBI nor local law enforcement has authority to compel cooperation with any investigation or require answers to questions, other than the name and address of the person speaking to the agent or officer.
- If the agent or officer presents a court order, the library director or officer should immediately refer the court order to the library's legal counsel for review.
- If the court order is a search warrant issued under the Foreign Intelligence Surveillance Act (FISA) (Patriot Act amendment): The recommendations for a regular search warrant still apply. However, a search warrant issued by a FISA court also contains a "gag order." That means that no person or institution served with the warrant can disclose that the warrant has been served or that records have been produced pursuant to the warrant. The library and its staff must comply with this order. ("Confidentiality and Coping with Law Enforcement Inquiries: Guidelines for the Library and Its Staff," January 23, 2002. www.ala.org/alaorg/oif/guidelineslibrary.html)

In addition to preparing guidelines for coping with the FBI, many libraries have concluded that they have an obligation to warn their patrons of the post-Patriot Act reality: compromised library confidentiality hidden under gag orders. Library patrons cannot be told of government surveillance *after* the fact—that would be a felony. But they can be warned in advance. Toward that end, libraries have begun posing warning signs, many of them quite imaginative. For example, the Santa Cruz (California) Public Library posted the sign shown in Figure 7 in all of their branches.

---

**WARNING**

Although the Santa Cruz Library makes every effort to protect your privacy, under the federal USA PATRIOT Act (Public Law 107-56), records of the books and other materials you borrow from this library may be obtained by federal agents. That federal law prohibits library workers from informing you if federal agents have obtained records about you. Questions about this policy should be directed to Attorney General John Ashcroft, Department of Justice, Washington, DC 20530.

---

Figure 7. Warning sign posted in the Santa Cruz, California, Library.

Not all librarians support the idea of posting warning signs about the Patriot Act. Judith Krug, Director of the ALA's Freedom to Read Foundation, says, "My concern with posting signs is that you terminate the reader's expectation that what they read in libraries is protected by statute. I think there are more effective ways [than signs] to raise awareness about the need to change this particular section of the PATRIOT Act" ("Libraries Warn of FBI Spying," *Newsletter on Intellectual Freedom*, May 2003, p. 94).

But Peter Simonson from the New Mexico chapter of the ACLU says,

This [posting of warning signs] is a unique way for us to demonstrate to the public how the Patriot Act can infringe on their private lives. We're concerned that as we get further and further away from the passage of the Patriot Act, the public becomes more apathetic and forgets about what we lost under that legislation. We're not trying in any way to scare the public into not using libraries. We want them to know about the radical and dramatic change that has affected their rights, and we hope to motivate them to demand a repeal from Congress. ("ACLU State Chapters Launch Campaign to Warn Patrons about Patriot Act," *American Libraries Online*, August 4, 2003. www.ala.org/alonline)

Anne Turner, director of libraries in Santa Cruz, California, said the response to their warning sign was community outrage, most of it directed against the Patriot Act rather than the library. "It's only recently that people have become aware just how pernicious it is," she said. "Our board decided to take a public stand" by posting warnings at its branches ("Calif. Libraries Warn Patrons about Government Monitoring," *Washington Post*, March 12, 2003, p. A22).

Catherine Wilken, a librarian in Guilford, Vermont, says, "I've been posting things since last fall about various aspects of the [Patriot] Act. What bothers me so much is that that person who might be investigated has no defense. They're not allowed to know they're being investigated. I'm not allowed to tell them" (Michael Neary, "Guilford Librarian Supports Free Thought, Study—Despite USAPA," *Brattleboro Reformer*, February 27, 2003, p. 1).

As the use of warning signs has become more common in libraries, some unusual choices are being offered on the Internet. A few examples are shown in Figure 8.

Even as they warn library patrons of the imminent threat to library confidentiality, libraries are seeking more proactive ways to deal with the Patriot Act. The most common approach is to recognize that the FBI cannot seize library records if those records don't exist. To accomplish this, libraries around the country are destroying library records before the FBI can get to them. For example, in Santa Cruz, California, librarians have decided to shred library records each day. "It used to be, a librarian would be pictured with a book," says branch manager Barbara Snider. "Now it is a librarian with a shredder" (Jeff Ballinger, "Opening the Book on Libraries," *San Luis Obispo Tribune*, January 11, 2003, p. 1).

During Attorney General Ashcroft's appearance before Congress on June 5, 2003, a sympathetic Republican congressman, Representative Jeff Flake (R-AZ), asked, "A lot of the librarians have made a practice of destroying computer records and other records in defiance of the Patriot Act. They are saying, we don't agree with it and therefore we'll make it more difficult for the Justice Department to come in and actually search those records. To your knowledge, has any investigation been stymied, has the Justice Department sought information that was then destroyed by any of the libraries?"

Ashcroft avoided answering the question, but Justice Department spokesman Marc Corallo acknowledges that librarians have accelerated the process of destroying library records since the passage of the Patriot Act.

## FURTHER READINGS

American Library Association. "Guidelines for Librarians on the USA Patriot Act: What to Do

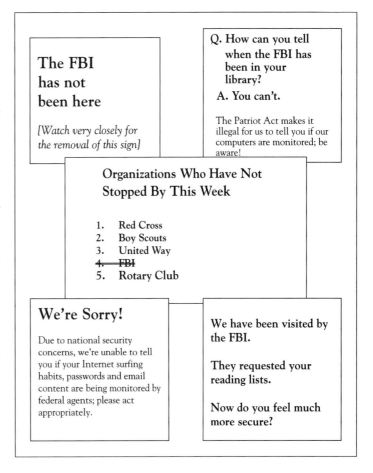

Figure 8. Sample signs suggested by Library.net. Reprinted from Herbert Foerstel's *Refuge of a Scoundrel* (Praeger, 2005).

Before, During, and After a 'Knock at the Door?" January 19, 2002. www.ala.org/wash off/patstep.pdf

Murphy, Dean E. "Librarians Use Shredder to Show Opposition to New F.B.I. Powers," *New York Times* (April 7, 2003), p. A12.

Rivard, Nicole. "USA Patriot Act: How to Be Response Ready," *University Business* (May 2002). www.universitybusiness.com/story/asp?txtFilename=archives/May2002/patriot.html

Smiley, Tavis. "Anne Turner and Carla Hayden Discuss the Impact of the USA Patriot Act on Their Customers," National Public Radio broadcast, April 14, 2003.

Strickland, Lee S. "Patriot in the Library: Management Approaches When Demands for Information Are Received from Law Enforcement and Intelligence Agencies," *Journal of College and University Law*, 30, no. 2 (2004), p. 363.

Tedeschi, Bob. "Patriot Act Curbing Data Retention," *NewYorkTimes.com* (October 13, 2003), p. 6. www.nytimes.com/2003/10/13/technology/13ecom.html?ex=1067053712&ei=1&en

# CHAPTER 5

# Detention, Deportation, Exclusion, and Expropriation

Figure 9. The Statue of Liberty. Courtesy of Shutterstock.

# Sacrificing Their Liberty
# for Our Security

- **Document:** Senator Russ Feingold's October 25, 2001 statement shortly before Passage of the Patriot Act
- **When:** October 25, 2001
- **Where:** U.S. Senate, Washington, DC
- **Significance:** Senator Feingold's predictions of abuse of new immigration authorities proved to be prescient.

---

# DOCUMENT

### Senator Feingold's October 25, 2001 Statement Prior to Final Vote on the Patriot Act

The bill continues to allow the Attorney General to detain persons based on mere suspicion. Our system normally requires higher standards of proof for a deprivation of liberty. For example, deportation proceedings are subject to a clear and convincing evidence standard. Criminal convictions, of course, require proof beyond a reasonable doubt.

The bill also continues to deny detained persons a trial or hearing where the government would be required to prove that the person is in fact, engaged in terrorist activity. This is unjust and inconsistent with the values our system of justice holds dear.

Another provision in the bill that deeply troubles me allows the detention and deportation of people engaging in innocent associational activity. It would allow for the detention and deportation of individuals who provide lawful assistance to groups that are not even designated by the Secretary of State as terrorist organizations, but instead have engaged in vaguely defined "terrorist activity" sometime in the past. To avoid deportation, the immigrant is required to prove a negative: that he or she did not know, and should not have known, that the assistance would further terrorist activity. This language creates a very real risk that truly innocent individuals could be deported for innocent associations with humanitarian or political groups that the government later chooses to regard as terrorist organizations....

Now here's where my cautions in the aftermath of the terrorists attacks and my concern over the reach of the anti-terrorism bill come together. To the extent that the expansive new immigration powers that the bill grants to the Attorney General are subject to abuse, who do we think is most likely to bear the brunt of that abuse? It won't be immigrants from Ireland, it won't be immigrants from El Salvador or Nicaragua, it won't even be immigrants from Haiti or Africa. It will be immigrants from Arab, Muslim, and South Asian countries. In the wake of these terrible events, our government has been given vast new powers and they may fall most heavily on a minority of our population who already feel particularly acutely the pain of this disaster.

When concerns of this kind have been raised with the Administration and supporters of this bill they have told us, "don't worry, the FBI would never do that." I call on the Attorney General and the Justice Department to ensure that my fears are not borne out.

*SOURCE:* "Statement of U.S. Senator Russ Feingold on the Anti-Terrorism Bill from the Senate Floor," October 25, 2001. www.senate.gov/-feingold/releases/01/10/102501at.html

---

# ANALYSIS

During the October 2001 congressional debate, when Senator Russ Feingold warned his Senate colleagues of the danger of abuse of the Patriot Act's controversial immigration provisions, supporters of the Act told him, "Don't worry, the FBI would never do that." But on the very day that the Patriot Act was signed into law, the prestigious Lawyers Committee for Human Rights issued a gloomy prediction: "In what is likely to be a significant number of cases the new law will result in long-term detention of non-citizens who have never been charged with a crime but who have violated their immigration status in some way.... This will be a likely result if a person has been certified by the Attorney General as a threat to U.S. national security" ("LCHR on Counter-Terror Bill," Center for Democracy and Technology, October 26, 2001, p. 2. www.cdt.org/security/0110261chr.shtml).

Most of the public controversy and criticism concerning the Patriot Act is directed toward its surveillance provisions, which critics say compromise the liberty and privacy of American citizens. But constitutional scholar David Cole charges that the worst provisions of the Patriot Act are the immigration provisions, which attract virtually no attention and little criticism. Cole says this is because of a double standard that allows American citizens to declare that they will accept any sacrifice of liberty that supports the war on terrorism, so long as that sacrifice is borne by noncitizens. This double standard could be seen in the list of "sunsetted" provisions of the Patriot Act, which were hotly debated during the 2005 reauthorization hearings. Not a single immigration provision was sunsetted, and their permanence has been accepted without debate.

Another example of the Patriot Act's double standard with respect to aliens can be seen in the Act's definition of "terrorism." For a U.S. citizen to be considered a terrorist he must commit "acts dangerous to human life that are a violation of the criminal law...[and] that appear to be intended...to influence the policy of a government by intimidation or coercion." But for aliens, "terrorist activity" is defined much more expansively, to include support of the otherwise lawful and nonviolent activities of any group that has previously used violence, and any use or threat to use a weapon against person or property other than for mere personal gain.

Thus, for American citizens, terrorism has a narrow definition corresponding to the common public understanding of the term, whereas for foreign nationals, terrorism includes ordinary crimes of violence or even wholly nonviolent activity. Neither the Justice Department nor Congress has bothered to explain why a particular act should be "terrorism" when committed by a foreign national but not when committed by an American citizen. This double standard can be seen throughout the Patriot Act, which applies its most severe measure to noncitizens.

The harsh immigration provisions of which Senator Feingold warned Congress can be found in several sections of the Patriot Act: Sections 315 and 319 increase the government's authority to seize foreign assets while Sections 805 and 805 criminalize "material support," including advice, to terrorist organizations. But the core of the powerful new authorities is found in Sections 411 and 412. Both sections are under "Subtitle B—Enhanced Immigration Provisions." Under "grounds of inadmissibility," Section 411 states that a foreign national may be excluded from the United States if he is a representative of:

1. A foreign terrorist organization, as designated by the Secretary of State, or
2. A political, social or other similar group whose public endorsement of acts of terrorist activity the Secretary of State has determined undermines United States efforts to reduce or eliminate terrorist activities.

Section 411 uses the redundant phrase "acts of terrorist activity" in defining the phrase "engaging in terrorist activities" and includes such acts as:

1. To gather information on potential targets for terrorist activity;
2. To solicit funds or other things of value for a terrorist activity or terrorist organization;
3. To solicit any individual to engage in such conduct or for membership in a terrorist organization; or
4. To commit an act that the actor knows, or reasonably should know, affords material support for the commission of a terrorist activity, or to any individual who the actor knows, or reasonably should know, has committed or plans to commit a terrorist activity, or to a terrorist organization.

The definitions and penalties prescribed in Section 411 are all *retroactive*, taking effect upon the enactment of the Patriot Act and applying to:

1. Actions taken by an alien before, on, or after such date; and
2. All aliens, without regard to the date of entry or attempted entry into the United States.

Section 412, "Mandatory Detention of Suspected Terrorists," was discussed in Chapter 3. It allows the Attorney General to take into custody "any alien who the Attorney General has reasonable grounds to believe is engaged in activity that endangers the national security of the United States." The alien may be held for unlimited additional periods of up to six months each "if the release of the alien will threaten the national security of the United States or the safety of the community or any person."

# FURTHER READINGS

Akram, Susan M. "Race, Civil Rights and Immigration Law after September 11, 2001: The Targeting of Arabs and Muslims," *New York University Annual Survey of American* Law, 58, no. 295 (2002).
Bali, Asli U. "Changes in Immigration Law and Practice After September 11: A Practitioner's Perspective," *Cardozo Public Law, Policy and Ethics Journal,* 2, no. 161 (2003).

Chin, Gabriel J. "The Civil Rights Revolution Comes to Immigration Law," *North Carolina Law Review*, 75, no. 273 (1996).

Johnson, Kevin R. "Immigration and Civil Rights after September 11: The Impact on California," *U.C. Davis Law Review*, 38, no. 3 (2005), p. 599.

Margulies, Peter. "Uncertain Arrivals: Immigration, Terror, and Democracy after September 11," *Utah Law Review*, no. 3 (2002), pp. 481–517.

Romero, Victor C. "Decoupling 'Terrorist' from 'Immigrant:' An Enhanced Role for the Federal Courts Post-9/11," *Journal of Gender, Race and Justice*, 7, no. 201 (Spring 2003).

Vandenberg, Quinn. "How Can the United States Rectify Its Post-9/11 Stance on Noncitizens' Rights?" *Notre Dame Journal of Law, Ethics, and Public Policy*, 18, no. 605 (2004).

# Deportation and Exclusion under the Patriot Act

- **Documents:** Speech by David Cole, author and legal scholar, on the Patriot Act's onerous immigration provisions; letter from Ziad Asali, Arab Anti-Discrimination Committee (ADC) to Attorney General John Ashcroft asking for termination of deportation prosecution against the "LA 8"
- **When:** Speech by David Cole: September 16, 2005; letter from Ziad Asali: May 22, 2003
- **Where:** David Cole speech delivered at Maryland Institute College of Art, Baltimore, MD; Asali letter reprinted on ADC web page
- **Significance:** David Cole points out the dangers of the Patriot Act's immigration provisions, ignored by much of Congress and the public because it does not significantly affect American citizens; Ziad Asali asks Attorney General Ashcroft to terminate the deportation prosecution against "the Los Angeles 8."

---

# DOCUMENT

### 1. Speech by David Cole on Patriot Act Immigration Provisions

Maher Arar is a Canadian citizen who was born in Syria, so he has Syrian citizenship as well as Canadian citizenship. He and his family have been living in Canada for the past 20 some years. He was returning to Canada from abroad when [American] immigration officials used the fact that he was changing planes at JFK to seize him, lock him up for two weeks, deny him access to a lawyer, and order him deported on the basis of secret evidence that he had no opportunity to see or confront. Arar said alright, deport me to Canada, I wasn't trying to come to the United States anyway. I just wanted to return home to Canada. But the immigration officials said, no, we're not going to put you on your connecting flight to Canada, we're going to charter a jet and take you to Syria.

Why would the government seize this person who had been living with his family in Canada for over 20 years, charter a jet and take him to Syria? The answer is, Canada does not have a record of torturing and arbitrarily detaining prisoners, and Syria does. Indeed, in

Syria, Maher Arar was locked up without charges for a year, ten months of which was spent in a jail cell the size of a coffin, and was tortured and interrogated, using a dossier of questions provided by the United States. He was eventually released by Syria and returned to Canada a free man.

We [the Center for Constitutional Rights] brought a law suit challenging the legality of sending someone to a third country in order to have him tortured. The government's response to the suit was to assert what is called "the state secrets privilege," under which it argues that the evidence as to why they sent Arar to Syria consists of secret communications between the United States, Syria, and Canada. Therefore, says the government, the entire case must be dismissed…. The whole reason why the government used immigration procedures rather than criminal procedures was to deny Arar the right to fair process.

SOURCE: David Cole. Speech on Constitution Day at Maryland Institute College of Art, Baltimore, MD, September 16, 2005.

---

## 2. Letter from ADC President Ziad Asali to Attorney General John Ashcroft

Dear Attorney General Ashcroft:

We write to urge you to terminate the government's longstanding efforts to deport a group of seven Palestinians and a Kenyan in Los Angeles. This case is notorious in the Arab community, because from the outset the government admitted that none of the individuals had committed any criminal, much less terrorist activity….

In 1989, a federal court declared unconstitutional the statutory provisions under which the eight were initially charged…. It also does not make sense to proceed against these individuals under the Patriot Act amendments to the INA [Immigration and Nationality Act]. As you know, those provisions make it a deportable offense to have provided material support to a terrorist organization, but where, as here, the organization was not designated as such when the support was allegedly provided, the alien may not be deported if he shows that he did not know nor reasonably should have known that his support would further the group's terrorist activity….

Is this really the case the government wants to make its first deportation case under the newly expanded Patriot Act provisions?

SOURCE: "ADC President Ziad Asali Urges Attorney General to Drop LA8 Case," ADC Kazoo, May 22, 2003. http://adckazoo.com/news-178.html

---

# ANALYSIS

The Patriot Act has made immigrants deportable for their political associations and excludable for pure speech. Before the Patriot Act, aliens were deportable for engaging in or supporting *terrorist activity*. Under the Patriot Act, they are deportable for virtually any *associational activity* with a designated "terrorist organization," even if the alien's support has no connection to an act of violence, much less terrorism. Aliens are deportable for asking people to join a designated "terrorist group," fundraising for it, or providing any kind of material support to it. The law extends even to those who support such a group in an effort to *prevent*

# IN HISTORY

## History of Ideological Exclusion

During the Cold War, laws were passed in the United States denying admission to foreigners on the basis of their political views. For example, the McCarran-Walter Act authorized federal officials to deny visas to anyone who had advocated certain political views, such as advocacy of communism. Hundreds of people were excluded under such laws, including Nino Pasti, a former NATO general; Tomas Borges, a leader of the Nicaraguan Sandinistas; and celebrated writers like Graham Greene, Carlos Fuentes, and Margaret Randall.

In 1986, Randall, a fifty-year-old poet, author, and grandmother, faced deportation under the McCarran-Walter Act for having espoused "the doctrines of world Communism" in her writings. Randall was born a U.S. citizen in New York City, but moved to Mexico in the 1960s where she married a Mexican poet. She became a Mexican citizen in order to facilitate finding work there, but the State Department declared that she had thereby forfeited her U.S. citizenship. She eventually prevailed in her deportation hearing, but only because the Board of Immigration Appeals said she was still a U.S. citizen.

The entrenched practice of ideological exclusion endured after the McCarthy period and even survived the Cold War itself. Finally, in 1990, with bipartisan expressions of America's commitment to freedom of speech, Congress repealed the laws authorizing ideological exclusion. This all changed after 9/11, as the Patriot Act denied admission to noncitizens who simply "endorse or espouse terrorist activity" or who "persuade others to support terrorist activity or a terrorist organization." Because of the breadth and ambiguity of the Patriot Act's definitions of "terrorist activity" and "terrorist organizations," the government is increasingly denying entry to noncitizens on ideological grounds. "The government is using ideological exclusion as a way of manipulating the political and economic debate," says the ACLU's Jameel Jaffer. "They are using the laws to deny Americans the right to hear views" ("Advocates Say U.S. Bars Many Academics," *Washington Post*, August 4, 2006, p. A7).

terrorism. This amounts to guilt by association, because it makes aliens culpable not for their own acts, but for the acts of those with whom their conduct is associated.

The Patriot Act also authorizes ideological exclusion, denying entrance to aliens who "endorse or espouse terrorist activity" or who "persuade others to support terrorist activity or a terrorist organization." It also excludes aliens who are members of groups that "endorse acts of terrorist activity in ways that similarly undermine U.S. efforts to combat terrorism." The case of Maher Arar, described above by David Cole, is a good example of the confusing new immigration authorities in the Patriot Act. One or more of the Patriot Act's provisions was undoubtedly implicated in Arar's deportation, but because the evidence in such cases is kept secret from defendants, lawyers, the press, even from Congress, no one can be quite sure of the legal basis for Arar's deportation.

Maher Arar was born in Syria but came to Canada in 1987. After earning bachelor's and master's degrees in computer engineering, he worked in Ottowa as a telecommunications engineer. In September 2002, as Arar was returning to Canada from a family vacation in Tunisia, he was seized by U.S. immigration officials when his plane made a stopover in New York. Arar was questioned at the airport for eight hours, and the next day was shackled and sent to a detention center in Brooklyn, New York, where he was locked in solitary confinement. Officials told him he had been seen with terrorist suspects in Canada.

Alhough he was a Canadian citizen carrying a Canadian passport, Arar was deported to Syria after U.S. officials claimed he had links to al Qaeda. He recalls, "When I saw FBI officials coming to me, my first reaction was to make a phone call to my family,...but they ignored my request. And then I asked for a lawyer, and they said, 'You are not an American citizen, you don't have a right to a lawyer'" ("The Price of Security: Ted Koppel on Discovery," Discovery Channel documentary, September 10, 2006).

In Syria, Arar was held in a cell the size of a coffin and tortured repeatedly. It was later revealed that the U.S. decision to deport Arar was based partly on an inaccurate tip from Canadian intelligence, but the American response to that tip was never discussed with Canada. Indeed, after Canadian officials determined that Arar was being held in a Syrian prison, the government issued a travel advisory to all Canadians born in Iran, Iraq, Libya, Sudan, or Syria, warning them against entering the United States. Finally, on October 5, 2003, Syria freed Arar after what the Canadian Foreign Affairs Department called "quiet Canadian diplomacy," and Arar returned to Canada 375 days after U.S. officials had arrested him.

Upon his return to Canada, Arar described the physical and psychological torture he endured during his year in Syria, and the Canadian government began an investigation into the abduction. The U.S. State Department declared that it would not provide any documents or cooperate in any way with the Arar inquiry, and U.S. federal judge David Trager dismissed Arar's law suit against American officials, saying he could not interfere in a case involving national security.

On October 27, 2005, the Arar inquiry released a report concluding that Arar had been tortured in Syria. On September 28, 2006, Canada's Commissioner of the Royal Mounted Police publicly apologized for Canada's role in the "terrible injustices" done to Arar, concluding: "Mr. Arar, I wish to take this opportunity to express publicly to you and to your wife and to your children how truly sorry I am." The Canadian House of Commons unanimously voted that "apologies should be presented" to Arar (Doug Struck, "Canadian Police Official Apologizes for Mistakes," *Washington Post*, September 29, 2006, p. A16).

Meanwhile, U.S. officials continued to stand by Attorney General John Ashcroft's original statement that the deportation of Arar was "fully within the law and applicable treaties and conventions that guide the activities of the United States."

On a September 10, 2006 television documentary commemorating the 9/11 attacks, Lanny Davis, vice-chairman of President Bush's own Privacy and Civil Liberties Oversight Board, told the audience, "We are all liberals, we are all conservatives tonight when we say, 'I am sorry,' as the American people to Mr. Arar. Why the President of the United States hasn't said 'I am sorry' to anyone innocent treated the way that man was treated is beyond me" ("The Price of Security: Ted Koppel on Discovery," Discovery Channel documentary, September 10, 2006).

Another high-profile deportation case that relied on the Patriot Act involves eight defendants in Los Angeles who came to be known as "the LA 8." In 1987, federal officials arrested eight student activists in Los Angeles,

## IN HISTORY

### Deportation on the Basis of Guilt by Association

For much of the twentieth century, U.S. immigration law authorized the deportation of foreign nationals for their political associations. For example, during the Cold War, noncitizens could be deported for mere membership in groups advocating communism or other proscribed political ideology. Nonetheless, in 1961 the Supreme Court declared: "In our jurisprudence, guilt is personal, and when the imposition of punishment on a status or on conduct can only be justified by a reference to the relationship of that status or conduct to other concededly criminal activity…that relationship must be sufficiently substantial to satisfy the concept of personal guilt in order to withstand attack under the Due Process Clause of the Fifth Amendment." The Court went on to say that guilt by association also violates the First Amendment right of association because it penalizes even those who support only a group's lawful ends (*Scales v. United States*, 367 U.S. 203 224-25 (1961)).

In 1982, the Supreme Court declared that guilt by association was "alien to the traditions of a free society and to the First Amendment itself" (*NAACP v. Claiborne Hardware*, 458 U.S. 886, 932 (1982)). Still, it was not until 1990 that Congress formally repealed the laws allowing deportation on the basis of guilt by association, and then, just eleven years later, the passage of the Patriot Act resurrected this practice. Indeed, the most significant new power in the Patriot Act's immigration provisions is the authority to deport noncitizens for their association with disfavored political organizations.

seven Palestinians and the Kenyan wife of one of them. They were charged with advocating "the doctrines of world Communism," their ideological connection being alleged support for the Popular Front for the Liberation of Palestine (PFLP). The government threatened the students with deportation, but then incarcerated them without bond while their deportation hearings proceeded. When the immigration judge requested the evidence to support the charges, the government said the classified nature of the evidence required it to be presented outside the presence of the students or their lawyers. The judge refused to accept the government's demands and ordered the defendants released.

Almost twenty years later, following legal procedures as arbitrary as their attempt to use secret evidence, the government continues their prosecution of the LA8. Government prosecutors have admitted from the outset that none of the LA8 had engaged in any criminal conduct, much less terrorist activity. The FBI acknowledged that they were arrested solely because of their alleged membership in a "world-wide Communist organization," which under the McCarran-Walter Act made them eligible for deportation, and that "if these individuals had been United States citizens, there would not have been a basis for their arrest" (*American-Arab Anti-Discrimination Comm. v. Reno*, 70 F.3d 1045, 1053 (9th Cir. 1995)).

David Cole filed a federal lawsuit arguing that the First Amendment equally protected the associational rights of citizens and foreign nationals living in the United States, but the government declared that it could deport foreign nationals for speech and associations that U.S. citizens could freely exercise. Indeed, the government's case against the LA8 consisted largely of PFLP newspapers and magazines seized in their homes or through the mails.

Then, on the eve of the court hearing on Cole's constitutional challenge, the INS dropped the "world communism" charges against six of the LA 8, retaining them against the other two defendants, Khader Hamide and Michel Shehadeh. Because Hamide and Shehadeh were both lawful permanent residents of the United States, the government could find no immigration violations to charge them with.

In January 1989, a federal district judge declared the McCarran-Walter Act provisions to be unconstitutional, ruling that the First Amendment protected all persons in the United States, citizen and noncitizen alike. The government appealed, but while the appeal was pending, Congress repealed the McCarran-Walter provisions, replacing them with a law making it a deportable offense to engage in terrorist activity. Despite the fact that FBI Director Webster had acknowledged that none of the LA8 had engaged in any terrorist activity, the INS continued to seek the deportation of the six defendants charged with technical visa violations and charged Hamide and Shehadeh, the two permanent residents, with having engaged in terrorist activities by providing "material support" to the PFLP.

Returning once more to court, David Cole argued that the LA8 had been singled out for deportation based on First Amendment-protected activities. The government argued once more that noncitizens could claim only diminished First Amendment rights and, hence, there was nothing unconstitutional about singling them out for their associations with a terrorist group, even though they had not sought to further any terrorist activity of that group. The district court and a unanimous court of appeals rejected the government's argument, concluding once more that noncitizens living in the United States are entitled to the same First Amendment rights as citizens. When the government did not seek Supreme Court review, it appeared that the LA8 had finally been vindicated, but there was more to come.

In 1996, the INS persuaded Congress to pass legislation removing the authority of federal courts to hear cases challenging selective enforcement of immigration law, allowing the government to continue prosecution of the LA8. The district court and the court of appeals again rejected the government's position, concluding that it would be unconstitutional to deny noncitizens a judicial forum to challenge action taken against them. The government now appealed to the Supreme Court. In an opinion authored by Justice Antonin Scalia, the Supreme Court ruled that, except in extreme situations, the issue of selective enforcement cannot be considered in the immigration setting. Thus, the Court concluded, it is permissible to deport a noncitizen for political associations that are freely exercised by citizens.

After almost twenty years, six of the LA8 had been granted residency status, and the government no longer seemed inclined to prosecute them. Only Khader Hamide and Michel Shehade remained the subject of deportation proceedings, despite the fact that they were legal permanent residents at the time of their alleged actions.

One would have thought that the FBI's admission that none of the LA8 had engaged in illegal or terrorist activity would undercut the case against the defendants, but here is where the Patriot Act finally enters the case. In September 2003, the government claimed that the FBI's admission was no longer relevant, because, under the Patriot Act, any "material support" to a "terrorist group," even to its wholly lawful activities, warrants deportation. The "material support" involved here—distributing Palestinian magazines and raising humanitarian aid in Los Angeles more than twenty years ago—was completely legal at the time, but the government now invokes the Patriot Act to authorize deportation. David Cole concludes, "The latest chapter in the LA8 case, courtesy of the Patriot Act, will do nothing to make us more secure—and much to make us less free" (David Cole, "9/11 and the LA8," *The Nation*, October 27, 2003).

Finally, on January 30, 2007, a federal immigration judge dismissed the twenty-year-old case against Shehade and Hamide. Judge Bruce Einhorn called the case "an embarrassment to the rule of law." Shehadeh said, "We did nothing wrong, but have a political view maybe contrary to that of the government." A government spokesperson said it was "considering its legal options" ("After 20 Years, Deportation Case against Palestinians Dismissed," *Washington Post*, January 31, 2007, p. A8).

The *Washington Post* editorialized: "It is high time for this to end. The government has until the end of the month to appeal the judge's ruling. It should, instead, drop this case, as it should have done years ago" ("Drop This Case," *Washington Post*, February 22, 2007, p. A18).

Another bizarre application of the Patriot Act's "material support" provision surfaced recently when it was used to deny asylum to health workers and doctors who had treated combatants in civil wars, American allies from past wars, and even former CIA employees. Examples include a nurse who was abducted and forced to treat a guerrilla fighter in Colombia, a woman in Liberia who was raped, her father killed, and her house occupied by rebel fighters, and several Montagnard and Hmong tribesmen from Vietnam who had fought the Viet Cong alongside American troops. Indeed, Anna Husarska of the International Rescue Committee says, "This absurd law…would seem to apply to those who helped overthrow Saddam Hussein" (Anna Husarska, "Old Allies Tagged 'Terrorist,'" *Washington Post*, December 16, 2006, p. A19).

Leonard Rubenstein, executive director of Physicians for Human Rights, says that, under the Patriot Act, the Department of Homeland Security is contesting asylum requests by health workers whose lives are at risk for having provided assistance to wounded members of rebel groups. "The government claims that providing such medical care amounts to 'material support' to terrorists," says Rubenstein. "Congress must revise the law to protect medical ethics and restore America's commitment to being a place of refuge for those fleeing persecution" (Leonard Rubenstein, "Doctors without Refuge," *Washington Post*, March 5, 2007, p. A15).

Conservatives and liberals in Washington were outraged, but the language of the "material support" provision placed the Department of Homeland Security in an impossible position. President Bush could do little more than promise to issue waivers on a case-by-case basis, leaving the bizarre Patriot Act provision unchanged. Indeed, by accepting the provision, the Administration was left with a policy that said, there is terrorism for a good cause and there is terrorism for a bad cause. Waivers would be issued for the former, not the latter.

Michael Horowitz, a fellow at the conservative Hudson Institute, reluctantly relies on a liberal Congress to change the law. "The key to ending these policies is in the hands of the new Democratic [congressional] majority. I do not think this is a sustainable policy" ("Conservatives Decry Terrorism Law's Impact on Refugees," *Washington Post*, January 8, 2007, p. A3).

On August 13, 2007, more than seven months after the Bush administration had promised waivers for asylum-seekers unfairly excluded under the Patriot Act, the *Washington Post* reported that "only a handful" of waivers had been granted. Senator Patrick Leahy (D-VT), the chief sponsor of legislation to correct the material support provisions, said, "It is unconscionable that the Bush administration has so meagerly used its waiver authority. These are victimized people who meet every other standard for admission as refugees…. If the Department of Homeland Security won't use the authority Congress gave it, then Congress needs to fix the law" ("U.S. Anti-Terrorism Laws Hold Up Asylum Seekers," *Washington Post*, August 13, 2007. p. A3).

# FURTHER READINGS

Ashar, Sameer M. "Immigration Enforcement and Subordination: The Consequences of Racial Profiling After September 11," *Connecticut Law Review*, 34, no. 4 (Summer 2002), pp. 1185–99.

Boswell, Richard A. "Racism and U.S. Immigration Law: Prospects for Reform after '9/11?'" *Journal of Gender, Race and Justice*, 7, no. 315 (Fall 2003).

Johnson, Kevin R. "The Antiterrorism Act, the Immigration Reform Act, and Ideological Regulation in the Immigration Laws," *Saint Mary's Law Journal*, 28, no. 833 (1997).

———. "The Case Against Racial Profiling in Immigration Enforcement," *Washington University Law Quarterly*, 78, no. 675 (Fall 2000).

Romero, Victor. "Race, Immigration, and the Department of Homeland Security," *Saint John's Journal of Legal Commentary*, 19, no. 51 (Fall 2004).

# Interrogation and Detention of Immigrants

- *Document:* Department of Justice Responses to Questions for the Record Concerning the USA PATRIOT Act, Committee on the Judiciary, U.S. House of Representatives
- *When:* June 5, 2003
- *Where:* Washington, DC
- *Significance:* Members of the House of Representatives question the preventive detention policies of the Department of Justice (DOJ) and the DOJ's defense of those policies.

---

# DOCUMENT

## Department of Justice Response to Questions from House Judiciary Committee

*Question:* The OIG report contains horrifying examples of mistreatment of detainees, including the taunting of detainees by calling them "Bin Laden junior" and telling them "you're going to die here," "someone thinks you have something to do with [9/11] so don't expect to be treated well." The detainees were physically abused as well—an inmate with a broken arm and injured finger had his wrist and finger twisted by officers, another was thrown in his cell naked without a blanket. They were deprived medical attention for injuries sustained in those assaults because, in the words of one physician's assistant, they "were not entitled to the same medical or dental care as convicted federal inmates." Your spokesperson said the Department makes "no apologies" for this conduct. Do you stand by her statement?

*Answer:* As the Attorney General indicated before the House Judiciary Committee on June 5, 2003 the Department of Justice does not condone the abuse or mistreatment of any person being held in federal custody. The Department takes such allegations seriously and if any such allegations are found to be true, appropriate action will be taken. The statement of the Department's spokesperson applied to the overall detention policy that we make no apologies that we detained illegal aliens when statistics show that 87 percent of them abscond when not detained. Again, it is not the policy of the Department to allow the mistreatment of anyone, particularly those persons in federal custody.

*SOURCE*: Department of Justice Responses to Questions for the Record concerning the USA PATRIOT Act, Committee on the Judiciary, U.S. House of Representatives, 108th Congress, June 5, 2003, pp. 129–30. Washington, D.C.: U.S. Government Printing Office, 2004.

---

# ANALYSIS

Immediately after 9/11, government agents across the United States began a roundup of foreign nationals as "suspected terrorists," a roundup that continues to this day. Attorney General John Ashcroft appeared regularly on television to announce the latest figures on how many "suspected terrorists" had been arrested. By early November 2001, Ashcroft announced that 1,152 suspected terrorists had been locked up, but when people began asking how many of those had actually been *charged* with terrorism, the Department of Justice announced that they would no longer keep a running total of suspected terrorists. Nonetheless, official reports and congressional testimony have revealed that the government has locked up over 5,000 foreign nationals under anti-terrorism preventive detention.

Many of these detainees were arrested with no charges whatsoever, picked up off the streets. If the wife of one of the detainees called the local police, FBI, or INS and asked if they had any record of her missing husband, she would be told no, even if he was sitting in a cell next to the person answering the phone, because the arrests were secret and remain secret to this day.

FBI Special Agent Coleen Rowly recognized the dangers of such a policy and expressed her concerns in a letter to FBI Director Robert Mueller:

> The vast majority of the one thousand plus persons "detained" in the wake of 9-11 did not turn out to be terrorists. They were mostly illegal aliens....[A]fter 9-11, Headquarters encouraged more and more detentions for what seem to be PR purposes. Field offices were required to report daily the number of detentions in order to supply grist for statements on our progress in fighting terrorism.... From what I observed, particular vigilance may be required to head off undue pressure (including subtle encouragement) to detain or "round up" suspects particularly those of Arab origin. (Letter from Coleen Rowly, FBI Special Agent, to Robert Mueller, FBI Director, February 26, 2003. www.nytimes.com/2003/03/05/politics/ROWLEY-LETTER.html)

## IN HISTORY

### Detention of Aliens in Times of Crisis

There is historic precedent for the post-9/11 roundup, detention, and deportation of foreign nationals. In 1919, cities across the United States were struggling with substantial unemployment and political unrest. On a single day, within the same hour, eight bombs were exploded in eight different American cities, one of them demolishing the front of the private home of Attorney General A. Mitchell Palmer in Washington, DC. The national hysteria that followed led to a government response that was quite similar to the post-9/11 roundups of foreign nationals.

The government did not locate and arrest the bombers. Indeed, the culprits were never identified or brought to justice. Instead, the government used immigration law to round up thousands of foreign nationals in coordinated raids that came to be known as the "Palmer Raids." The aliens who were picked up were held incommunicado, often without charges, interrogated without lawyers present. Many were eventually deported, based not on any criminal activity or involvement in the bombings, but on their political affiliation with communist organizations. There was no evidence that the bombers were foreign nationals or that they were in any way connected with the Communist Party. But the government *could* round up foreign nationals and hold them without charges, whereas it *could not* do so with American citizens.

Louis Post, acting Secretary of Labor at the time, would later write that "the delirium caused by the bombings turned in the direction of a deportation crusade with all the spontaneity of water seeking out the course of least resistance" (David Cole, "No More Roundups," *Washington Post*, June 16, 2004, p. A27).

How were these detainees initially identified as potential terrorists? The Inspector General of the Justice Department has said they were targeted on the basis of evidence such as an anonymous tip that there were too many Middle Eastern men working at a local convenience store. The FBI would then interview such men, and if they could not prove that they had no terrorist connections, they would be locked up. Many of those picked up in the sweeps had overstayed their visas or committed some other immigration violation. Normally, such matters would be quickly resolved, because the purpose of any immigration investigation is to determine whether a person has violated the terms of his visit to this country. If so, he would be deported. But here, because the immigration charges were just a ruse used to pick up "suspected terrorists," the purpose is not to send them out of the country—we wouldn't want a terrorist to be free to threaten us from abroad—but to incarcerate them here until it can be determined that they pose no threat to national security.

Under the Patriot Act, such detentions can be *indefinite*. The Act authorizes the attorney general to detain any immigrant whom he certifies as a "suspected terrorist." It gives the attorney general unilateral authority to detain aliens without any opportunity for the alien to respond to the charges. David Cole says the Patriot Act defines a "suspected terrorist" so broadly that it includes virtually every immigrant who has been involved in a barroom brawl or domestic dispute, as well as aliens whose only crime was providing humanitarian aid to an organization disfavored by the government. It mandates preventive detention of persons who pose no threat to national security or risk of flight, and without any hearing, allowing the INS to detain such aliens *indefinitely*, even when they prevail in their removal proceedings. Cole says, "This is akin to detaining a prisoner even after he has been pardoned" (David Cole, "Terrorizing Immigrants in the Name of Fighting Terrorism," *Human Rights*, Winter 2002, pp. 12–13).

Al Gore, the presidential candidate who won the 2000 vote but lost the election, has been speaking out against the arbitrary roundups and detention of foreign nationals, particularly Arabs and Muslims. In a speech on November 9, 2003, Gore decried the "constant violation of civil liberties" since 9/11, noting, "I believe the Patriot Act has turned out to be, on balance, a terrible mistake, and that it became a kind of Tonkin Gulf Resolution conferring Congress' blessing for this President's assault on civil liberties."

Gore characterized the treatment of immigrants as the worst example of the post-9/11 assault on civil liberties, saying, "More than 90 percent of the mostly Arab-background men who were rounded up had merely overstayed their visas or committed some other minor offense.... But they were used as extras in the Administration's effort to give the impression that they had caught a large number of bad guys. And many of them were treated horribly and abusively" ("Freedom and Security," remarks by Al Gore at Constitution Hall, Washington, DC, November 9, 2003. www.acslaw.org/files/2003%20programs_Gore_speech%20transcript.pdf).

Gore's critical remarks drew little attention in the United States until he repeated them in February 2006 in Saudi Arabia. Gore was quoted as saying that Arabs in the United States had been "indiscriminately rounded up...and held in conditions that were just unforgivable." Gore concluded, "Unfortunately, there have been terrible abuses, and it's wrong. I do want you to know that it does not represent the desires or wishes or feelings of the majority of the citizens of my country" (Chris Cillizza and Dan Balz, "Politics," *Washington Post*, February 20, 2006, p. A6).

# FURTHER READINGS

Carey, Michelle. "You Don't Know If They'll Let You Out in One Day, One Year, or Ten Years," *Chicano-latino Law Review*, 24, no. 12 (Spring 2003).

Cole, David. "In Aid of Removal: Due Process Limits on Immigration Detention," *Emory Law Journal*, 51 (2002), pp. 1003–39.

Engle, Karen. "Constructing Good Aliens and Good Citizens: Legitimizing the War on Terrorism," *University of Colorado Law Review*, 75, no. 59 (Winter 2004).

"Indefinite Detention of Immigrant Parolees: An Unconstitutional Condition?" *Harvard Law Review*, 116, (2003), pp. 1868–88.

Miller, Teresa A. "Blurring the Boundaries between Immigration and Crime Control after September 11th," *Boston College Third World Law Journal*, 25, no. 81 (Winter 2005).

Twibell, Ty S. "The Road to Internment: Special Registration and Other Human Rights Violations of Arabs and Muslims in the United States," *Vermont Law Review*, 29, no. 408 (Winter 2005).

# Seizing Assets under the Patriot Act

- **Document:** A passage from David Cole's book, *Enemy Aliens: Double Standards and Constitutional Freedoms in the War on Terrorism*
- **When:** Published 2003
- **Where:** The New Press, New York City
- **Significance:** Cole argues that "fungibility" of money is no legal basis for punishing donors to charities or members of political organizations that use both legal and illegal means.

---

## DOCUMENT

### Excerpt from *Enemy Aliens: Double Standards and Constitutional Freedoms in the War on Terrorism* by David Cole

The government has argued that the threat from terrorist organizations abroad and the fungibility of money require adjustments to the constitutional prohibition on guilt by association, permitting the punishment of "material support" where one could not punish mere membership [in a terrorist organization]....The fungibility argument is flawed as a factual and a legal matter. It maintains that because money is fungible, even a donation of blankets to a hospital will ultimately support terrorism, by freeing up resources that will then be devoted to terrorism. But this argument assumes that a group engaged in a political struggle that uses both legal and illegal means will divert legal donations to its illegal means. On this assumption, every dollar donated to the ANC [African National Congress] for its non-violent opposition to apartheid freed up a dollar that the ANC then spent on violent terrorist ends....

The fungibility argument also proves too much as a legal matter. The Supreme Court has repeatedly struck down or narrowly construed laws that penalized association with the Communist Party absent proof that the individual specifically intended to further the group's illegal ends. The government insists that money is different, but the Supreme Court has also repeatedly recognized that the rights of speech and association would mean little without the right to raise and spend money for those purposes, and accordingly has protected fundraising and donations as acts of association and speech....

If the provision of material support to a group were somehow constitutionally different from membership, all of the anti-communist measures declared invalid by the Supreme Court could simply have been rewritten to make punishment contingent on the payment of dues, the volunteering of time, or any of the other material manifestations of political association. The right of association would be left a meaningless formality.... In short, penalizing material support for terrorist groups resurrects guilt by association under a different label. It is no coincidence that its genesis was in immigration laws directed exclusively at foreign nationals, and the Patriot Act has now extended the concept to its limit through the immigration law.

SOURCE: David Cole, *Enemy Aliens: Double Standards and Constitutional Freedoms in the War on Terrorism*, New York: The New Press, 2003, pp. 60–64. Reprinted with permission.

## IN HISTORY

### Is Halliburton a Terrorist Organization?

OMB Watch, this nation's premier government watchdog organization, has charged that Muslim charities are being shut down on scanty evidence, while giant corporations like Halliburton are being treated gently, despite having broken U.S. law by doing business with Iran, a designated sponsor of terrorism. OMB Watch reports, "Even though little is known about the evidence the Treasury's Office of Foreign Assets Control (OFAC) relied on to freeze and seize assets of Muslim charities, it appears there is much stronger evidence against Halliburton."

OMB Watch says Halliburton, the giant defense contractor once headed by Vice President Dick Cheney, has been treated with a "velvet glove" by the government. Rather than freezing and seizing its assets pending an investigation, as is done with Muslim charities, the Justice Department has been quietly investigating Halliburton since 2001 for breaking U.S. sanctions against Iran. DOJ sent a polite inquiry to Halliburton requesting "information with respect to compliance." Halliburton responded by explaining that because its dealings with Iran were done through its Cayman Islands subsidiary, not its U.S.-based entity, it was in compliance with the law.

OMB Watch asks, "If U.S. [Muslim] charities formed Cayman Island subsidiaries, could they avoid the USA PATRIOT ACT, IEEPA, and Executive Order restrictions on dealings with groups or countries linked to terrorism?" ("Muslim Charities and the War on Terror," OMB Watch, February 2006. www.ombwatch.org/pdfs/muslim_charities.pdf#search=%22OMB).

## ANALYSIS

The broad and vaguely defined concept of "material support" for terrorism was introduced in Section 805 of the Patriot Act to make virtually any association with a designated terrorist group punishable under the immigration laws. Shortly after 9/11, President Bush had issued Executive Order (EO) 13224 authorizing the blocking of assets of particular individuals or groups designated as Specially Designated Global Terrorists (SDGTs). Such individuals or groups were specified for posing "a significant risk of committing acts of terrorism" or for being "otherwise associated" with designated individuals or groups. Thus, the Executive Order designates SDGTs on the basis of their propensity to commit terrorism or their association with someone who is perceived to have that propensity. The passage of the Patriot Act on October 26, 2001 essentially permanently codified EO 13224 into existing law, creating a SDGT list that blocks "all property and interests in property" of designated terrorists and individuals who "materially support" them. The Patriot Act also amended the International Emergency Economic Powers Act (IEEPA), the civil forfeiture statute authorizing seizure of assets (1) belonging to anyone engaged in terrorism, (2) affording a "source of influence" over a terrorist organization, or (3) derived from or used to commit an act of terrorism.

The government can support the seizure with secret evidence that the designated group has no opportunity to see. Indeed, DOJ spokesperson Stefan Cassella says that forfeiture under IEEPA, as amended by the Patriot Act, is "specifically exempted...from virtually all of the other evidentiary and due process requirements of federal forfeiture law" (Jenifer Van Bergen, "How

Government Forfeitures Are Shutting Down U.S.-based Muslim Charities," *FindLaw*, May 1, 2006. http://writ.news.findlaw.com/commentary/20060501). No criminal charges need ever be filed for forfeitures to occur, and, under the Patriot Act, law enforcement can give away those seized assets to any agency or person designated by the President "for the benefit of the United States."

After 9/11, Muslim charities quickly came under suspicion as funders of terrorism, resulting in prominent charities being closed down, their assets seized, and needy recipients denied their assistance. Early in December 2001, just two months after the Patriot Act was signed into law, the Treasury Department froze the assets and accounts of the Holy Land Foundation for Relief and Development, based in Richardson, Texas, charging that the organization was a front for the Palestinian group Hamas. That same month, Customs and Internal Revenue Service (IRS) agents seized financial records from the Benevolence International Foundation in Newark, New Jersey and the Global Relief Foundation near Chicago, Illinois.

The Treasury Department announced that all financial assets of the two foundations had been blocked. The Global Relief Foundation issued a statement strongly denying any connection with terrorism, but said it had already been forced to shut down its worldwide humanitarian operations. The Benevolence Foundation also announced that the asset freeze had ended its relief to the poor.

All of the foundations raided by the government complained that the seizures were timed for the end of Ramadan, the biggest period of charitable giving for Muslims, and the government has consistently denied requests to have the confiscated funds released to other charities doing similar work. The evidence on which these charities were closed was often kept secret, even from the targeted charities, but the Patriot Act's notion of "material support" was usually invoked, authorizing the government to close down charities the moment an investigation is begun.

None of the Muslim charities closed down since 9/11 has had employees or board members convicted of terrorism, and the government has never been able to document a money trail from the charities to actual terrorists. American Muslims suspect they and the beneficiaries of their charity are being targeted because of their religion or ethnicity. The Treasury Department told two board members of a Muslim humanitarian organization, "There are folks here who look at you guys like notches on their belts...just waiting to take the next one out." Laila al-Marayati, a board member of KinderUSA, a Muslim-American nonprofit humanitarian organization, has written, "[T]he message we are hearing is this: 'All Muslims are suspected of supporting terrorism. Your charities are guilty of this crime until proven innocent. But don't bother trying to prove your innocence because you won't have the chance'" (Laila al-Marayati, "The Crime of Being a Muslim Charity," *Washingtonpost.com*, March 12, 2006, p. B07. www.washingtonpost.com/wp-dyn/content/article/2006/03/10/). Most disturbing to people like al-Marayati is the fact that the government has not taken action against any

---

## IN HISTORY

### Material Support as a Basis for Exclusion

Donations to Muslim charities that are under investigation for links to terrorism are increasingly used as a basis for excluding foreign nationals from the United States. On September 25, 2006, the government rejected the visa application of Tariq Ramadan, one of Europe's most prominent Muslim intellectuals, saying he had supported a terrorist group. The American Civil Liberties Union (ACLU) said the government had notified Ramadan that he was being excluded because he donated $765 to French and Swiss organizations that provide humanitarian aid to Palestinians. The organizations are legitimate charities in France, but the Bush administration said some of the money donated by Ramadan ended up in the hands of the Palestinian group Hamas, making him guilty of "material support" to terrorism under the Patriot Act, which requires that a donor "reasonably should have known" that a charity would provide money for terrorism.

Ramadan explains: "[M]y donations were made between December 1998 and July 2002, and the United States did not blacklist the charities until 2003. How should I reasonably have known of their activities before the U.S. government itself knew?" (Tariq Ramadan, "Why I'm Banned in the USA," *Washington Post*, October 1, 2006, p. B2). Ramadan adds, "I am excluded not because the government truly believes me to be a national security threat, but because of my criticisms of American foreign policies in the Middle East; because of my opposition to the invasion of Iraq; and because of my criticism of some of the Bush administration's policies with respect to civil liberties" (Larry Neumeister, "Leading Muslim Scholar Is Denied U.S. Travel Visa," *Washington Post*, September 26, 2006, p. A11).

non-Muslim charities working in the same geographical areas as were the Muslim charities accused of financing terrorism.

Muslim charities have seen a precipitous decline in contributions since the passage of the Patriot Act. The Muslim philanthropic community has asked the Treasury Department to issue a "white list" of "approved" charities to which they could legally donate. The government responded: "Our role is to prosecute violations of criminal law. We're not in a position to put out lists of any kind, particularly of organizations that are good or bad" (William Fisher, "In Terror War, Not All Names Are Equal," *Common* Dreams, April 20, 2006. ww.commondreams.org/headlines06/0420-06.html).

# FURTHER READINGS

Benthall, Jonathan. *The Charitable Crescent: The Politics of Aid in the Muslim World.* New York: I.B. Tauris, 2003.

Burr, J. Millard. *Alms for Jihad: Charity and Terrorism in the Islamic World.* New York: Cambridge University Press, 2006.

"The Hamas Asset Freeze and Other Government Efforts to Stop Terrorist Financing." Hearing before the Subcommittee on Oversight and Investigations of the Committee on Financial Services. U.S. House of Representatives, 108th Congress, 1st Session, September 24, 2003. Washington, DC: GPO, 2004.

Levitt, Matthew. *Hamas: Politics, Charity, and Terrorism in the Service of Jihad.* New Haven, CT: Yale University Press, 2006.

Pieth, Mark. *Financing Terrorism.* Dordrecht, Netherlands: Kluwer Academic Publishers, 2003.

# Measuring Patriot Act Success: Harassing Aliens or Catching Terrorists?

- **Documents:** The Justice Department telling Congress that the Sami al-Arian indictment was a triumph of the USA Patriot Act; statement released by ACLU saying that the al-Arian case has nothing to do with 9/11 or al Qaeda and the Patriot Act was unnecessary to the case
- **Date:** February 13, 2004: the DOJ sent answers to questions from the House Judiciary Committee; June 4, 2003: ACLU memo on al-Arian case
- **Where:** Washington, DC
- **Significance:** The Justice Department claims that the prosecution of Sami al-Arian is among the most significant success stories of the Patriot Act. The ACLU says that the al-Arian case has little to do with America's War on Terror and that the Patriot Act had little to do with the prosecution of al-Arian. In any case, al-Arian was eventually acquitted on all charges, though he was subsequently deported under a plea agreement.

---

# DOCUMENTS

## 1. Justice Department Response to Question from House Judiciary Committee

*Question:* Can you tell us which [Patriot Act] authorities have proven most useful and why?

*Answer:* Prior to the [Patriot] Act, intelligence and law enforcement agencies and personnel were discouraged from sharing certain types of information.... Provisions of the Act, such as sections 203, 218, 403, 504, and 905, have enabled the intelligence arm and the law enforcement arm of the U.S. government to coordinate their efforts by breaking down the "wall".... Sections 218 and 504 were essential to the success of the Sami Al-Arian investigation in Tampa, Florida. Al-Arian was indicted on conspiracy charges related to his involvement with the North American cell of the Palestinian Islamic Jihad (PIJ) cell. Sections 218 and 504 enabled prosecutors to consider all evidence against the defendant, Sami Al-Arian, including evidence obtained pursuant to FISA. By considering the intelligence and law enforcement information together, prosecutors were able to create a complete history for the case and put each piece of evidence in its proper context. This comprehensive approach enabled prosecutors to build their case and pursue the proper charges. Thus, sections 218 and 504 were essential in allowing prosecutors to fully consider all evidence in this particular case and then move forward in an appropriate manner.

SOURCE: Hearing before the Committee on the Judiciary, House of Representatives, 108th Congress, 1st Session, June 5, 2003, Washington, DC: U.S. Government Printing Office, 2004.

---

## 2. ACLU Memo on Sami al-Arian Case

The DOJ discloses that, after September 11, 2001, the Attorney General ordered a review of almost "4,500 intelligence files" to determine whether any of the files contained information of relevance to a criminal prosecution.... The only case that is identified as resulting from the review of intelligence files has nothing to do with September 11 or Al Qaeda. Instead, the case is that of Sami Al-Arian, an Arab American leader in Tampa, Florida who has been accused of raising funds for Palestinian terrorism abroad. The accusations concerning Mr. Al-Arian…have been well known for almost a decade. In fact, virtually all of the FISA intercepts that form the basis of the indictment against Mr. Al-Arian were approved prior to the passage of the USA PATRIOT Act.... Still, high-ranking DOJ officials, including Attorney General Ashcroft and Assistant Attorney General Viet Dinh, still insist on claiming (1) that the Al-Arian indictment relies on intelligence information "previously unavailable" to prosecutors and (2) that the USA PATRIOT Act made such information available.

SOURCE: Timothy Edgar, "Interested Persons Memo on Congressional Oversight of the USA PATRIOT Act and Department of Justice Anti-Terrorism Policies," American Civil Liberties Union, June 4, 2003, pp. 3–4. www.aclu.org/safefree/general/172150leg20030604.html

---

# ANALYSIS

David Cole has written extensively on America's post-9/11 willingness to sacrifice the rights of aliens in order to ensure the security of our citizens. But he asks,

What are the results from this set of sacrifices? What are the gains we've made?... What concrete results do we see from this use of the coercive force of law in the name of a preventive paradigm, future-directed? There are some objective measures that we can look to. Of those 5,000 foreign nationals locked up in anti-terrorism preventive detention since 9/11, how many have been convicted of a terrorist crime? Zero. Not one. Zero for 5,000. Of the 8,000 called in for FBI interviews because they were from Muslim or Arab countries and therefore were presumably more likely to be terrorists, how many have been charged with a terrorist crime? Zero. Zero for 8,000. And for the 80,000 who were called in for special registration, fingerprinting, photographing and interviews, again because they were from Arab and Muslim countries, none have been charged or convicted of a terrorist crime. Those are pretty stark figures.

Cole points out that even the statistics on the DOJ Web page showing 500 deportations resulting from anti-terrorism investigations are an admission of failure, because, under the Patriot Act, the DOJ follows a policy of "hold until cleared." This means that the United States does not deport a detained alien until it has been determined that he has no connection to terrorism. "So these are misses, not hits, in terms of finding any actual terrorists," concludes Cole (David Cole, Speech on Constitution Day at Maryland Institute College of Art, Baltimore, MD, September 16, 2005).

Despite such discouraging statistics, the Bush Administration can offer simple and indisputable proof of the success of the Patriot Act and other new law enforcement powers in protecting America: There has not been another al-Qaeda attack on America since the passage of the Patriot Act. This positive analysis requires two assumptions: (1) the threat of terrorism against the United States remains high, and (2) the government's aggressive use of anti-terrorism tools like the Patriot Act has succeeded in capturing terrorists before they can act against us.

A recent study of DOJ investigations of international terrorism cases since 9/11 provides a comprehensive picture that seems to contradict both of these assumptions. The study by the independent Transactional Records Access Clearinghouse (TRAC) in late 2006 showed that DOJ prosecutions of terrorism cases surged after 9/11 but then dropped dramatically to pre-9/11 levels. The study also revealed that as many as nine out of ten terrorism investigations do not result in prosecutions, that most charges eventually brought are not related to terrorism, and that only about one-third of those prosecuted end up in prison.

The data show that in 2002, federal prosecutors filed charges against 355 defendants in international terrorism cases, but in 2005 the number had fallen to just forty-six, fewer than in 2001, and the numbers continue to drop. Only nineteen cases were prosecuted during the first nine months of 2006. The TRAC study found that federal prosecutors declined to bring charges in about two-thirds of the nearly 1,400 international terrorism cases over the five years since 9/11, often because of weak evidence. In 2006, nine out of ten terrorism cases had no charges brought against suspects.

The final TRAC report concluded: "Considering the numerous warning statements from [the] President and other federal officials about the continuing nature of the terrorism threat… the gradual decline in these cases since the FY2002 high point and the high rate at which prosecutors are declining to prosecute terrorism cases raises questions" (Dan Eggen, "Terrorism Prosecutions Drop," *Washington Post*, September 4, 2006, p. A6).

The major question posed by these statistics is, of course, whether the broad program of detention, interrogation, and deportation of foreign nationals has been productive. The DOJ points to some high-profile court cases testing the Patriot Act's power to identify and prosecute terrorists. For example, the case of Sami al-Arian has been characterized by Attorney General John Ashcroft as a triumph of the Patriot Act.

On February 20, 2003, Florida professor Sami al-Arian was arrested and imprisoned on terrorism charges after ten years of intensive surveillance that included 20,000 intercepted phone calls and faxes. The various wiretaps and surveillance orders used against al-Arian were authorized under the FISA years before the passage of the Patriot Act. Nevertheless, the Justice Department trumpeted al-Arian's indictment as a "triumph of the Patriot Act." None of the crimes listed in the indictment were covered in the Patriot Act's new definition of "domestic terrorism" and none of the massive surveillance that produced the evidence against al-Arian was authorized by the Patriot Act. How, then, could this case be celebrated as a triumph of the Patriot Act? The answer is found in what many feel is the centerpiece of the Patriot Act, the new authority to share investigative information between law enforcement and intelligence agencies, and perhaps more important, to prosecute criminal cases using evidence collected through foreign intelligence investigations. The latter is a powerful new authority, because the legal standards that must be satisfied before conducting foreign intelligence surveillance are less restrictive than those required for criminal investigations. Thus, under the Patriot Act, information acquired through methods that would never be authorized in a criminal *investigation* can nonetheless be used in a criminal *prosecution*. Such is the convoluted new legal environment in which Sami al-Arian found himself indicted.

Dr. al-Arian, a professor of computer science at the University of Southern Florida, had been placed on forced leave and banned from the university campus during the post-9/11 roundups and interrogations of Muslims, largely on the basis of a series of incendiary television commentaries on Fox News. He was arrested on February 20, 2003, held mostly in solitary confinement for more than two years until his trial began in June 2005. The charge against him was that he had supported the Palestinian Islamic Jihad, a group designated as a terrorist organization by the State Department.

At his indictment, the evidence presented against him consisted primarily of intercepted phone conversations and magazines seized from his office, all of which demonstrated vocal support for the Palestinian cause but no connection to terrorist acts. During his trial, the prosecution witnesses were mostly Israeli citizens brought in to testify about terrorist attacks they said were committed by the Palestinian Islamic Jihad in Israel. None of the testimony suggested that al-Arian was connected to such attacks or that he even knew of them.

Finally, on December 6, 2005, al-Arian was acquitted of all charges. The jury found him not guilty on eight of seventeen counts and deadlocked on the other counts. David Cole, the Georgetown University law expert who represented one of the other defendants, said the prosecutors in the al-Arian case had proceeded "on a kind of extremely sweeping guilt-by-association theory…without any showing that he specifically furthered or sought to further any violent act of any kind.…They have long proclaimed this as Exhibit A in the successful use of the Patriot Act and as one of their most important prosecutions in the war on terror ("Fla. Professor is Acquitted in Case Seen as Patriot Act Test," *Washington Post*, December 7, 2005, p. A15).

Despite the failure of its case, the government continued to detain al-Arian pending a decision to appeal. Finally, after being imprisoned for over three years and facing indefinite detention, al-Arian agreed to a deal with the Justice Department. He would plead guilty to supporting the Palestinian Islamic Jihad and the prosecution would specify that his actions did not contribute directly or indirectly to violence. The government agreed that it would impose no other conditions on al-Arian and would recommend that he be given the minimal prison sentence allowed by law and credit for time served. This would effectively allow him to avoid serving any time, releasing him into the custody of immigration officers for probable deportation.

At the time of his sentencing, everything changed. The judge ignored the terms of the plea agreement, chastised al-Arian for promoting violence and death—despite the fact that the jury had found him not guilty of such actions—and imposed the *maximum* prison sentence allowed by law, fifty-seven months. As a result, even with credit for time served, al-Arian was faced with another year and a half of prison, with deportation awaiting his release.

To make matters worse, the government reneged on its plea agreement by demanding that al-Arian appear before a grand jury in Virginia. When al-Arian refused to testify, citing his agreement with federal prosecutors, he was given an eighteen-month prison sentence for contempt of court. Each time a new grand jury was empanelled, al-Arian's prison sentence was renewed, effectively making his period of incarceration indefinite.

On January 21, 1007, al-Arian began a hunger strike to protest the government's actions and the conditions of his imprisonment. After the twenty-third day without food, he collapsed and was moved to a medical facility in North Carolina, where he was kept in twenty-four-hour solitary confinement. Amnesty International sent a letter to Attorney General Alberto Gonzales protesting al-Arian's treatment, saying it was "in breach of the USA's obligations under international standards and treaties" ("Why Is Dr. Sami Al-Arian Still in Prison? An Open Letter to Attorney General Alberto Gonzales," *Washington Post*, March 5, 2007, p. A13).

Attorney General Gonzales still regards the Sami al-Arian case as a Patriot Act victory, declaring: "We have a responsibility not to allow our nation to be a safe haven for those who provide assistance to the activity of terrorists. Sami Al-Arian has already spent significant time behind bars and will now lose the right to live in the country he calls home" ("Former Fla. Professor to Be Deported," *Washington Post*, April 14, 2006, p. A6).

# FURTHER READINGS

"Ashcroft: Patriot Act Is a Success," *St.Petersburg Times* (November 8, 2003). www.sptimes. com/2003/11/08/State/Ashcroft_Patriot_Act.shtml

Demleitner, Nora V. "Immigration Threats and Rewards: Effective Law Enforcement Tools in the 'War' on Terrorism?" *Emory Law Journal*, 51 (2002), pp. 1059–94.

Johnson, Kevin R. "Immigration, Civil Rights, and Coalitions for Social Justice," *Hastings Race and Poverty Law Journal*, 1, no. 181 (2003).

McDonnell, Thomas M. "Targeting the Foreign Born by Race and Nationality: Counter-Productive in the 'War on Terrorism?'" *Pace International Law Review*, 16, no. 19 (Spring 2004).

"The Patriot Act: Justice Department Claims Success," *NPR.org*, October 1, 2006. www.npr.org/templates/story/story.php?storyId=4756706

CHAPTER **6**

# Congressional Oversight of the Patriot Act

Figure 10. U.S. Capitol Building. Images of American Political History.

# Congress Includes Oversight Requirements in the Patriot Act

- **Documents:** Oversight provisions in Sections 215, 411, 412, and 1001 of the USA PATRIOT Act
- **When:** Signed October 26, 2001
- **Where:** Washington, DC
- **Significance:** Though Congress overwhelmingly passed the Patriot Act, it was aware that the sweeping new powers conferred on the executive branch would require strong congressional oversight. Several sections of the Patriot Act contained oversight provisions, some of which were retained from laws amended by the Patriot Act.

---

## DOCUMENTS

### 1. Oversight Provision in Section 215: Access to Records and Other Items under the Foreign Intelligence Surveillance Act

CONGRESSIONAL OVERSIGHT

(a) On a semiannual basis, the Attorney General shall fully inform the Permanent Select Committee on Intelligence of the House of Representatives and the Select Committee on Intelligence of the Senate concerning all requests for the production of tangible things....

(b) On a semiannual basis, the Attorney General shall provide to the Committees on the Judiciary of the House of Representatives and the Senate a report setting forth with respect to the preceding 6-month period—

(1) the total number of applications made for orders approving requests for the production of tangible things...; and

(2) the total number of such orders either granted, modified, or denied.

## 2. Oversight Provision in Section 411: Definitions Relating to Terrorism

NOTICE

(i) TO CONGRESSIONAL LEADERS—Seven days before making a designation under this subsection, the Secretary shall, by classified communication, notify the Speaker and Minority Leader of the House of Representatives, the President pro tempore, Majority Leader, and Minority Leader of the Senate, and the members of the relevant committees of the House of Representatives and the Senate, in writing, of the intent to designate an organization under this subsection, together with the findings made under paragraph (1) with respect to that organization, and the factual basis therefore.

## 3. Oversight Provision in Section 412: Mandatory Detention of Suspected Terrorists; Habeas Corpus; Judicial Review

(c) REPORTS—Not later than 6 months after the date of the enactment of this Act, and every 6 months thereafter, the Attorney General shall submit a report to the Committee on the Judiciary of the House of Representatives and the Committee on the Judiciary of the Senate, with respect to the reporting period, on—

(1) the number of aliens certified under section 236A(a)(3) of the Immigration and Nationality Act, as added by subsection (a);

(2) the grounds for such certifications;

(3) the nationalities of the aliens so certified;

(4) the length of detention for each alien so certified; and

(5) the number of aliens so certified who—

(A) were granted any form of relief from removal;

(B) were removed;

(C) the Attorney General has determined are no longer aliens who may be so certified; or

(D) were released from detention.

## 4. Section 1001: Review of the Department of Justice

The Inspector General of the Department of Justice shall designate one official who shall

(6) review information and receive complaints alleging abuses of civil rights and civil liberties by employees and officials of the Department of Justice;

(7) make public through the Internet, radio, television, and newspaper advertisements information on the responsibilities and function of, and how to contact, the official; and

(8) submit to the Committee on the Judiciary of the House of Representatives and the Committee on the Judiciary of the Senate on a semi-annual basis a report on the implementation of this subsection and detailing any abuses described in paragraph (1), including a description of the use of funds appropriations used to carry out this subsection.

SOURCE: USA PATRIOT Act (H.R. 3162). www.epic.org/privacy/terrorism/hr3162.html

# ANALYSIS

Section 215 of the Patriot Act authorizes the Director of the FBI to order the production of "any tangible thing (including books, records, papers, documents, and other items) for an investigation to protect against international terrorism or clandestine intelligence activities." The congressional oversight provision of Section 215 (see above) requires the Attorney General to inform the appropriate House and Senate committees on a semi-annual basis of the number of applications for such orders and the number of such orders granted, modified, or denied.

Section 411 of the Patriot Act defines a "foreign terrorist organization" and authorizes the Secretary of State to designate such organizations. The oversight provision of Section 411 requires that seven days before designating a terrorist organization, the Secretary of State notify House and Senate leaders and the relevant House and Senate committees of the intent to designate that organization, together with factual basis for the designation.

Section 412 of the Patriot Act authorizes the detention of aliens who are certified by the Attorney General as representing a danger to national security. The oversight provision of Section 412 requires the Attorney General to report every six months to the Judiciary Committees of the House and Senate on the number of aliens so certified; the grounds for certification; the nationalities of those certified; the length of detention; and the number of certified aliens who were granted relief from removal, removed, released from detention, or determined to be no longer subject to certification.

Section 1001 of the Patriot Act is, in its entirety, an oversight provision, requiring the Inspector General of the Department of Justice (DOJ)to designate an official to receive information and complaints of abuse of civil rights and civil liberties by employees and officials of the Department of Justice, publicize contact information, and submit to Congress on a semi-annual basis a report describing any such abuses.

In addition to the oversight provisions in the original Patriot Act, new requirements were added in the Improvement and Reauthorization Act of 2006. A new Section 106A requires the DOJ's Inspector General to conduct an audit on the effectiveness and use of Section 215 of the Patriot Act (the "tangible things" section) and submit an unclassified report of the audit to the House and Senate Committees on the Judiciary and Intelligence.

Section 107 of the Reauthorization Act requires the Attorney General to report annually to the Judiciary Committees of the House and Senate and to set forth the number of accounts subject to Section 212 disclosures and the basis for disclosure in certain circumstances (Section 212 of the original Patriot Act allows Internet service providers to disclose the contents of electronic communications, as well as subscriber information, in emergency situations).

Section 118 of the Reauthorization Act requires the Attorney General to submit to Congress the annual aggregate number of National Security Letter (NSL) requests concerning U.S. persons. Section 119 requires the Inspector General of the DOJ to conduct an audit of the effectiveness and the use of the NSL authority and report on the specific functions and characteristics of the NSLs issued.

The inclusion of oversight requirements in the Patriot Act was a small victory for those members of Congress who recognized that they were granting vast powers to the executive branch with little or no role for the courts. Only congressional oversight could prevent the arbitrary exercise of Executive power.

During the Senate debate on the Patriot Act in October 2001, Senator Maria Cantwell (D-WA) addressed Judiciary Committee Chairman Patrick Leahy: "May I ask the Chairman, do you agree that, under these circumstances it is incumbent upon the committee which has jurisdiction over the Department of Justice to maintain vigilant oversight of the department in its use of FISA authorities after the enactment of this legislation?"

Leahy answered,

> I agree with you completely, and you can rest assured that the Judiciary Committee under my chairmanship will conduct meaningful oversight.... Section 306 of

FISA…provides for semiannual reports from the Attorney General for physical search orders made, granted, modified or denied, and the number of physical searches which involved the property of United States persons. The Judiciary Committee's responsibility will be greater under [Patriot Act] amendment to FISA, because of the greater authority to use FISA for law enforcement purposes.

Cantwell responded,

I would like to suggest to the chairman…that the General Accounting Office provide to the Senate Judiciary Committee every six months a report on the use of the FISA wiretap authorities, and the expanded pen register and trap-and-trace authorities, by the Federal Bureau of Investigation or other agencies within the Department of Justice.…[O]nly with such oversight can we reasonably assure our constituents that the use of these new authorities is not impinging on our fourth amendment rights." (*Congressional Record—Senate*, October 11, 2001, S.10593-594)

The oversight provisions in the Patriot Act require only the submission of reports and statistics, leaving congressional hearings as the only method by which DOJ officials could be directly confronted. The ineffectiveness of written inquiries became painfully clear during the first few months after the passage of the Patriot Act, when the DOJ showed itself to be unresponsive to congressional requests for information. Judiciary Committee Chairman Leahy's early assurance of "meaningful oversight" was never put to the test. By 2002, Republican majorities had taken over both the House and Senate, resulting in new chairmanships for all committees. Congressional oversight understandably suffered as a single party took control of both Congress and the White House.

---

**IN HISTORY**

**The Church Committee: A Model for Congressional Oversight**

In the early 1970s, the Senate Select Committee to Study Government Operations with Respect to Intelligence Activities, chaired by Sen. Frank Church (D-ID), soon became known as the "Church Committee." The Committee's final report, submitted on April 26, 1976, was circumscribed by Central Intelligence Agency (CIA) pressure, but it nonetheless shocked Congress and the nation with its revelations of intelligence abuses, ranging from poison pen letters to recruitment of journalists to assassination plots.

The report was the result of more than 800 interviews, over 250 executive hearings, and documentation in excess of 110,000 pages. The Committee was never allowed to examine CIA files on its own, leading Church to complain,

[D]ocuments and evidence have been presented through the filter of the agency itself. Although the Senate inquiry was congressionally ordered, and although properly constituted committees under the Constitution have the right of full inquiry, the Central Intelligence Agency and other agencies of the executive branch have limited the Committee's access to the full record. (*Foreign and Military Intelligence Activities of the United States*, Final Report of the Select Committee to Study Governmental Operations with Respect to Intelligence Activities, April 26, 1976)

Despite these restraints, the Church Committee report revealed more information about American intelligence agencies, their powers and abuses, than all the oversight committees that would follow it. Indeed, the Church Committee revelations forced the CIA to renounce a number of its more controversial programs, including the use of American journalists as intelligence agents.

---

## FURTHER READINGS

Aberbach, Joel D. *Keeping a Watchful Eye: The Politics of Congressional Oversight*. Washington, DC: Brookings Institution, 1990.

Center for Democracy and Technology. "Congressional Oversight, Hearings and Legislation Introduced After the PATRIOT Act," December 30, 2006. www.cdt.org/security/usa patriot/hearings.shtml

Hamilton, Lee. *How Congress Works and Why You Should Care*. Bloomington, IN: Indiana University Press, 2004.

Krent, Harold J. *Presidential Powers*. New York: New York University Press, 2005.

Rosen, Bernard. *Holding Government Bureaucracies Accountable*. Westport, CT: Praeger, 1998.

Savage, Charlie. "Bush Shuns Patriot Act Requirement," *Boston.com News* (March 24, 2006). www.boston.com/news/nation/articles/2006/03/24

Weissman, Robert. "Oversight in the Republican Congress: Hearing Loss," *The American Prospect* (November 1998).

# Senate Faces Difficulties in Oversight of the Justice Department

- **Documents:** Statement in support of congressional oversight by Robert S. Mueller at his confirmation hearings as new FBI Director; *Interim Report on FBI Oversight*, Senate Judiciary Committee, describing lack of cooperation by the Department of Justice
- **When:** Mueller confirmation hearing held July 3–31, 2001; Senate Judiciary Committee *Interim Report* dated February 2003
- **Where:** Washington, DC
- **Significance:** Despite the supportive statements of incoming FBI Director Mueller at his confirmation hearings, the lack of subsequent cooperation from the Justice Department made effective congressional oversight of the Patriot Act virtually impossible.

## DOCUMENTS

### 1. Statement before Senate Judiciary Committee by FBI Director Robert S. Mueller

I understand, firmly believe in the right and the power of Congress to engage in its oversight function. It is not only a right, but it is a duty.... I absolutely agree that Congress is entitled to oversight of the ongoing responsibilities of the FBI and the Department of Justice. You mentioned at the outset the problems that you have had over a period of getting documents in ongoing investigations. And as I stated before and I'll state again, I think it is incumbent upon the FBI and the Department of Justice to attempt to accommodate every request from Congress swiftly and, where it cannot accommodate or believes that there are confidential issues that have to be raised, to bring to your attention and articulate with some specificity...why producing the documents would interfere with either that trial or for some other reason.

SOURCE: Confirmation Hearing on the Nomination of Robert S. Mueller, III to be Director of the Federal Bureau of Investigation, Senate Committee on the Judiciary, 107th Congress, 2nd Session, July 30–31, 2001.

---

## 2. Statement of Senator Patrick Leahy Concerning Failure of Congressional Oversight

Vigorous oversight is instrumental to ensuring that our law enforcement officials are effective and accountable, both in fighting crime and in preventing acts of terrorism. The lack of attention this Justice Department has given to oversight by the Senate Judiciary Committee regarding issues of national importance, including implementation of the USA PATRIOT Act, is, quite frankly, appalling. Reticence by the Nation's chief law enforcement officer to appear before the authorizing committee of the Senate would be disappointing any time. During these trying times in which the administration has chosen unilateral action it is inexcusable.

The written questions I posed to General Ashcroft in connection with last year's hearing did not get any response for 9 months, and even then, the so-called answers were incomplete and unresponsive. In fact, the Justice Department has delayed answering numerous written oversight requests until answers are moot or outdated, or they respond in vague and evasive terms. This approach stymies our constitutional system of checks and balances. The checks and balance on the executive intended by the founders and embodied in the Constitution are being put to the test by a secretive administration. More importantly, such flagrant avoidance of accountability fuels the sort of public distrust that is now associated with federal law enforcement and, in particular, with this Attorney General and his department.... We in Congress have the constitutional obligation and public responsibility to oversee the Department of Justice's operations. After September 11, after we expressed our sorrow for the victims and our determination to respond while preserving American freedoms, I publicly noted my regret that we had not performed more effective and thorough oversight of the Department of Justice in the years before 2001. During the 17 months in 2001 and 2002 when I chaired the Judiciary Committee I worked with all Members, Republicans and Democrats, to provide real oversight. There were times when the Attorney General used our hearings as a forum to attack us and our patriotism but we persisted to perform our constitutional duties. It is with deep regret that I report to this Senate and the American people that it is now more than a year since the Attorney General of the United States last appeared before the Senate Judiciary Committee. It is with sadness that I note the lack of effective oversight the Committee and the Senate are conducting on matters that threaten the freedoms and security of the American people.

SOURCE: *Congressional Record—Senate*, April 8, 2004, pp. S4012–13. www.fas.org/irp/congress/2004_cr/s040804.html

---

# ANALYSIS

Within weeks after the passage of the Patriot Act, the Senate Judiciary Committee, chaired by Democratic Senator Patrick Leahy (see Figure 11), convened hearings with senior officials from the Department of Justice (DOJ) on its implementation of the new authorities.

On November 28, 2001, the Committee heard testimony from Assistant Attorney General Michael Chertoff and on December 6, 2001 from Attorney General John Ashcroft.

The DOJ soon made clear that it wished additional improvements to anti-terrorism laws, including an expansion to the definition of "foreign power" to include non-U.S. persons who engaged in international terrorism. Committee Chairman Leahy, joined by colleagues Charles Grassley and Arlen Specter, complained,

> Shortly after the Committee initiated oversight hearings and had confirmed the new Director of the FBI, the Nation suffered the terrorist attacks of September 11, 2001.... In the immediate aftermath of the attacks, the Congress and, in particular, the Senate Judiciary Committee responded to demands by the Department of Justice (DOJ) and the FBI for greater powers to meet the security challenges posed by international terrorism. We worked together to craft the USA PATRIOT Act to provide such powers. With those enhanced powers comes an increased potential for abuse and the necessity of enhanced congressional oversight.... At times, the DOJ and FBI have been cooperative in our oversight efforts. Unfortunately, however, at times the DOJ and FBI have either delayed answering or refused to answer fully legitimate oversight questions. Such reticence only further underscores the need for continued aggressive congressional oversight. Out constitutional system of checks and balances and our vital national security concerns demand no less. In the future, we urge the DOJ and FBI to embrace, rather than resist, the healthy scrutiny that legitimate congressional oversight brings. ("Interim Report on FBI Oversight in the 107th Congress by the Senate Judiciary Committee," February 2003, p. 8. www.fas.org/irp/congress/2003_rpt/fisa.html)

Figure 11. Senator Patrick Leahy (D-VT).

DOJ cooperation with the Senate Judiciary Committee would continue to worsen. During the first ten months after the passage of the Patriot Act, the Committee sent twenty-seven unanswered letters to the Justice Department seeking information on the Patriot Act and related matters. Committee Chairman Leahy commented, "Since I've been here, I have never known an administration that is more difficult to get information from that the oversight committees are entitled to" (Adam Clymer, "Justice Dept. Balks at Effort to Study Antiterror Powers," *NYTimes.com*, August 15, 2002, p. 2).

In addition, the DOJ responded to some of the questions by providing information not to the Judiciary Committee which had requested it, but to the Intelligence Committee, leading Leahy to complain: "Such attempts at forum shopping by the Executive Branch are not a productive means of facilitating legitimate oversight" ("Interim Report on FBI Oversight in the 107th Congress by the Senate Judiciary Committee," February 2003, p. 10).

During oversight hearings on May 8, 2002, June 6, and September 10, Justice Department officials and FBI Director Mueller were questioned extensively, often in writing, but were frequently unresponsive. A Judiciary Committee report stated,

> Particularly with respect to our FISA oversight efforts, we are disappointed with the non-responsiveness of the DOJ and FBI. Although the FBI and the DOJ have sometimes cooperated with our oversight efforts, often, legitimate requests went unanswered or the DOJ answers were delayed for so long or were so incomplete that they were of minimal use in the oversight efforts of this Committee. The difficulty in obtaining responses from DOJ prompted Senator Specter to ask the Attorney General directly, "how do we communicate with you and are you really too busy to respond?" (ibid.)

The Judiciary Committee report concluded,

> [T]he FBI have made exercise of our oversight responsibilities difficult. It is our sincere hope that the FBI and DOJ will reconsider their approach to congressional oversight in the future. The Congress and the American people deserve to know what their government is doing. Certainly, the department should not expect Congress to be a "rubber stamp" on its request for new or expanded powers if requests for information about how the Department has handled its existing powers have either been ignored or summarily paid lip service. (ibid., 11)

Finally, on December 23, 2002, Assistant Attorney General Daniel Bryant provided a response to a question Leahy had asked at the May 8, 2002 Judicial Committee hearing. Leahy had asked:

(A)  Has the FBI requested records from a library or bookstore under section 215 of the Patriot Act?

(B)  Can the FBI serve such an order on a public library requiring it to produce records about patron Internet use?

(C)  Do library and bookstore patrons have a "reasonable expectation of privacy" in the titles of books they have purchased or borrowed?

The Department of Justice answered the questions as follows:

(A)  Any information about the implementation of Section 215 was classified "at the SECRET level" and would have to be provided under separate cover.

(B)  "Such an order could conceivably be served on a public library" but "the more appropriate tool for requesting electronic communication transactional records would be a National Security Letter (NSL)."

(C)  "Any right of privacy possessed by library and bookstore patrons in such information is necessarily and inherently limited since, by the nature of these transactions, the patron is reposing that information in the library or bookstore and assumes the risk that the entity may disclose it to another. Whatever privacy interests a patron may have are outweighed by the Government's interest in obtaining the information in cases where the FBI can show the patron's relevance to an authorized full investigation to protect against international terrorism or clandestine intelligence activities." (Letter from Daniel J. Bryant, Assistant Attorney General, to Senator Patrick J. Leahy, Chairman, Senate Judiciary Committee, in response to May 8, 2002, Judiciary Committee hearing, December 23, 2003. www.fas.org/irp/agency/doj/fisa)

On the same day, December 23, but in a separate mailing, Assistant Attorney General Bryant sent Leahy responses to a few of the questions submitted to Attorney General Ashcroft almost five months earlier at a Senate oversight hearing. Once again, the questions related primarily to the seizure of library records. Question 14 asked:

(A)  Please clarify what the government is doing to impose secrecy on its demands for information from libraries.

(B)  How many demands for library information has the Department made since enactment of the USA PATRIOT Act, as well as the legal authority that was used to require secrecy?

(C)  How many libraries has the FBI visited (as opposed to presented with court orders) since passage of USA PATRIOT Act?

(D)  Is the decision to engage in surveillance subject to any determination that the surveillance is essential to gather evidence on a suspect [who]...may be engaged in terrorism-related activities and that it could not be obtained through any other means?

In answering part A, the DOJ described the gag order imposed by Section 215 and NSLs, each of which imposes secrecy on "officers, employees or agents" of the companies or institutions receiving such orders. The only distinction made between the two types of gag order was with respect to whom the FBI's action could not be disclosed. The exercise of a Section 215 order may not be disclosed "to the target or to persons outside the company or institution" served with an order. The issuance of an NSL may not be disclosed "to any person."

Question 15 asked the Attorney General what precautions he was taking to ensure the security and confidentiality of records seized under Section 215 that do not relate to the target of the investigation. The DOJ responded that obtaining records under Section 215 of the Patriot Act requires a showing that "the individual for whom the records are being sought is related to an authorized investigation" (Letter from Daniel J. Bryant, Assistant Attorney General, to Senator Patrick J. Leahy, Chairman, Senate Judiciary Committee, in response to July 25, 2002 Judiciary Committee hearing, December 23, 2003. www.fas.org/irp/agency/doj/fisa).

No further answers to the many questions submitted by the Senate Judiciary Committee were forthcoming, but there was a DOJ letter sent on December 23, 2002 to Senator Russ Feingold, Chairman of the Subcommittee on the Constitution which responded to a few of the questions he had posed to Attorney General Ashcroft five months earlier. Question 2 asked about the implementation of Section 215:

a. Please provide the number of instances in which the FBI or other federal agencies have invoked this subpoena power and indicate the type of businesses served with the subpoena …

b. How many entities have challenged the subpoena and the information sought? … [W]hat has been the nature of the objection?

c. How many of these subpoenas has resulted in the collection of information that would otherwise be protected by state or federal privacy protection laws?

d. How many of these subpoenas have directly led to the prosecution of terrorists or the prevention of acts of terrorism? … [P]lease describe the prosecution or act of terrorism that was prevented.

e. How many subpoenas have been sought or granted to obtain the records of persons not the target of an investigation? … [P]lease explain why the Department sought the subpoenas.

f. Please provide copies of all policy directives or guidance issued to law enforcement officials about requesting subpoenas pursuant to Section 215.

The DOJ responded evasively to Feingold's questions, stating that information pertaining to the implementation of Section 215 "is classified at the SECRET level" and would accordingly be delivered under separate cover. The Department did, however, attach a revealing policy memo in response to Feingold's inquiry about guidance to FBI agents. The memo, dated October 26, 2001, was addressed to all FBI divisions. It advised all agents that the old standard for seizing library and other business records ("specific and articulable facts giving reason to believe that the target of the subpoena was an agent of a foreign power") had been replaced by Section 215, which required only "simple relevance." The memo explained,

In the past the FBI has encountered situations in which the holders of relevant records refused to produce them absent a subpoena or other compelling authority. When those records did not fit within the defined categories for National Security Letters or the four categories then defined in the FISA business records section, the FBI had no means of compelling production. With the new language the FBI can seek a FISA court order for any such materials. (Letter from Daniel J. Bryant, Assistant Attorney General, to Senator Russell D. Feingold, Chairman, Subcommittee on the Constitution, Senate Judiciary Committee, December 23, 2003. www.fas.org/irp/agency/doj/fisa)

In short, FBI agents are now advised that if a librarian refuses to divulge patron records without a proper subpoena, the Patriot Act gives them automatic and unchallengeable authority to compel disclosure.

When Republicans took control of both houses of Congress in 2002, the conflict between Congress and the White House was at least expected to be muted, but new Judiciary Committee Chairman, Republican Arlen Specter, was almost as outspoken in criticizing Executive arrogance as was his Democratic predecessor. Even after the Democrats took control of Congress in 2006, there was little promise that Congress would reassert its oversight authority. As is the case in the broader society, rights easily given away cannot easily be reclaimed.

# FURTHER READINGS

FBI Oversight: Terrorism and Other Topics. Hearing before the Committee on the Judiciary, United States Senate, 108th Congress, 2nd Session, May 20, 2004.

Johnson, Loch K. *A Season of Inquiry: The Senate Intelligence Investigation.* Lexington, KY: University Press of Kentucky, 1985.

Oversight of the USA PATRIOT Act. Hearing before the Committee on the Judiciary, United States Senate, 109th Congress, 1st Session, April 5 and May 10. 2005.

Sundquist, James L. *The Decline and Resurgence of Congress.* Washington, DC: Brookings Institution, 1981.

"Transcript: Bill Moyers Interviews Chuck Lewis," *NOW*, February 7, 2003, Public Affairs Television. www.pbs.org/now/transcript_lewis2.html

# The House of Representatives Demands Answers from the Justice Department

- *Documents:* Cover letter from House Judiciary Committee to Attorney General John Ashcroft, describing the need for answers to fifty questions concerning the Patriot Act; three cover letters from Assistant Attorney General Daniel Bryant to Judiciary Committee James Sensenbrenner, describing attached answers to the committee's questions
- *When:* Judiciary Committee letter dated June 13, 2002; Daniel Bryant's letters dated July 26, 2002, August 26, 2002, and September 20, 2002
- *Where:* Washington, DC
- *Significance:* The questions submitted by the House Judiciary Committee to Attorney General Ashcroft were the first congressional attempt to acquire detailed information on the conduct of the Patriot Act. The Justice Department's incomplete response and frequent resort to classified answers set the tone for future cooperation between Congress and the Bush Administration on Patriot Act issues.

## DOCUMENTS

### 1. Letter from House Judiciary Committee to Attorney General John Ashcroft

June 13, 2002

Dear Attorney General Ashcroft:

As the Chairman and Ranking Member of the House Committee on the Judiciary, it is our responsibility to conduct oversight of the Department of Justice's implementation of the USA PATRIOT Act ("Act"), signed into law by President Bush on October 26, 2001. The Act gave the government new investigative tools to combat new terrorist threats against the United States made all too evident by the attacks of September 11, 2001.

The Committee is interested in hearing from you and FBI Director Robert F. Mueller concerning the Department of Justice's use of these new tools and their effectiveness. In light of the broad scope of the Act, we are initially seeking written responses to the following questions, and we plan to schedule a hearing in the near future to allow further public discussion of these and other issues relating to the Department of Justice's activity in investigating terrorists or potential terrorist attacks.

Unless otherwise indicated, please provide data to the Committee current through May 31, 2002. In addition, if any answer requires the disclosure of classified material, please provide those answers under separate cover to the Committee in accordance with appropriate security procedures....

| F. James Sensenbrenner, Jr. | John Conyers, Jr. |
|---|---|
| Chairman | Ranking Member |

SOURCE: House Judiciary Committee, letter to Chairman F. James Sensenbrenner and Ranking Member John Conyers to Attorney General John Ashcroft, June 13, 2002. www.house.gov/judiciary/ashcroft061302.html

---

## 2. Letter from House Judiciary Committee Chairman F. James Sensenbrenner and Ranking Member John Conyers to Attorney General John Ashcroft

April 1, 2003

Dear Attorney General Ashcroft:

As the Chairman and Ranking Member of the House Committee on the Judiciary, it is our responsibility to conduct oversight of the Department of Justice's efforts to combat terrorism, which includes implementation of the USA PATRIOT Act signed into law by President Bush on October 26, 2001. In response to our letter of June 13, 2002, you provided us with information regarding the use of these new tools, which helped us to understand the complexity and extensive scope of the effort to implement the law.

The Department of Justice has also been faced with significant new challenges to which it has responded using existing authorities as well as those contained in the Act. This letter seeks information regarding the use of preexisting authorities and the new authorities conferred by the Act....

Sincerely,

| F. James Sensenbrenner, Jr. | John Conyers, Jr. |
|---|---|
| Chairman | Ranking Member |

SOURCE: House Judiciary Committee, letter from Chairman F. James Sensenbrenner and Ranking Member John Conyers to Attorney General John Ashcroft, April 1, 2003.

---

# ANALYSIS

Public hearings are the most visible and powerful form of congressional oversight, but quiet correspondence between Judiciary Committees and the DOJ has been arguably more effective in extracting information from the executive branch. The response to questions submitted to DOJ has been fitful and tardy, but persistence has occasionally produced valuable details on the implementation of the Patriot Act. On June 13, 2002, the House Judiciary Committee sent a letter to Attorney General John Ashcroft asking for a response to fifty questions pertaining to the implementation of the Patriot Act. The questions covered virtually the entire Patriot Act, including sections 103, 106, 203, 205–207, 211, 214–216, 218–220, 223–224, 310, 313–314, 401–405, 411–418, 421–422, 424–427, 806, 908, 1001, 1005, and 1007–1009.

The letter, signed by Chairman Sensenbrenner and Ranking Member Conyers, concluded: "Please forward your responses to these questions to the Committee at the address on this letter not later than 5:00 p.m. on Tuesday, July 9, 2002 (see Document 1 above).

On July 26, 2002, the DOJ responded to twenty-eight of the fifty questions. Of those twenty-eight, six were claims that such information required a classified answer. Of the twenty-two unclassified answers, many were simply boilerplate restatements of statutory language and others claimed that no relevant data were available. For example, Question 14 asked whether surveillance now authorized under the lower standard of Section 218 (requiring that foreign intelligence be only "a significant purpose" of an investigation rather than "the purpose") had resulted in surveillance that could not have been approved under prior law.

The DOJ responded:

> Because we immediately began using the new "significant purpose" standard after passage of the PATRIOT Act, we had no occasion to make contemporaneous assessments on whether our FISAs would also satisfy a "primary purpose" standard. Therefore, we cannot respond to the question with specificity.

DOJ was more responsive to questions related to the Patriot Act's immigration provisions. Question 35A asked if the Immigration and Naturalization Service (INS) has used the Patriot Act's definitions of "terrorism" to file new charges against aliens. The DOJ answered: "Although no additional charges have been filed as a result of the changes to Section 411, we have and will continue to carefully assess each case for the potential of adding additional charges created by the Patriot Act."

Question 35B asked if any alien had been denied admission based on the Patriot Act's new grounds of inadmissibility. The DOJ answered: "One alien has been denied admission under these new provisions. He was refused admission under the VISA Waiver Program as there is reason to believe that he is a money launderer."

Question 35C asked about the effect that Section 411 has had on ongoing investigations. The DOJ answered: "Section 411's expanded definition of 'engage in terrorist activity,' as well as the new definitions of 'terrorist organization' should enable the INS to charge more

## IN HISTORY

### The Demise of Congressional Oversight

During 2006, concerns over lax congressional oversight of the Bush Administration erupted in an unusual confrontation between a Republican Congress and a Republican president. On May 18, Peter Hoekstra, Chairman of the House Intelligence Committee and a staunch supporter of President Bush's anti-terrorism initiatives, wrote directly to the president to complain that the administration was preventing congressional oversight by withholding information on its domestic surveillance programs. Hoekstra wrote that the secrecy "may represent a breach of responsibility by the Administration, a violation of law and…a direct affront to me and the Members of this committee."

One week later, Senate Judiciary Committee Chairman Arlen Specter (R-PA) protested what he called "the administration's policy of not informing the Congress…in a way which enables the Congress and the Judiciary Committee to do our constitutional job on oversight" ("Bush Is Pressed on Reporting Domestic Surveillance," *Washington Post*, July 9, 2006, p. A6).

Today, members of Congress, past and present, are quick to acknowledge the demise of congressional oversight of the executive branch. On July 12, 2006, Thomas Foley, the last Democratic speaker of the House, and Newt Gingrich, the man who ousted him to become the first Republican speaker of the House in half a century, spoke together at the American Enterprise Institute on the topic, "How Congress Is Failing America."

Gingrich, still a conservative icon, urged Congress to rediscover its power to supervise the administration, arguing, "Congress really has to think about how wrong the current system is…. [I]t's important to have an informed, independent legislative branch coming to grips with this reality and not sitting around waiting for presidential leadership." He concluded, "The failure to do effective, aggressive oversight disserves the president."

Foley agreed, declaring, "It's the obligation of Congress to decide how far they want executive power to be exercised" ("The Ex-Speakers Speak with One Voice on the Sorry State of Congress," *Washington Post*, July 13, 2006, p. A2).

aliens with the security-related grounds of removal.... The INS is currently examining each potential terrorist-related investigation for appropriate use of the additional tools added by Section 411."

Question 35D asked if the Attorney General has used Section 411 to exclude any alien who has "used his position of prominence within any country to endorse or espouse terrorist activity or to persuade others to support terrorist activity or a terrorist organization." The DOJ said it was awaiting information from the Department of State on this issue.

Question 35E asked if any aliens had been found inadmissible because of an association with a terrorist organization. The DOJ said no aliens had been excluded under that provision of Section 411, but that "since inception of the USA PATRIOT Act, and due to the new provisions, the names of 304 aliens...have been added to the counter-terrorism database, TIPOFF."

Question 35F asked if there had been any challenges to the constitutionality of the charges added in Section 411. DOJ answered: "No, the charges have not been used. As a result, there have not been any federal suits."

Question 36 asked about the use of the Patriot Act's mandatory detention provision in Section 412. The DOJ answered: "Since September 11 and enactment of the PATRIOT Act, the INS has detained numerous aliens for violations of immigration law and who also present national security risks. It has been unnecessary, however, to use the new certification procedure added by the PATRIOT Act ..." (Letter from Daniel J. Bryant, Assistant Attorney General, to F. James Sensenbrenner, Chairman, House Committee on the Judiciary, July 26, 2002).

More than two months had passed since the Judiciary Committee had submitted its fifty questions to Attorney General Ashcroft. A month and a half had passed since the July 9 deadline by which the Committee had requested answers from DOJ, and unclassified responses had been received for less than half of the questions. Ranking Member John Conyers appeared on a National Public Radio program to discuss the continuing delays and the broader problems of oversight of the Patriot Act. When asked what he would do if the Justice Department continued to ignore the Judiciary Committee's requests for information, he answered, "I'll call up the attorney general and remonstrate with his secretary for ignoring my letters. I won't tolerate this." But in the absence of subpoena power, Conyers admitted, "If the attorney general continues to thumb his nose at me and everybody in the Congress, then I'm in the same place as 275 million other people" (*The Marc Steiner Show*, WNPR National Public Radio, August 21, 2002).

Only after House Judiciary Committee Chairman Sensenbrenner publicly stated that he would subpoena the requested information did the DOJ provide a response to the remainder of the fifty questions. In addition, as had been the case with the Senate Judiciary Committee, the DOJ responded to some of the questions by providing information not to the requesting committee, but to the Intelligence Committee.

On August 26, 2002, the DOJ finally responded to the remainder of the fifty questions. Question 13 asked for the number of "roving" pen register and trap and trace orders issued under Section 216. DOJ answered: "Section 216 does authorize a court to order 'the installation and use of a pen register or trap and trace device anywhere within the United States.' Although the exact number of pen/trap orders that have been executed outside of the district of the authorizing magistrate is unknown, such orders have proved to be critically important in a variety of terrorist and criminal investigations."

Question 24 asked: "[P]lease advise the Committee as to how many terrorist attacks have been prevented since September 11, 2001, how... were they prevented, and where were these terrorist attacks planned to have taken place?" DOJ answered: "It is impossible to know exactly how many terrorist attacks have been prevented, but the FBI, Department of Justice, and all relevant Federal agencies, along with our international allies and colleagues in State and local government have been aggressively working to prevent another attack."

Question 49 addressed the power to seize civil assets under Section 806 of the Patriot Act. It asked, "Has the Department of Justice used this power? If so, what is the status of the seized assets? Have any seizures under this section been challenged in court?" DOJ answered: "Currently, there is a single case ongoing, which is not a matter of public record. The assets have been seized pursuant to a court authorized seizure warrant.... No seizures under this section have been challenged in court."

Question 50 addressed Section 1001 of the Patriot Act, which requires the DOJ Inspector General (OIG) to investigate complaints of civil rights and civil liberties abuses by the DOJ. It asked, "How many such complaints have been received? How many investigations have been initiated? What is the status of those investigations?" DOJ answered: "As of June 15, 2002, the OIG had received approximately 450 complaints by letter, e-mail, telephone, or by referral from the Civil Rights Division" (Letter from Daniel J. Bryant, Assistant Attorney General, to F. James Sensenbrenner, Chairman, House Committee on the Judiciary, August 26, 2002).

In late August, 2002, Judiciary Committee staff submitted a series of follow-up questions to DOJ which were answered in a September 20 letter to Chairman Sensenbrenner. The most significant of these were Questions 10 and 11, which asked DOJ to describe the precautions taken to avoid Sections 214 and 215 of the Patriot Act being used against individuals solely because of their First Amendment activities. DOJ used identical language in answering both. First, the answer to Question 10:

> A great deal of care is given to ensure that an order authorizing the installation and use of a pen register or trap and trace device is not sought solely on the basis of activities protected by the First Amendment. In each case in which an order is sought from the Foreign Intelligence Surveillance Court, the attorney for the government conducts a review of the factual basis underlying the investigation and the request for pen/trap authority. The Attorney General or his designee, the Counsel for Intelligence policy..., personally approves the filing of every application with the Court. A brief statement of facts in each case is then presented to the Court, along with the Government's certification, signed by the individual applicant, that the order is not being sought solely for activities protected by the First Amendment.

The answer to Question 11 used the same language, simply substituting "the production of tangible things" for "the installation and use of a pen register or trap and trace device."

The most recent Patriot Act-related correspondence between the House Judiciary Committee and the Department of Justice began with an April 1, 2003, letter to Attorney General Ashcroft posing thirty-eight questions regarding "the use of preexisting authorities and the new authorities conferred by the [Patriot] Act." The DOJ referred several of those questions to the Department of Homeland Security (DHS) and said four other questions required a classified response. Of those that were answered, the first two concerned Section 215, authorizing the seizure of "any tangible thing."

The DOJ said such seizures "are conducted under the Attorney General Guidelines for FBI Foreign Intelligence Collection and Foreign Counterintelligence Investigation," but added, "These guidelines are classified at the Secret level."

Question 9 concerned Section 213, which allows a court to order a delay in notice of the execution of a search warrant. DOJ said such delays were ordered forty-seven times as of April 1, 2003.

Question 20 asked if the INS has relied on the Patriot Act's new definition of "terrorism" to deny admission to aliens. DOJ answered, "Prior to the transfer of the INS to DHS, at least three aliens had been denied admission under these new provisions.

Question 37 asked for details on "three successive FBI sweeps" of aliens since September 11 "to monitor, question, arrest, detain, or deport various immigrants." DOJ said: "The answers relating to these questions are classified" (Letter from Daniel J. Bryant, Assistant Attorney General, to F. James Sensenbrenner, Chairman, House Committee on the Judiciary, September 20, 2002).

How should we judge the effectiveness of almost two years of correspondence between the House Judiciary Committee and the DOJ, involving over a hundred questions and answers concerning the implementation of the Patriot Act? In June 2003, the American Civil Liberties Union (ACLU) released a statement suggesting that the questions and answers had been revealing, but not encouraging. It concluded:

(1) The DOJ did not need many of the powers it obtained in the USA PATRIOT Act or through new regulations and changes in longstanding government policies, such as the Attorney General's investigative guidelines;

(2) DOJ cited fears of terrorism to get powers without adequate debate which were then used in ordinary criminal cases;

(3) DOJ has failed to answer many of the legitimate questions Congress has posed about its use of the USA PATRIOT Act and other new powers; and

(4) DOJ has been deceptive in describing the scope of the powers it has been granted, apparently to mollify widespread public concern. ("Interested Persons Memo on Congressional Oversight of the USA PATRIOT Act," American Civil Liberties Union, www.aclu.org/safefree/general/17215leg20030604.html)

# FURTHER READINGS

Epstein, Edward. "Bush to Face Tough Questions Over Patriot Act," *San Francisco Century*, SFGate.com, December 24, 2005. www.sfgate.com/cgi-bin/article.cgi?f=/c/a/2005/12/24/MNGBOGD4FF1.DTL

Farnam, Julie. *U.S. Immigration Laws under the Threat of Terrorism*. New York: Algora Publications, 2005.

Feuerherd, Joe. "Congress Questions Patriot Act Policies," *National Catholic Reporter* (September 6, 2002). www.findarticles.com/p/articles/mi_m1141/is_38_38/ai_91566310

McCullagh, Declan. "DOJ Responds to House on Patriot Act," *CNET News.com* (October 17, 2002). http://news.com.com/2100-1023-962468.html

Murray, Frank. "Patriot Act of 2001 Casts Wide Net," *Washington Times* (June 15, 2003). http://washingtontimes.com/national/20030615-123422-5163r.html

# The Attorney General and Deputy Attorney General on the Congressional Hot Seat

- *Documents*: Opening statement of Attorney General John Ashcroft at hearing before the, 108th Congress, 1st Session, June 5, 2003; Opening statement of Deputy Attorney General James Comey at hearing before the House Judiciary Committee, 109th Congress, 1st Session, June 8, 2005
- *When*: June 5, 2003; June 8, 2005
- *Where*: Washington, DC
- Significance: In these two public hearings, Congress confronted Attorney General John Ashcroft and Deputy Attorney General James Comey on the implementation of the Patriot Act.

---

## DOCUMENTS

### 1. Opening Statement of Attorney General John Ashcroft

Chairman Sensenbrenner, thank you very much. And Ranking Member Congressman Conyers, thank you very much.... Twenty months ago you understood what was needed to preserve freedom. You understood that our Nation's success in this long war on terrorism demanded that the Justice Department continuously adapt and improve its capabilities to protect Americans from a fanatical, ruthless enemy. That's why you worked so hard together with us to shape an anti-terrorism law housed in the framework of American freedom, guided by the Constitution of the United Sates....I thank you for this opportunity to testify today. I thank you for the constitutional weapons that you have provided that make the war against those who fight freedom a war whose conflict will be resolved in victory. And I thank the American people for their support and their faith in the justice of our cause. I would be happy to answer questions.

*SOURCE*: Hearing before the Committee on the Judiciary, House of Representatives, 108th Congress, 1st Session, June 5, 2003.

---

## 2. Opening Statement of Deputy Attorney General James Comey

Thank you Mr. Chairman, Mr. Conyers, Members of the Committee. Thank you for this opportunity to come and talk, but most importantly to listen and to respond to concerns and questions.

I believe that people should question authority; that people should be skeptical of Government power; people should demand answers about how the Government is using its power. Our country, I was taught, was founded by people who had a big problem with Government power and worried about Government power, and so divided our powers and then added a Bill of Rights to make sure that some of their concerns were set out in writing.

I think it's incumbent upon the Government to explain how it's using power, how its tools have been important, how they matter; and to respond especially to the oversight of the legislative branch. I think citizens should question authority, and should demand the details about how the Government is using its power.

I worried very much a year ago that we were never going to find the space in American life to have debate, a real informed discussion about the PATRIOT Act.... I needn't have worried. Thanks largely to the work of this Committee and to your colleagues in the Senate, we have had, as you said, Mr. Chairman, a robust discussion and debate about these tools over the last months. And I think the American people understand them better. I think all of us have had an opportunity to demand details and respond to the questions.

*SOURCE:* Hearing before the Committee on the Judiciary, House of Representatives, 109th Congress, 1st Session, June 8, 2005.

---

# ANALYSIS

The pattern of continuous correspondence between congressional oversight committees and the DOJ that began almost immediately after the passage of the Patriot Act played an important role in informing Congress and the public about its implementation. But the Government's response to the many written questions submitted by the House and Senate Judiciary Committees had been slow and evasive. Information and data had occasionally been grudgingly released through written responses to the congressional correspondence, but by 2003, the soft approach of letter writing had run its course. It was time for Congress to confront the DOJ officials in person through public hearings. With no opportunity to delay their answers and no place to hide from television cameras, perhaps the Attorney General and his representatives would be more responsive.

Important hearings were held in June 2003 and 2005. At the first hearing, Attorney General John Ashcroft gave an impassioned defense of the Patriot Act. At the 2005 hearing, new Attorney General Alberto Gonzalez sent his Deputy Attorney General James Comey to quiet the growing congressional concern about the excesses of the Patriot Act. What a difference two years makes. Comey's tone was conciliatory, emphasizing the need of the people to "question authority" and "be suspicious of Government power." In particular, he welcomed congressional oversight of the Patriot Act.

Ashcroft's tone and message in 2003 were aggressive and exultant, confident in the righteousness of the executive branch and the new powers bestowed on it by the Patriot Act. He began his testimony with a stirring call to battle:

> The United States Department of Justice has been called to defend America. We
> accept that charge. We fight in the tradition of all great American struggles with

resolve, with defiance and honor. We fight to secure victory over the evil in our midst. We fight to uphold the liberties and ideals that define a free and brave people. Every day the Justice Department is working tirelessly, taking this war to the hideouts and havens of our enemies so that this never again touches the hearts and homes of America. (Hearing before the Committee on the Judiciary, House of Representatives, 108th Congress, 1st Session, June 5, 2003, p. 9)

Not all of the Committee members were impressed with the attorney general's patriotic rhetoric. Representative Maxine Waters (D-CA), the first committee member recognized by the chairman, addressed Ashcroft:

[W]e are concerned about the way that you have used your power, the way that you have detained immigrants, and we are increasingly concerned about the way that you have used the Foreign Intelligence Surveillance Act.... [Y]ou state that the United States has deported 5,145 individuals linked to the September 11 terrorism investigation.... [I]sn't it a fact that after you rounded up these individuals, you found that they had no involvement with terrorist activity, but found the problem with their immigration status that provided you with a simple legal basis to deport them? Is that what you mean when you say that these individuals were linked to the September 11 investigation? (ibid., 13)

This was a rude awakening for the attorney general. The collegial niceties of formal correspondence were gone. Ashcroft responded, "You raised the question about individuals who were deported who had—who were individuals that were linked to the terrorism investigation. There are individuals who had strong links to the terrorists against whom we did not have a case that was sufficient to bring criminal charges, or about whom the bringing of the case might result in the revelation of material in court which would be against the national security interest of the United States. And certain of those cases we have to make a considered judgment about what's in the best interest of the United States" (ibid., 14).

A similar confrontation occurred between Ashcroft and Representative William Delahunt (D-MA), who began:

Mr. Attorney General, you last appeared before this Committee some 18 months ago and asked us to enact the PATRIOT Act. At that time we were all struggling to absorb the magnitude of the assault on the country and the loss of innocent lives....

Now today, the reality is that many Americans are increasingly uneasy about some of these measures. As you indicated, libraries and book stores have launched a campaign to overturn section 215, and scores of cities and towns across America have adopted resolutions opposing the PATRIOT Act.... It appears that...the American people feel that the Government is intent on prying into every nook and cranny of people's private lives while, at the same time, doing all it can to block access to Government information that would inform the American people as to what is being done in their name....

You said in your statement, "We must not forget that our enemies are ruthless fanatics," and you are right. We all agree with that. But the solution is not for us to become zealots ourselves so that we remake our society in the image of those that would attack us. Then we have given them the victory that no one here wants them to achieve.

Ashcroft responded: "First of all, the rationale for not releasing anything is the national interest. There are lots of times, especially in international intelligence, security matters, when we don't release things because it is not in the national interest to do so." He concluded, "I tend to find it amusing when it is suggested to me in the Congress that I have a secret plan to change the law....I can assure you that in the event that the law is changed, this Congress will be involved in it and I won't have a vote on it" (ibid., 22–23).

By 2005, relations between Congress and the Justice Department, headed by Attorney General Alberto Gonzales, had warmed considerably. When Deputy Attorney General James Comey appeared before the Judiciary Committee on June 8, 2005, he was greeted warmly by Chairman Sensenbrenner, who opened the questioning in a supportive way: "Do you believe that section 218 [of the Patriot Act] helped tear down the wall that prevented communications between agencies? Should we make this section permanent? And can you give us some specific details on why we had problems before 9/11, and how this was solved?"

Comey responded amiably:

> Yes, Mr. Chairman, I'd be glad to, and thank you for the question. Section 218 changed our world. It is the one part of the PATRIOT Act that is groundbreaking, earthshaking, breathtaking to those of us who have devoted our lives to this work, because it broke down that wall....That is the absolutely most important part of the PATRIOT Act. And if it were to go away, we would go back to a place that people don't want us to be. That changed our world for the better, Mr. Chairman.

Some of the Democrats on the Committee, led by Ranking Member Conyers, had tough questions for Comey, but they seemed satisfied with his answers. By the end of the hearing a palpable sense of optimism about cooperation between Congress and the DOJ seemed to have emerged. This was summed up by Chairman Sensenbrenner in his final remarks:

> I believe that in the last year and a half the Justice Department has been much more forthcoming on the PATRIOT Act and on other issues than in the two and a half years prior to that. And this Chair has both publicly and privately expressed to former Attorney General John Ashcroft that an "I've got a secret" attitude on legitimate oversight that does not involve classified information is self-defeating.
>
> I would like to salute both you and Attorney General Gonzales. I think that there has been a change in attitude that has been particularly marked in the hearings that we've had on this. You help your cause by coming up here and answering questions in the way that you did, and the way that your boss did a couple of months ago. And I hope that continues. (ibid., 52)

Unfortunately, the honeymoon was short-lived. Less than a year later, Committee Chairman Sensenbrenner had an opportunity to question Attorney General Gonzales directly during another Judiciary Committee hearing. At that time, Gonzales evaded most of the questions asked by Republican and Democratic committee members, claiming either secrecy or ignorance. For example, when Representative Jerrold Nadler (D-NY) asked Gonzales about the highly publicized case in which a Canadian citizen was kidnapped by U.S. agents in a New York airport and whisked off to Syria for torture (see Chapter 7), it produced the following exchange.

> *Gonzales:* Well, I'm not comment[ing] on what may or may not have—
> *Nadler:* Do we claim the right to do that?
> *Gonzales:* I don't know, but I would be happy to get back to you on that....
> *Nadler:* The Government defended that in court, your Department defended that in court.
> *Gonzales:* Before I comment any further on that, Congressman, I'd like the opportunity to get back to you.

*Nadler:* Okay. And let me further ask, since we have done this, and since your Department has defended this in court…is this practice limited only to airports, or do we claim the right to take people going about their business, walking on the street, grocery shopping, window shopping, at the mall, suddenly and unexpectedly to grab them and to deport them to places like Syria without any evidence, without any due process?

*Gonzales:* Mr. Congressman, I'm not going to get into specific, what we do, what we don't do. What I can say is that we understand what our legal obligations are, we follow the law.…

*Nadler:* Can you assure this Committee that the United States Government will not grab anybody at an airport or any place in U.S. territory, and send them to another country without some sort of due process?

*Gonzales:* Well, what I can tell you is that we're going to follow the law.…

*Nadler:* Well, does the law permit us to send someone to another country without any due process, without a hearing before an administrative, an immigration judge or somebody?.…

*Gonzales:* I'm not going to confirm that we've done that.

Eventually, Chairman Sensenbrenner himself had to lecture Gonzales on his stonewalling: "I'm afraid that you have caused more questions to be put out for debate within the Congress and in the American public as a result of your answers. We have not been treated as partners for whatever reason.…I am really concerned that the Judiciary Committee has been kind of put in the trash heap" (Hearing before the Committee on the Judiciary, House of Representatives, 108th Congress, 2d Session, April 6, 2006, Serial No. 109-137, U.S. Government Printing Office, Washington: 2006).

# FURTHER READINGS

Arar, Maher. "We All Have a Right to the Truth." www.maherarar.ca/

De Young, Karen. "Gonzales Revisits Deportation Remarks," *Washington Post* (September 22, 2006), p. A14. www.washingtonpost.com/wp-dyn/content/article/2006/09/21/AR2006092101504.html

DOJ Oversight: Terrorism and Other Topics. Hearing before the Committee on the Judiciary, United States Senate, 108th Congress, 2d Session, June 8, 2004.

House Judiciary Committee. Letter to Attorney General Alberto Gonzales on NSA Surveillance (February 8, 2006). www.fas.org/irp/congress/2006/04/gonzales-doj-oversight-hearing-us.php

Prepared Remarks of Attorney General Alberto R. Gonzales at the House Judiciary Committee Oversight Hearing (April 6, 2006). Washington, DC: U.S. Department of Justice. www.usdoj.gov/ag/speeches/2006/ag_speech_060406

# Inspector General Reports Find Fault with Patriot Act Implementation

- **Document:** Question from Representative Linda Sanchez (D-CA) and answer from Office of the Inspector General (OIG) Department of Justice concerning the 2003 report
- **When:** June 5, 2003 Hearing before the Committee on the Judiciary, House of Representatives, 108th Congress, 1st Session
- **Where:** Washington, DC
- **Significance:** The semi-annual reports of the OIG, required by Section 1001 of the USA PATRIOT Act, exposed abuses in its implementation, particularly with respect to its treatment of immigrants and foreign nationals.

---

## DOCUMENT

### Question from Representative Linda Sanchez and Answer from Department of Justice

*Sanchez:* The OIG report contains horrifying examples of mistreatment of detainees, including the taunting of detainees by calling them 'Bin Laden junior' and telling them "you're going to die here," "someone thinks you have something to do with [9/11] so don't expect to be treated well." The detainees were physically abused as well—an inmate with a broken arm and injured finger had his wrist and finger twisted by officers, another was thrown in his cell naked without a blanket. They were deprived medical attention for injuries sustained in those assaults because, in the words of one physician's assistant, they "were not entitled to the same medical or dental care as convicted federal inmates." Your spokesperson said the Department makes "no apologies" for this conduct. Do you stand by her statement?

*Department of Justice:* As the Attorney General indicated before the House Judiciary Committee on June 5, 2003, the Department of Justice does not condone the abuse or mistreatment of any person being held in federal custody. The Department takes such allegations seriously and if any such allegations are found to be true, appropriate action will be taken. The statement of the Department's spokesperson applied to the overall detention policy: that we make no apologies that we detained illegal aliens when statistics show that 87 percent of them abscond when not detained. Again, it is not the policy of the department to allow the mistreatment of anyone, particularly those persons in federal custody.

SOURCE: Hearing before the Committee on the Judiciary, House of Representatives, 108th Congress, 1st Session, June 5, 2003, pp. 129–30.

---

# ANALYSIS

Of the several provisions in the Patriot Act relating to congressional oversight, perhaps the most significant is Section 1001, which requires semi-annual reports from the Justice Department's Office of the Inspector General (OIG) to the Judiciary Committees on "abuses of civil rights and civil liberties by employees and officials of the Department of Justice." A list of the complaints submitted and published in the OIG reports since passage of the Patriot Act appears in Table 6.1.

Some of the complaints investigated by the OIG had no direct connection to the Patriot Act and others were related to statutes amended by the Patriot Act, but all were part of the oversight requirements of Section 1001 of the Act. The very first OIG report explained that it was examining three primary issues:

- The detainees' ability to obtain legal counsel;
- The government's timing for issuance of criminal or administrative charges; and
- The general conditions of detention experienced by the detainees, including allegations of physical and verbal abuse, restrictions on visitation, medical care, duration of detention, confinement policies, and housing conditions.

Among the new investigations described in the first OIG report was one involving allegations that an individual detained shortly after the 9/11 attacks "was repeatedly slammed against a wall by unidentified correctional officers." Three other detainees were alleged to have been injured by the officers. The report concluded: "The OIG investigation has identified the correctional officers allegedly involved in the abuse. In addition, the OIG has interviewed the alleged victims and is reviewing their medical records" (U.S. Department of Justice, Office of the Inspector General, "Report to Congress on Implementation of Section 1001 of the USA PATRIOT Act," July 15, 2002, p. 5. www.usdoj.gov/oig/special/0207/index.html).

The second OIG report, covering the period from June 16 to December 15, 2002, stated: "During this reporting period, the OIG opened 6 new Patriot Act-related investigations, continued 11 ongoing Patriot Act-related investigations, and closed 4 investigations, 3 of which we discussed in our previous semi-annual report to Congress." Among the new cases was one involving an INS officer who allegedly held a loaded gun to an alien detainee's head and threatened him ("Report to Congress on Implementation of Section 1001 of the USA PATRIOT Act," January 22, 2003, p. 5. www.usdoj.gov/oig/special/0301a/index.html).

The third OIG report, covering December 16, 2002 through June 15, 2003, described six new Patriot Act-related investigations, eight ongoing Patriot Act-related cases, and three closed investigations. The first of the new cases concerned allegations by twenty inmates that a correctional officer engaged in abusive behavior toward Muslim inmates. A Bureau of Prisons witness provided the OIG with a sworn statement confirming the allegations, which were then corroborated by six inmates. Another investigation concerned claims by an Egyptian national that the FBI improperly arrested him immediately after 9/11, subjected him to multiple invasive body cavity searches, denied him access to counsel and the right to practice

TABLE 6.1 Complaints Submitted to the Justice Department about Civil Rights Abuses

| Date of Report (Period Covered) | Number of Patriot Act-Related Complaints | Number of Complaints within OIG Jurisdiction | Types of Complaints | Number of Complaints Warranting Review |
|---|---|---|---|---|
| June 15, 2002 (October 26, 2001–June 15, 2002) | 458 | 87 | Excessive force; illegal detention; denied access to attorney; detention under adverse conditions | N/A |
| January 22, 2003 (June 16, 2002–December 15, 2002) | 783 | 167 | Excessive force; verbal abuse; rude treatment; forced feeding against religious custom | 33 |
| July 17, 2003 (December 16, 2002–June 15, 2003) | 1,073 | 272 | Excessive force; verbal abuse; rude treatment; unwarranted cell searches; illegal searches of residences and property | 34 |
| January 27, 2004 (June 14, 2003–December 15, 2003) | 1,266 | 162 | Excessive force; verbal abuse; unwarranted cell searches; retaliatory action; illegal searches of property; fabrication of evidence | 17 |
| September 13, 2004 (December 16, 2003–June 21, 2004) | 1,613 | 208 | Excessive force; verbal abuse; religious discrimination; retaliation; illegal search and seizure; racial profiling | 13 |
| March 11, 2005 (June 22. 2004–December 31, 2004) | 1,943 | 195 | Sexual harassment; excessive force; verbal abuse | 12 |
| August 15, 2005 (January 1, 2005–June 30, 2005) | 834 | 210 | Verbal abuse; religious discrimination; physical and mental abuse; denying medical care | 13 |
| March 8, 2006 (June 1, 2005–December 31, 2005) | 701 | 131 | Religious discrimination; verbal and physical abuse | 4 |
| August 15, 2006 (January 1, 2006–June 30, 2006) | 803 | 156 | Verbal abuse; religious discrimination; no access to attorney; illegal search of family homes and businesses | 8 |

his religion, forced him to consume food prohibited by his religion, and denied him access to the Egyptian Consulate.

By this time, members of Congress were beginning to respond to the OIG reports. During the June 5, 2003 hearings on the Patriot Act, Representative Robert C. Scott (D-VA) asked Attorney General John Ashcroft: "The IG report on the 9/11 detainees, do you agree that that report suggests that crimes may have been committed by Government officials, including obstruction of justice, criminal assaults and intentional denial of civil rights and, if so, are you going to appoint a special prosecutor, or special counsel?"

Ashcroft answered: "We are aware of 18 cases that were alleged to be abuse cases.... I have no plan at this time to employ a special counsel in this matter."

Representative Howard Berman (D-CA) pressed the issue with Ashcroft, declaring:

[W]hat concerns me, when the Inspector General provides a list of institutional failures at DOJ, prolonged detentions without charges; a policy referred to as hold until cleared that led to average detentions of 80 days, but sometimes up to 200 days; a policy of obstruction of access to counsel; and an unwritten policy of denying bond for all aliens, a policy not restricted to suspected terrorists....

The Department of Justice spokesman says, in quite a defensive articulation, "The Inspector General report is fully consistent with what courts have ruled over and over, that our actions are fully within the law and necessary to protect the American people. We make no apologies for finding every legal way possible to protect the American public from further terrorist acts."

I find that kind of response troubling. (Hearing before the Committee on the Judiciary, House of Representatives, 108th Congress, 1st Session, June 5, 2003, pp. 18, 38–39)

The fifth OIG report, covering December 16, 2003 through June 21, 2004, documented the highly publicized investigation of Brandon Mayfield, whose fingerprints were falsely identified by the FBI on a bag containing bomb detonators. On the basis of the fingerprints, the Government detained Mayfield on a material witness warrant in connection with a train bombing in Spain. The FBI later discovered that the prints on the bag did not match Mayfield's, and he was released. Mayfield alleged that the FBI inappropriately conducted a surreptitious search of his home based on the faulty fingerprint analysis and motivated by his Muslim faith.

The OIG pursued the Mayfield investigation until early 2006, when it concluded that Mayfield's religion was "not the sole or primary cause of its misidentification of his fingerprints." It added, "However, we believe that Mayfield's representation of a convicted terrorist and other facts developed during the field investigation, including his Muslim religion, also likely contributed to the examiners' failure to sufficiently reconsider the identification after legitimate questions about it were raised by the Spanish National Police."

The 2006 OIG report said the FBI's ability, under the Patriot Act, to share information gathered from FISA surveillance with law enforcement officials contributed to the case against Mayfield, but it also noted an awkward conflict between the OIG and the DOJ, the very target of their oversight authority. The report stated:

> The OIG initially had intended to investigate the entire Mayfield matter, including the conduct of the DOJ attorneys working with the FBI.... However, DOJ OPR [Office of Professional Responsibility] disagreed. It contested our attorneys in the Mayfield case, and asserted jurisdiction over the entire matter.... It also disagreed with our position that Section 1001 provided us the authority to review the conduct of attorneys. Eventually the Deputy Attorney General resolved the matter by ruling that...the OPR should investigate the conduct of attorneys and the OIG should investigate the conduct of FBI agents in the Mayfield case. As a result of its investigation, DOJ OPR concluded that the DOJ attorneys assigned to the Mayfield matter did not commit misconduct. ("Report to Congress on Implementation of Section 1001 of the USA PATRIOT Act," March 8, 2006, pp. 8–9. www.usdoj.gov/oig/special/s0603/index.html)

The U.S. government agreed to pay $2 million to Mayfield and his family, apologized for the suffering it had caused them, and allowed Mayfield to proceed with a legal challenge to the constitutionality of the Patriot Act. The challenge produced a district court decision on September 26, 2007, in which Judge Ann Aiken ruled the Patriot Act to be in violation of the Constitution because it "permits the executive branch of government to conduct surveillance and searches of American citizens without satisfying the probable cause requirements of the Fourth Amendment.... A shift to a nation based on extra-constitutional authority is prohibited, as well as ill-advised" ("Patriot Act Provisions Voided," *Washington Post*, September 27, 2007, p. A2).

At a press conference, Mayfield said, "This is a momentous occasion and decision....The Fourth Amendment has been restored to its rightful place..., and now I do feel there is a sense of balance between privacy and security" (*NewsHour with Jim Lehrer*, PBS, September 28, 2007).

In response to the decision, the Justice Department said it would consider all its options.

This same OIG report had much to say about other possible abuses of authority by the DOJ, citing cases in which FBI agents tapped the wrong telephone, intercepted the wrong e-mails or continued to listen to conversations after a warrant had expired. In one case, the FBI obtained the *contents* of 181 telephone calls, rather than the billing records authorized under the law. In another case, communications were monitored for more than one year after surveillance should have ended. Representative John Conyers (D-MI), ranking member on the House Judiciary Committee, said the OIG report was

> yet another vindication for those of us who have raised concerns about the administration's policies in the war on terror....Despite the Bush administration's attempt to

demonize critics of its anti-terrorism policies as advancing phantom or trial concerns, the report demonstrates that the independent Office of Inspector General has found that many of these policies indeed warrant full investigations. ("FBI Cites More Than 100 Possible Eavesdropping Violations," *Washington Post*, March 9, 2006, p. A9)

# FURTHER READINGS

"ACLU Leadership Meets with Justice Department Inspector General to Inquire about Long-Overdue Report on Detainee Abuses," American Civil Liberties Union, May 9, 2003. www.aclu.org/safefree/general/17270prs20030509.html

Eggen, Dan. "Justice Department to Examine Its Use of NSA Wiretaps," *Washington Post* (November 28, 2006), p. A10. www.washingtonpost.com/wp-dyn/content/article/2006/11/27/AR2006112701063.html

"Publications and Products, Office of the Inspector General (OIG), Department of Justice." www.fas.org/irp/agency/doj/oig/product.html

Report to Congress on Implementation of Section 1001 of the USA PATRIOT Act: (as Required by Section 1001 (3) of Public Law 107-56). U.S. Department of Justice, Office of the Inspector General, 2003. http://purl.access.gpo.gov/GPO/LPS34056

Talanian, Nancy. "What the Justice Department Inspector General's Report Doesn't Tell Us," CommonDreams.org News Center. www.commondreams.org/views04/0204-11.html

U.S. Department of Justice, Office of the Inspector General (OIG). www.usdoj/oig/

# CHAPTER 7

# Amendments and Legal Challenges to the Patriot Act

Figure 12. Senator Bernie Sanders (I-VT).

# The Freedom to Read Protection Act

- *Document:* Text of the Freedom to Read Protection Act
- *When:* Bill introduced in the House of Representatives on March 6, 2003
- *Where:* Washington, DC
- *Significance:* The Freedom to Read Protection Act, introduced by then Representative Bernie Sanders (I-VT), was the first major attempt to roll back some of the powerful surveillance powers granted in the USA PATRIOT Act.

---

## DOCUMENT

### Text of the Freedom to Read Protection Act (H.R.1157)

108th CONGRESS
1st Session

#### H.R. 1157

To amend the Foreign Intelligence Surveillance Act to exempt bookstores and libraries from orders requiring the production of any tangible things for certain foreign intelligence investigations, and for other purposes.

IN THE HOUSE OF REPRESENTATIVES
March 6, 2003

Mr. SANDERS (for himself, Mr. PAUL, Mr. DEFAZIO, Mr. BLUMENAUER, Mr. OWENS, Ms. LEE, Mr. FARR, Mr. TOWNS, Mr. GRIJALVA, Mr. CONYERS, Mr. McDERMOTT, Ms. JACKSON-LEE, Mr. HINCHEY, Mr. OLVER, Ms. WOOLSEY, Mr. FRANK of Massachusetts, Mr. JACKSON of Illinois, Mr. McGOVERN, Ms. BALDWIN, Ms. WATERS, Mr. FORD, Mr. LIPINSKY, Mr. STARK, and Mr. UDALL of Colorado) introduced the following bill; which was referred to the Committee on the Judiciary, and in addition to the Select Committee on Intelligence (Permanent Select), for a period to be subsequently determined by the Speaker, in each case for consideration of such provisions as fall within the jurisdiction of the committee concerned.

## A BILL

To amend the Foreign Intelligence Surveillance Act to exempt bookstores and libraries from orders requiring the production of any tangible things for certain foreign intelligence investigations, and for other purposes....

### Section 1. Short Title

This Act may be cited as the "Freedom to Read Protection Act of 2003."

### Section 2. Exemption of Bookstores and Libraries from Orders

Requiring the Production of Any Tangible Things for Certain Foreign Intelligence Investigations.

Section 501 of the Foreign Intelligence Surveillance Act of 1978 (50 U.S.C. 1861) is amended by adding at the end the following new subsection:

(f)(1) No application may be made under this section with either the purpose or effect of searching for, or seizing from, a bookseller or library documentary materials that contain personally identifiable information concerning a patron of a bookseller or library.

(2) Nothing in this subsection shall be construed as precluding a physical search for documentary materials referred to in paragraph (1) under other provisions of law, including under section 303.

(3) In this subsection:

(A) The term "bookseller" means any person or entity engaged in the sale, rental or delivery of books, journals, magazines or other similar forms of communication in print or digitally.

(B) The term "library" has the meaning given that term under section 213(2) of the Library Services and Technology Act (20 U.S.C. 9122(2)) whose services include access to the Internet, books, journals, magazines, newspapers, or other similar forms of communication in print or digitally to patrons for their use, review, examination or circulation.

(C) The term "patron" means any purchaser, renter, borrower, user or subscriber of goods or services from a library or bookseller.

(D) The term "documentary materials" means any document, tape or other communication created by a bookseller or library in connection with print or digital dissemination of a book, journal, magazine, newspaper, or other similar form of communication, including access to the Internet.

(E) The term "'personally identifiable information" includes information that identifies a person as having used, requested or obtained specific reading materials or services from a bookseller or library.

### SEC. Section 3. Expansion of Reporting Requirements under FISA

Section 502 of the Foreign Intelligence Surveillance Act of 1978 (50 U.S.C. 1862) is amended by striking subsections (a) and (b) and inserting the following:

(a) On a semiannual basis, the Attorney General shall fully inform the appropriate congressional committees concerning all requests for the production of tangible things under section 501, including with respect to the preceding 6-month period—

(1) the total number of applications made for orders approving requests for the production of tangible things under section 501; and

(2) the total number of such orders either granted, modified, or denied.

(b) In informing the appropriate congressional committees under subsection (a), the Attorney General shall include the following:

(1) A description with respect to each application for an order requiring the production of any tangible things for the specific purpose for such production.

(2) An analysis of the effectiveness of each application that was granted or modified in protecting citizens of the United States against terrorism.

(c) In a manner consistent with the protection of the national security of the United States, the Attorney General shall make public the information provided to the appropriate congressional committees under subsection (a).

(d) In this section, the term "appropriate congressional committees" means—

(1) the Permanent Select Committee on Intelligence of the House of Representatives and the Select Committee on Intelligence of the Senate; and

(2) the Committees on the Judiciary of the House of Representatives and the Senate.

SOURCE: Freedom to Read Protection Act, http://thomas.loc.gov/cgi-bin/query/z?c108: H.R.1157

---

# ANALYSIS

On March 6, 2003, Independent Congressman Bernie Sanders, now serving as Vermont's senator, introduced the first major legislative attempt to roll back some of the vast powers granted to the executive branch in the USA PATRIOT Act. The Freedom to Read Protection Act (H.R. 1157) was actually drafted in response to an "open letter" signed by two-thirds of Vermont's independent booksellers and nearly 200 librarians from across the state. Not only was H.R. 1157 introduced at the behest of librarians and booksellers, but that constituency was responsible for publicizing the bill and its target, Section 215 of the Patriot Act, which was seen as the single greatest threat to library and bookstore confidentiality.

Thirty-two groups representing booksellers, librarians, book publishers, authors, and others joined several companies, including Barnes and Noble and Borders, in issuing a statement supporting H.R. 1157. Judith Krug, executive director of the American Library Association's (ALA's) Office for Intellectual Freedom, said, "Protecting the confidentiality of one's use of the library is of primary concern to librarians. Representative Sanders' bill would restore this core value of librarianship." Chris Finan, president of the American Booksellers for Free Expression (ABFFE), echoed that view: "The book community is united in believing that Section 215 of the Patriot Act threatens First Amendment freedom by making people afraid that their purchase or borrowing records may be monitored by the government" ("Book Groups Call for Patriot Act Amendment," American Booksellers Foundation for Free Expression, May 15, 2003).

Finan said that librarians and booksellers were mobilizing congressional and public support for H.R. 1157. "The rapid increase in the number of cosponsors is very encouraging," he said. "In addition, we are seeing a spike in the amount of press coverage that the issue is getting. Hopefully, this will enable us to maintain our momentum, but it is crucial that booksellers continue to contact their representatives in the House" ("Sanders Bill to Amend Patriot Act Attracts Seven More Co-Sponsors," April 4, 2003, http://news.bookweb.org/1314.html).

The Sanders bill would modify Section 215 by returning to the standard under which the Federal Bureau of Investigation (FBI) could obtain library and bookstore records prior to the passage of the Patriot Act. The FBI would still have access to such records through the usual court-ordered search warrant or subpoena, but it would be required to provide "specific and articulable facts" supporting the belief that the target of the search was an agent of a foreign power. The Patriot Act lowered that standard by allowing the FBI to seize "any tangible thing" from anyone, not just a foreign agent, and requiring the FBI to show only that the warrant was "relevant" to a counterintelligence investigation.

Sanders explained,

> Few who voted for the Patriot Act—I did not—knew that among its provisions was one that gave FBI agents the authority to engage in fishing expeditions to see what Americans read.... To remedy the excesses of the Patriot Act that threaten our right to read, I have introduced the Freedom to Read Protection Act. The bill, which has the support of Democrats and Republicans, progressives and conservatives, will establish once again that libraries and bookstores are no place for fishing expeditions. (Rep. Bernie Sanders, "Pulling FBI's Nose Out of Your Books," *Los Angeles Times*, May 8, 2003, pp. 1–2)

In a 2003 interview, Joel Barkin, Representative Sanders' press secretary, gave me an optimistic assessment of the chances for passage of the Sanders bill. "I think there's a real chance that we could win this," he said.

> The great thing about our bill is that it's very comprehensible. People understand it. It spells out very clearly the proper protection of their confidentiality in the use of libraries and book stores, something they do every day. The Patriot Act, on the other hand, is a confusing piece of legislation. (Author interview with Rep. Bernie Sanders (I-VT), May 29, 2003)

## IN HISTORY

### Senate Companion to the Sanders Amendment

Because of his early initiative and the strong support of the library and bookseller communities, Representative Sanders' House bill (H.R. 1157) attracted far more publicity than its companion bill in the Senate, Barbara Boxer's Library and Bookseller's Protection Act (S.1158), introduced on May 23, 2003. Still, many saw the Boxer bill as the stronger of the two, because it addressed both Section 215 and the National Security Letter (NSL) provision of the Patriot Act.

The text of the Boxer bill stated that it would:

(1) exempt bookstores and libraries from FISA court orders (Section 215 of the Patriot Act) that require the production of "tangible things" for intelligence investigations and (2) exempt libraries from being considered "wire or electronic service providers" under Section 2709 of Title 18 of the U.S. Code, which provides for counterintelligence access to records.... The FBI has told Congress that it is more likely to use NSLs to get at the electronic records...in libraries than Section 215 of the Patriot Act.

Sanders' House bill came closer to passage than its Senate companion, which never reached markup. Ultimately, both the House and Senate bills failed to overcome the Republican majority, which continued to regard any change to the Patriot Act as a threat to national security.

Despite acquiring over 150 co-sponsors, H.R.1157 languished in two different House committees for more than a year. Finally, on July 8, 2004, Representative Sanders tried an end run around hostile Republican chairmen by inserting language into a $39.8-billion appropriations bill that would bar the use of any of those funds to conduct surveillance under Section 215 of the Patriot Act. Despite a threatened White House veto, the Sanders provision, called the Freedom to Read Amendment, appeared to have broad support on the House floor, leading at one point in the voting by 219 to 210, but Republican leaders resorted to an unusual tactic, arbitrarily extending the allotted voting time to allow them to reign in dissident party members. Irate Democrat members shouted in unison, "Shame, shame, shame," but the Republican leadership succeeded in bringing the vote down to a 210 to 210 tie, defeating the Sanders amendment.

A disconsolate Sanders said, "I find it ironic that, on an amendment designed to protect American democracy and our constitutional rights, the Republican leadership in the House had to rig the vote and subvert the democratic process in order to prevail." Representative Butch Otter, a conservative Republican from Idaho who co-sponsored the amendment, said, "You win some, and some get stolen" ("House Rejects Effort to Curb Patriot Act's Section

215," American Libraries Online, July 9, 2004. www.ala.org/ala/alonline/currentnews/news-archive/alnews2004).

The defeat of the Freedom to Read Amendment foreshadowed a major battle in Congress during the 2005 debate on reauthorization of the Patriot Act's sunsetted provisions, including Section 215. When Sanders announced on March 9, 2005 that he would reintroduce the original Freedom to Read Protection Act, few thought that he could resurrect the support needed for passage. Yet, on June 15, 2005, the House approved the Sanders bill 238 to 187, with the support of thirty-eight Republicans.

The ALA's Emily Sheketoff declared, "Library patrons should be thrilled that their champion, Congressman Sanders, has finally prevailed. People from every political persuasion supported this amendment, and we are grateful that members of the House listened to librarians' concerns"("House Votes to Limit Patriot Act's Section 215," American Library Association, June 17, 2005. www.ala.org/historyTemplate.cfm?Section=Professional).

The Sanders victory was short-lived. Formidable obstacles remained. The Senate had not even begun to consider a companion bill, and as Congress began hearings on reauthorization of the full Patriot Act, concerns about Section 215 were lost in the patriotic debate. On July 21, 2005, the House approved legislation that would make permanent 14 of the 16 expiring provisions of the Patriot Act. Section 215 was not made permanent in the House bill, but it was given a lengthy ten-year sunset and none of the changes sought by Sanders were approved. This was essentially the end of the trail for the Freedom to Read Protection Act. The Senate would later make minor changes to the House bill, but the controversial provisions of Section 215 would remain unscathed.

# FURTHER READINGS

"Rep. Bernie Sanders Talks with BTW." *Bookselling This Week* (May 23, 2005). http://news.bookweb.org/freeexpression/3569.html

Sanders, Bernie. "Pulling the FBI's Nose Out of Your Books," *CommonDreams.org* (May 8, 2003). www.commondreams.org/views03/0508-10.html

———. "Republican Leadership Hijacks U.S. House to Defeat Sanders' Patriot Act Amendment," Bernie.House.Gov, July 8, 2004. www.law.harvard.edu/students/orgs/crcl/vol41_1/herman

"Sanders Attempts to Overturn Part of Patriot Act," *Democracy Now*, June 15, 2005. www.democracynow.org/article.pl?sid=05/06/15/134

Weinberg, Anna. "Second Time's the Charm for Rep. Bernie Sanders and American Booksellers," *Book Standard*, June 16, 2005. www.thebookstandard.com/bookstandard/news/author/article_display.jsp?.vnu

# Amendments Languish in Committee, But Their Language Influences Events

- *Document:* Text of the Benjamin Franklin True Patriot Act
- *When:* September 24, 2003
- *Where:* Washington, DC
- *Significance:* The Benjamin Franklin Real Patriot Act, introduced by Representative Dennis Kucinich (D-OH) and others, was the most ambitious amendment proposed to modify the powerful surveillance powers granted in the USA PATRIOT Act. Like the other attempts to amend the Patriot Act, this bill was buried in committee, but would later influence congressional action during the 2005 reauthorization of the Patriot Act.

---

## DOCUMENT

### Benjamin Franklin True Patriot Act

108th CONGRESS
1st Session

#### H.R.3171

To provide for an appropriate review of recently enacted legislation relating to terrorism to assure that powers granted in it do not inappropriately undermine civil liberties.

#### IN THE HOUSE OF REPRESENTATIVES
#### September 24, 2003

Mr. KUCINICH (for himself, Mr. PAUL, Mr. CONYERS, Mr. GEORGE MILLER of California, Mr. SERRANO, Mrs. JONES of Ohio, Mr. MCGOVERN, Mr. ABERCROMBIE, Ms. LEE, Mr. STARK, Mr. FILNER, Mr. GRIJALVA, Ms. JACKSON-LEE of Texas, Mr. HINCHEY, and Mr. FARR) introduced the following bill; which was referred to the Committee on the Judiciary, and in addition to the Select Committees on Intelligence (Permanent Select), Education and the Workforce, Government Reform, and Transportation and Infrastructure, for a period to be subsequently determined by the Speaker, in each case for consideration of such provisions as fall within the jurisdiction of the committee concerned.

## A BILL

To provide for an appropriate review of recently enacted legislation relating to terrorism to assure that powers granted in it do not inappropriately undermine civil liberties.

*Be it enacted by the Senate and House of Representatives of the United States of America in Congress assembled.*

### Section 1. Short Title.
This Act may be cited as the "Benjamin Franklin True Patriot Act."

### Section 2. Findings.
Congress finds the following:

(1) Benjamin Franklin stated: "Those who would give up essential Liberty, to purchase little temporary Safety, deserve neither Liberty nor Safety."

(2) The First, Fourth, Fifth, Sixth, Eighth, and Fourteenth Amendments to the United States Constitution were established to protect the civil rights and liberties of all Americans in perpetuity.

(3) Federal policies adopted since September 11, 2001, including provisions in the USA PATRIOT Act (Public Law 107-56) and related executive orders, regulations, and actions threaten fundamental rights and liberties, including the First, Fourth, Fifth, Sixth, Eighth, and Fourteenth Amendments to the Constitution by—

(A) authorizing the indefinite incarceration of noncitizens based on mere suspicion, and the indefinite incarceration of citizens designated by the President as "enemy combatants" without access to counsel or meaningful recourse to the Federal courts;

(B) limiting the traditional authority of Federal courts to curb law enforcement abuse of electronic surveillance in antiterrorism investigations and ordinary criminal investigations;

(C) expanding the authority of Federal agents to conduct so-called "sneak and peek" or "black bag" searches, in which the subject of the search warrant is unaware that his or her property has been searched;

(D) granting law enforcement and intelligence agencies broad access to personal, medical, financial, library, and education records with little if any judicial oversight;

(E) chilling constitutionally protected speech through overbroad definitions of "terrorism";

(F) creating divisions between immigrant communities and the police that protect them by encouraging involvement of State and local police in enforcement of Federal immigration law; and the police that protect them;

(G) permitting the FBI to conduct surveillance of religious services, internet chatrooms, political demonstrations, and other public meets of any kind without having any evidence that a crime has been or may be committed; and

(H) mandating the closure of certain immigration removal hearings, including denying judges the authority to reject stays of release where bond has been ordered and denying noncitizens the right to a bond hearing.

(4) Future legislation, such as legislation drafted entitled the Domestic Security Enhancement Act (DSEA) or Patriot II, contains a multitude of new and sweeping law enforcement and intelligence gathering powers many of which are not related to

terrorism, and would severely dilute and undermine many basic constitutional rights as well as disturb our unique system of checks and balances by—

(A)  diminishing personal privacy by removing important checks on government surveillance authority;

(B)  reducing the accountability of government to the public by increasing government secrecy;

(C)  expanding the definition of "terrorism" in a manner that threatens the constitutionally protected rights of Americans; and

(D)  seriously eroding the right of all persons to due process of law.

(5)  The above new and unprecedented powers pose threats to all Americans and particularly to the civil rights and liberties of the residents of our Nation who are Arab, Muslim, or of South Asian descent.

### Section 3. Ninety-Day Review Period.

Each provision of law, regulation, or other policy directed listed in sections 4 through 10, and any amendments made by that provision, shall cease to have effect 90 days after the date of the enactment of this Act. During this 90-day period, the Congress may, at the request of the President, hold hearings to determine whether a particular section should be removed from the list in section 4.

### Section 4. Provisions in the USA PATRIOT Act.

The provisions in the USA PATRIOT Act (Public Law 107-56) to which section 3 applies are:

(1)  Section 213, relating to "sneak and peek searches."

(2)  Section 214, relating to the use of pen registers for foreign intelligence purposes.

(3)  Section 215, relating to the obtaining by the Government of certain business records.

(4)  Section 216, relating to the use of pen registers in criminal cases.

(5)  Section 218, relating to the Foreign Intelligence Surveillance Act.

(6)  Section 411, relating to new grounds for deportation.

(7)  Section 412, relating to mandatory detention of certain aliens.

(8)  Section 505, relating to national security letters.

(9)  Section 507, relating to educational records.

(10)  Section 508 relating to collection and disclosure of individually identifiable information under the National Education Statistics Act of 1994.

(11)  Section 802, relating to the definition of domestic terrorism.

### Section 5. Provisions of Aviation Security Act Excluding Permanent Resident Aliens from Being Baggage Checkers.

Section 3 also applies to section 44935(e)(2)(A)(ii) of title 49, United States Code.

### Section 6. Homeland Security Act of 2002 PROVISIONS.

Section 3 also applies to the following provisions of the Homeland Security Act of 2002.

(1)  Section 14, relating to an exemption from the Freedom of Information Act.

(2)  Section 871, relating to an exemption from the Federal Advisory Committee Act.

### Section 7. Immigration Regulations Provisions.

Section 3 also applies to the following provisions of regulations:

(1) The regulation found at 66 Federal Register 48334-35 (September 20, 2001) relating to time held without charges.

(2) The regulation found at 66 Federal Register 54909-12 (October 31, 2001) relating to automatic stays for the Government in immigration hearings.

(3) The so-called "Creppy memo" that mandates closed immigration hearings in certain cases, and 67 Federal Register 54878 (August 26, 2002) relating to restructuring appeals.

(4) Any legal opinion or regulation that increases the powers of the Attorney General to authorize State or local law enforcement officers to exercise Federal immigration enforcement beyond those given in 8 CFR Part 2 or 28 CFR Part 65.

(5) The regulation found at 67 Federal Register 52584 (August 12, 2002), relating to registration and monitoring of certain aliens, and all notices published pursuant to that regulation.

### Section 8. Attorney-Client Monitoring.

Section 3 also applies to the regulation found at 66 Federal Register 55063, relating to monitoring conversations between attorneys and clients.

### Section 9. Secrecy Orders.

Section 3 also applies to the memorandum of Attorney General Ashcroft dated October 12, 2001 and relating to the disclosure of documents under the Freedom of Information Act.

### Section 10. Thornburg Guidelines on Religious Institution Spying.

Section 3 also applies to any regulations having the effect of changing the effect of the Attorney General's Guidelines on General Crimes, Racketeering Enterprise and Domestic Security/Terrorism Investigations approved by Attorney General Dick Thornburg for the Department of Justice on March 21, 1989.

*SOURCE:* Benjamin Franklin True Patriot Act, www.theorater.com/bills/hr3171.html

---

# ANALYSIS

Even the strongest supporters of the Patriot Act acknowledged that the sense of urgency after 9/11 imposed extraordinary pressures on Congress to limit debate and swiftly pass the Administration's anti-terrorism bill. Yet not until 2003 was Congress willing to consider amending that hastily passed legislation. Representative Bernie Sanders' Freedom to Read Protection Act, analyzed earlier in this chapter, amended Section 215 of the Patriot Act, as did Senator Russ Feingold's Library and Personal Records Privacy Act, introduced on July 30, 2003.

On July 31, Senators Lisa Murkowski (R-AK) and Ron Wyden (D-OR) introduced the Protecting the Rights of Individuals Act, a bipartisan bill that would:

- Narrow the government's authority to conduct secret "sneak and peek" searches by requiring that they be conducted only in terrorism investigations and only when revealing the search would endanger the life or safety of an individual, result in flight from prosecution, or destroy evidence sought under the warrant.
- Narrow the definition of "domestic terrorism."
- Limit access to business records, including library and bookstore records, under Section 215.
- Limit the FBI's ability to use roving wiretaps.

- Increases judicial review for telephone and Internet monitoring.
- Require prior congressional approval for "data mining."
- Require public disclosure of basic information about the FBI's otherwise secret intelligence investigations.
- Apply traditional discovery procedures to evidence used in court proceedings.
- Raise the standard of review for seizing educational records.

On October 1, 2003, Senators Larry Craig (R-ID), Patrick Leahy (D-VT), John Sununu (R-NH), Richard Durbin (D-IL), and Harry Reid (D-NV) introduced the PATRIOT Oversight Restoration Act of 2003 (S.1695), which sought to sunset some of the more controversial sections of the Patriot Act, including:

- Portions of Section 203 authorizing disclosure of grand jury information to government officials.
- Sections 210 and 211, which broaden the types of information that law enforcement may obtain from electronic service providers.
- Section 213, which authorizes "sneak and peek" search warrants.
- Sections 216 and 222, which expand government authority to obtain pen register or trap and trace orders.
- Section 412, which grants the Attorney General authority to "certify," and therefore detain, an alien as a threat to national security.
- Section 505, which expands FBI authority to use National Security Letters.
- Sections 507 and 508, which remove privacy protections for educational records.
- Section 802, which broadly defines "domestic terrorism."

## IN HISTORY

### Floor Amendments

Most significant amendments to existing law are carefully drafted and publicly introduced before ever reaching the floor of Congress for a vote. Time is required to assemble a list of prominent sponsors and to allow appropriate committees the opportunity to approve the amendment and report it out to the floor. Frequently, the committees to which amendments are sent become their graveyard. Indeed, having an amendment "referred to committee" can be the kiss of death.

Not all amendments reach a committee. Many appear for the first time on the House or Senate floor, usually as part of the general debate on pending legislation. As we saw in Chapter 2, floor amendments to the Patriot Act were discouraged during the October 2001 debates, and only the persistence of Senator Russ Feingold allowed any amendments to be considered. They were all soundly defeated.

During the 2005 debate on reauthorization of the Patriot Act (see Chapter 8), a number of amendments were offered. The more substantial ones, such as the SAFE Act and the Benjamin Franklin True Patriot Act, had been introduced earlier and sent to committee, but others were more spontaneous responses to a flawed reauthorization conference report. Most of the amendments failed, but portions of a few emerged in the final reauthorization package.

Surely the most ambitious amendment proposed during 2003 was the Benjamin Franklin True Patriot Act (H.R. 3171), introduced on September 24. The amendment, cosponsored by Representatives Dennis Kucinich (D-OH) and Ron Paul (R-TX), would repeal eleven different sections of the Patriot Act, two provisions of the Homeland Security Act, and a variety of post-9/11 federal regulations. The full text of H.R. 3171 was presented above, but its major provisions would:

- Repeal searches of library, medical, and financial records without judicial warrant.
- Repeal detention and deportation of non-citizens without careful judicial review.
- Establish the fundamental right of attorney-client privilege.
- Restore transparency to DOJ and Department of Homeland Security procedures by revoking Freedom of Information Act (FOIA) secrecy orders and exemption from the Federal Advisory Committee Act.

Representative Jim McDermott (D-WA), an original cosponsor of H.R.3171, said:

> The Benjamin Franklin True Patriot Act seeks to repeal the unconstitutional provisions of the Patriot Act and to protect the Constitution…I am proud to be a cosponsor of this bill, and I will continue to oppose the Bush Administration's efforts to steal our civil liberties. Congress must not sit by while the Administration uses fear and the threat of terrorism to tread on our constitutionally guaranteed civil liberties. ("Congressman Jim McDermott Co-Sponsors the Benjamin Franklin True Patriot Act," September 29, 2003. www.house.gove/mcdermott/pr030929.html)

Representative Pete Stark (D-CA), another cosponsor of the True Patriot Act, said,

> Attorney General Ashcroft has used the Patriot Act to engage in an out-and-out assault on basic civil liberties. He has made a mockery of due process, violated basic privacy protections, and authorized federal agents to spy and snoop under a shroud of absolute secrecy…. Repealing the worst provisions of the Patriot Act will reign in this gross abuse of power and restore to everyone our basic constitutional rights. (Representative Pete Stark, press release, September 24, 2003. www.house.gov/stark/news/news_2003-09-24_PatAct.html)

On October 22, Representative C. L. "Butch" Otter (R-ID) introduced the Security and Freedom Ensured (SAFE) Act in the House after its earlier introduction in the Senate. The SAFE Act, which had bipartisan cosponsors in both the House and Senate, would:

- Limit the government's authority to conduct secret "sneak and peek" to situations where informing the subject would endanger the life or safety of an individual, result in flight from prosecution, or destroy evidence sought under the warrant.
- Limit the FBI's ability to use roving wiretaps.
- Limit access to library, bookseller, and other business records.
- Prevent the FBI from using National Security Letters to obtain transactional records from library computers.
- Sunset Section 213, the "sneak and peek" provision, and other provisions expanding the FBI's ability to obtain records without a court order.
- Narrow the overly broad definition of "domestic terrorism" to serious federal crimes like bombing, kidnapping, and hijacking.

All of the amendments to the Patriot Act proposed in 2003 were "referred to committee," the congressional action that keeps bills from full consideration and an ultimate vote. In a Republican Congress with Republican committee chairmen, there was little chance that any bill designed to roll back the Administration's anti-terrorism powers would escape the committees. But the language and intent of these amendments could not be bottled up. In particular, the language of the SAFE Act became the basis for virtually every reform proposed to the Patriot Act during the 2005 reauthorization debate. As will be seen in the next chapter, some of those reforms were codified and passed in the final version of the reauthorized Patriot Act.

# FURTHER READINGS

"Benjamin Franklin True Patriot Act," *Answers.com*, 2005. www.answers.com/topic/benjamin-franklin-tru-patriot-act

"EFF Analysis of the Security and Freedom Ensured Act (S.1709)." Electronic Frontier Foundation, 2005. www.eff.org/patriot/safe_act_analysis.php

"Resolution in Support of Benjamin Franklin True Patriot Act." American Civil Liberties Union (December 16, 2003). www.aclu.org/safefree/resources/16916res20031216.html

A Review of Counter-terrorism Legislation and Proposals, Including the USA PATRIOT Act and the SAFE Act. Hearing before the Committee on the Judiciary, United States Senate, 108th Congress, 2d Session, September 22, 2004.

"The SAFE Act of 2005." American Civil Liberties Union, 2005. http://action.aclu.org/reformthepatriotact/safe.html

# Secret FISA Court Renders Unprecedented Rebuff to the Patriot Act

- *Document:* Text of U.S. Foreign Intelligence Surveillance Court decision
- *When:* May 17, 2002
- *Where:* Washington, DC
- *Significance:* The proceedings of the secret FISA Court had never been revealed to Congress or the public since its inception in 1979, but in August 2002 a conflict between the court and the Justice Department over the implementation of the Patriot Act was revealed to the Senate Judiciary Committee. When the FISA court ruled that the government was inappropriately combining criminal investigations with foreign intelligence investigations, the Justice Department appealed, constituting the first formal challenge to the court in its history.

---

## DOCUMENT

### Foreign Intelligence Surveillance Court Memorandum Opinion

The Department of Justice has moved this Court to vacate the minimization and "wall" procedures in all cases now or ever before the Court, including this court's adoption of the Attorney General's July 1995 intelligence sharing procedures, which are not consistent with new intelligence sharing procedures submitted for approval with this motion. The Court has considered the Government's motion, the revised intelligence sharing procedures, and the supporting memorandum of law as required by the Foreign Intelligence Surveillance Act (hereafter the FISA or the Act) at 50 U.S.C. §1805(a)(4) and §1824(a)(4) (hereafter omitting citations to 50 U.S.C.) to determine whether the proposed minimization procedures submitted with the Government's motion comport with the definition of minimization procedures under §1801(b) and §1821(4) of the Act. The Government's motion will be GRANTED, EXCEPT THAT THE PROCEDURES MUST BE MODIFIED IN PART....

THEREFORE, because

- the procedures implemented by the Attorney General govern the minimization of electronic surveillance searches of U.S. persons;

- such intelligence and criminal investigations both target the same U.S. person;
- the information collected through FISA surveillances and searches is both foreign intelligence information and evidence of crime, depending upon who is using it;
- there are pervasive and invasive techniques for electronic surveillances and physical searches authorized under the FISA;
- surveillances and searches may be authorized for extensive periods of time;
- notice of surveillances and searches is not given to the targets unless they are prosecuted;
- the provisions in FISA constrain discovery and adversary hearings and require ex parte, in camera review of FISA surveillances and searches at criminal trial;
- the FISA, as opposed to TITLE III and Rule 41 searches, is the only tool readily available in these overlapping intelligence and criminal investigations;
- there are extensive provisions in the minimization procedures for dissemination of FISA intercepts and seizures to criminal prosecutors and for consultation and coordination with intelligence officials using the FISA;
- criminal prosecutors would, under the proposed procedures, no longer be prohibited from "directing or controlling" counterintelligence investigations involving use of the FISA toward law enforcement objectives; and
- criminal prosecutors would, under the proposed procedures, be empowered to direct the use of FISA surveillances and searches toward law enforcement objectives by advising FBI intelligence officials on the initiation, operation, continuation and expansion of FISA authority from this Court,

The Court FINDS that parts of section II.B of the minimization procedures submitted with the Government's motion are NOT reasonably designed, in light of their purposes and technique, "consistent with the need of the United States to obtain, produce, or disseminate foreign intelligence information" as defined in §1801(h) and §1821(4) of the Act.

THEREFORE, pursuant to this Court's authority under §1805(a) and §1824(a) to issue ex parte orders for electronic surveillances and physical searches "as requested or as modified," the Court herewith grants the Government's motion BUT MODIFIES the pertinent provisions of sections II.B. of the proposed minimization procedures as follows:....

> Notwithstanding the foregoing, law enforcement officials shall not make recommendations to intelligence officials concerning the initiation, operation, continuation or expansion of FISA searches or surveillances. Additionally, the FBI and the Criminal Division shall ensure that law enforcement officials do not direct or control the use of the FISA procedures to enhance criminal prosecution, and that advice intended to preserve the option of a criminal prosecution does not inadvertently result in the Criminal Division's directing or controlling the investigation using FISA searches and surveillances toward law enforcement objectives.

These modifications are intended to bring the minimization procedures into accord with the language used in the FISA, and reinstate the bright line used in the 1995 procedures, on which the Court has relied. The purpose of minimization procedures as defined in the Act, is not to amend the statute, but to protect the privacy of Americans in these highly intrusive surveillances and searches, "consistent with the need of the United States to obtain, produce, and disseminate foreign intelligence information."

SOURCE: Foreign Intelligence Surveillance Court Memorandum Opinion, May 17, 2002. www.fas.org/irp/agency/doj/fisa/fisc051702.html

# ANALYSIS

Since the passage of the Patriot Act, the Justice Department has exalted its new "intelligence sharing" authority into the essential centerpiece of the anti-terrorism legislation. Imagine their shock when the ultrasecret Foreign Intelligence Surveillance Court ruled on May 17, 2002 that the Justice Department's use of this new power had inappropriately combined intelligence gathering and law enforcement in violation of FISA and the Constitution. In its entire twenty-five-year history, up until its 2002 ruling, the FISA court had approved over 13,000 surveillance orders and, according to available records, had *never* refused an application for surveillance!

The proceedings of the secret FISA court had remained hidden from the public and even from Congress until this legal conflict was revealed in Senate Judiciary Committee hearings. The case began in May 2002, when the FBI secretly sought two wiretap orders from the FISA court, which issued a confidential ruling denying the applications and setting out guidelines to separate intelligence gathering from criminal prosecutions. The crux of the dispute centered on the provision in the Patriot Act that allows FISA surveillance orders to be issued if foreign intelligence gathering is "a significant purpose" of the investigation. Previously, FISA orders could only be approved in investigations whose primary purpose was foreign intelligence gathering. The Justice Department interpreted the Patriot Act provision to mean that a FISA order could now be issued even if its primary purpose was a criminal investigation, an approach the court said contradicted the very purpose of the FISA statute.

In its May 17 opinion (see text above), the court scaled back the Patriot Act's information-sharing provisions, allowing criminal prosecutors to consult with intelligence investigators, but not allowing them to steer investigations to further prosecutions or to control or direct foreign intelligence investigations. It said the Department had not complied with the FISA's minimization procedures (the process by which surveillance information inadvertently acquired on nontargeted individuals is isolated and destroyed), whose purpose is "to protect the privacy of Americans in these highly intrusive surveillances and searches, 'consistent with the need of the United States to obtain, produce, and disseminate foreign intelligence information.'"

In announcing its intention to appeal the FISA court's ruling, the Justice Department declared: "We believe the court's action unnecessarily narrowed the Patriot Act and limited our ability to fully utilize the authority Congress gave us" ("Secret Court Rebuffs Ashcroft," *Washington Post*, August 23, 2002, p. A01. www.washingtonpost.com/ac2/wp-dyn?pagename).

To what court was DOJ appealing the FISA ruling? By statute, there exists a United States Foreign Intelligence Surveillance Court of Review (FISCR), but in its twenty-five years of existence, it had never issued a ruling. This secret FISA Court of Review consisted of three semi-retired appeals court judges selected by Supreme Court Chief Justice William Renquist. The FISCR accepted the government's claim that the Patriot Act allows it to obtain a FISA surveillance order even where its primary purpose is a criminal investigation. The review court said,

## IN HISTORY

### The Foreign Intelligence Surveillance Court

The Foreign Intelligence Surveillance Act (FISA) of 1978 created a secret court that approves or denies the use of electronic surveillance for foreign intelligence purposes. Originally consisting of 7 judges, the court was increased to 11 judges by the Patriot Act. The judges, who come from different federal circuits, meet twice a month in Washington, D.C., and three judges are always available in Washington.

The FISA court decides its cases in secret, and the U.S. citizens who are targeted by its warrants are never informed of its surveillance and are not represented before the court. The court is not required to reveal its legal opinions, resulting in a secret body of case law unprecedented in American jurisprudence. If the court denies an application for surveillance, the government may appeal to the Foreign Intelligence Surveillance Court of Review, a panel of three federal judges appointed by the Chief Justice of the Supreme Court. Each of the current review court judges was originally appointed to the federal judiciary by President Ronald Reagan.

Not surprisingly this case raises important questions of statutory interpretation, and constitutionality. After a careful review of the briefs filed by the government and amici, we conclude that FISA, as amended by the Patriot Act, supports the government's position, and that the restrictions imposed by the FISA court are not required by FISA or the Constitution.

The reasoning by which the FISCR reversed the FISA court seemed to be the notion that 9/11 had imposed a virtually permanent state of emergency on the American people, forcing the judicial system to accept standards for surveillance that need only "come close" to meeting Fourth Amendment requirements. The FISCR concluded:

FISA's general programmatic purpose, to protect the nation against terrorists and espionage threats directed by foreign powers, has from its outset been distinguishable from "ordinary crime control." After the events of September 11, 2001, though, it is hard to imagine greater emergencies facing Americans than those experienced on that date.... Our case may well involve the most serious threat our country faces. Even without taking into account the President's inherent constitutional authority to conduct warrantless foreign intelligence surveillance, we think the procedures and government showings required under FISA, if they do not meet the minimum Fourth Amendment warrant standards, certainly come close. We, therefore, believe firmly, applying the balancing test drawn from *Keith*, that FISA as amended is constitutional because the surveillances it authorizes are reasonable. (United States Foreign Intelligence Surveillance Court of Review, November 18, 2002. www.fas.org/irp/agency/doj/fisa/fisc111802.html)

Under normal circumstances, the public would have no knowledge of the FISCR ruling or its deliberations. But because the initial FISA case had been revealed to Congress, the FISCR reversal was, in part, made public. The extraordinary ex parte proceedings were particularly interesting, and disturbing to legal scholars. Only the Justice Department representatives and the three judges were allowed to participate. In the course of the proceedings, even the presiding FISCR judge, Ralph B. Guy, Jr., observed, "This is a strange proceeding because it is not adversarial. If one were to just read the transcript of the hearing today, one might think that the adversary, if there is one, is the lower body in this matter."

The record of the proceeding is unique because of the absence of an opposing view. Civil liberties groups were allowed to submit written "amicus" briefs, but the judges left it to the Justice Department to decide whether those briefs should be considered at all. At one point, Judge Laurence H. Silberman asked the DOJ representatives, "Do you have a view what we should do with amicus briefs?"

Solicitor General Ted Olson responded generously to the judge's deferential inquiry: "Our position is we have no objection to the Court receiving amicus briefs" ("Transcript Shines Light on FISA Review Court," *Secrecy News*, FAS Project on Government Secrecy, 2003, no. 10, February 6, 2003, p. 1).

And so the briefs were received, but probably never read. Under these circumstances, how could the FISCR be expected to do other than endorse the DOJ's desire for broader surveillance authority?

# FURTHER READINGS

"Foreign Intelligence Surveillance Act: Frequently Asked Questions (and Answers)." Electronic Frontier Foundation, September 27, 2001. www.eff.org/Censorship/Terrorism_militias/fisa_faq.html
Implementation of the USA PATRIOT Act: Sections of the Act That Address the Foreign Intelligence Surveillance Act (FISA. Hearings before the Subcommittee on Crime,

Terrorism, and Homeland Security of the Committee on the Judiciary. House of Representatives, 108th Congress, 1st Session, April 26 and 28, 2005.

Musch, Donald J. *Civil Liberties and the Foreign Intelligence Surveillance Act*. Dobbs Ferry, NY: Oceana Publications, 2003.

Poole, Patrick S. *Inside America's Secret Court: The Foreign Intelligence Surveillance Court*. 2002. http://home.hiwaa y.net/-pspoole/fiscshort.html

S.2586 and S.2659, Amendments to the Foreign Intelligence Surveillance Act. Hearing before the Select Committee on Intelligence of the United States Senate, 107th Congress, 2d Session, July 31, 2002.

The USA PATRIOT Act in Practice; Shedding Light on the FISA Process. Hearing before the Committee on the Judiciary, United States Senate, 107th Congress, 2d Session, September 10, 2002.

# ACLU FOIA Suits Shed Light on Implementation of the Patriot Act

- **Documents:** DOJ Motion for Summary Judgment in American Civil Liberties Union (ACLU) Freedom of Information Act (FOIA) suit; ACLU reply to DOJ motion; opinion of District Judge William J. vanden Heuvel on ACLU FOIA suit
- **When:** DOJ Motion submitted March 28, 2003; ACLU reply on April 4, 2003; Judge vanden Heuvel's opinion rendered on May 19, 2003
- **Where:** Washington, DC
- **Significance:** The DOJ was claiming a broad national security exemption from the ACLU FOIA request. The ACLU was claiming the public's need to be informed of the government's action under the Patriot Act. Judge William J. vanden Heuvel ruled for the DOJ, but acknowledged the public interest in the implementation of the Patriot Act.

---

## DOCUMENTS

### 1. Department of Justice Motions for Summary Judgment, March 28, 2003

#### Introduction

At issue in this FOIA case are the Department of Justice's ("DOJ") claims that certain classified information is protected by FOIA's Exemption 1 and that certain deliberative, predecisional information is protected by FOIA's Exemption 5. The information that plaintiffs' seek, and that DOJ has properly withheld, relates to the frequency with which the Government has sought to use particular investigative and surveillance techniques authorized by the Foreign Intelligence surveillance Act ("FISA"), as amended by the USA PATRIOT Act. This information has long been treated by the Government as classified, for good reason, and now is no time to change that well-established practice. If released to the public, the information would provide our nation's adversaries with critical information about the Government's counterintelligence capabilities, targets and areas of relative safe harbor, and allow them to avoid and defeat our counterintelligence efforts. This information is rightly classified in the interests of protecting our national security.

Plaintiffs' opposition to DOJ's motions for summary judgment fails to refute the Government's sound rationale for classifying the withheld information and for withholding deliberative, predecisional material. Much of plaintiffs' argument is simply irrelevant to the narrow issues before the Court. The Court should grant summary judgment in DOJ's favor.

*SOURCE:* "Legal Papers Relating to August 2002 FOIA Request." American Civil Liberties Union, www.aclu.org/safefree/patriot_foia/2003/doj_sj_reply_032803.pdf

---

## 2. Plaintiff's (ACLU et al.) Reply, April 4, 2003

### Introduction

Remaining at issue in this case is Defendant's assertion that certain information that would otherwise have to be released under the Freedom of Information Act ("FOIA"), 5 U.S.C. §552, may be withheld from the public on the authority of Exemptions 1 and 5 of that Act. The records consist principally of aggregate, statistical data indicating the extent to which the Federal Bureau of Investigation ("FBI") has relied on controversial new surveillance powers authorized by the USA PATRIOT Act ("Patriot Act").... Neither Exemption 1 nor Exemption 5 authorizes the government to withhold this basis information from the public.

### Argument

The records sought by Plaintiffs in this case are critical to the public's ability to evaluate new surveillance authorities and the government's use of them. Americans cannot evaluate government conduct if they are not permitted to know what the government's policies are....

In arguing that the public has no right to know the extent to which the FBI has relied on new surveillance authorities, Defendant repeatedly insists that this Court should defer to the government's own determination that disclosure of the information would jeopardize national security. While Plaintiffs do not dispute that a certain degree of deference is appropriate, the question whether particular records fall within the ambit of Exemption 1 is a question ultimately to be answered by the courts, *not* by the executive branch.

*SOURCE:* "Legal Papers Relating to August 2002 FOIA Request." American Civil Liberties Union, www.aclu.org/safefree/patriot_foia/2003/reply_sj_040403.pdf

---

## 3. Opinion of Judge William J. vanden Heuvelle, May 19, 2003

In response to the events of September 11, 2001, Congress enacted the USA PATRIOT Act, which gave federal officials greater power to conduct surveillance within the United States for purposes of both preventing terrorism and monitoring the activity of foreign intelligence agents. In this case plaintiffs have brought an action under the Freedom of Information Act, 5 U.S.C. §552 ("FOIA"), seeking information about how the Department of Justice ("DOJ") has used this new authority. As helpfully narrowed by the parties, the instant dispute centers on certain records that DOJ claims are protected from disclosure by two FOIA exemptions. Specifically, the information at issue concerns the number of times DOJ has used the particular surveillance and investigatory tools authorized by the Patriot Act since the statute took effect....

Both parties have now moved for summary judgment on these issues. For the reasons given below, the Court concludes that DOJ's assertion of Exemption 1 is appropriate, and the dispute about Exemption 5 is largely illusory.... Accordingly, the Court will grant defendant's motions for summary judgment, and deny plaintiffs' motion.

SOURCE: *American Civil Liberties Union, et al. v. U.S. Department of Justice*, 265 F.Supp. 2d 20.

---

# ANALYSIS

As we have seen, Congress was not only ineffective in overseeing the implementation of the Patriot Act, but failed to acquire even the most basic data necessary for the public to judge that implementation. As a result, the American citizenry, through various civil liberties organizations, has asserted their own "right to know" by way of FOIA suits. This form of public oversight, initiated primarily by the ACLU allied with other public service organizations, has succeeded in acquiring statistical data on the Patriot Act.

As the court documents shown above indicate, the ACLU suit resulted in a lengthy and contentious court battle. Although the case was eventually decided in favor of the DOJ, numerous heavily redacted documents were released in the process of the litigation. The initial FOIA request, submitted on August 21, 2002 by the ACLU, the Freedom to Read Foundation, the Electronic Privacy Information Center, and the American Booksellers Foundation for Free Expression, sought data on the number of times the government had directed a library, bookstore, or newspaper to produce "tangible things" under Section 215 of the Patriot Act; initiated surveillance of Americans under the expanded FISA regulations; conducted "sneak and peek" searches; authorized monitoring of telephone calls and e-mails of people not suspected of a crime; or investigated American citizens or permanent legal residents on the basis of activities protected by the First Amendment.

In a September 3, 2002 ruling, The court granted the ACLU's request for "expedited review" of materials sought, and the DOJ conceded that the documents concerned "a matter of widespread and exceptional media interest in which there exist possible questions about the government's integrity which affect public confidence" ("ACLU Asks Government to Account for Its Use of Vast New Surveillance Powers," American Civil Liberties Union, October 24, 2002. www.aclu.org/Privacy/Privacy.cfm?ID=11048&c=130).

ACLU attorney Jameel Jaffer said,

> As the Justice Department has conceded, there is widespread public concern about the scope of the new surveillance powers and the possibility that the government is abusing them. The records we have identified would enable the public to judge for itself whether these new surveillance powers are necessary and whether they are being used as they should be.

Finally, on January 17, 2003, the Justice Department released a batch of mostly blacked-out documents to the ACLU. Despite the heavy-handed censorship of the released materials, the ACLU was able to draw some conclusions about the use of the Patriot Act, including evidence that the government was

- Conducting wiretaps and secret searches in criminal investigations without meeting probable cause requirements.
- Using Section 215 of the Patriot Act to acquire "tangible things."
- Using pen registers and trap and trace devices to track phone calls and e-mails.
- Planning to use Patriot Act surveillance powers against American citizens and permanent residents.

### Freedom of Information Act Exemptions

The Freedom of Information Act (FOIA), passed in 1966 and amended in 1974, 1976, 1986, and 1996, contains nine basic exemptions from disclosure under the Act, summarized as follows:

1. *Matters specifically authorized by Executive Order to be kept secret and are properly classified pursuant to such an order.*
2. *Matters related solely to the internal personnel rules and practices of an agency.*
3. *Matter specifically exempted from disclosure by statute, providing that such statute leaves no discretion on the issue or establishes particular criteria or types or material for withholding.*
4. *Trade secrets and commercial or financial information that is privileged or confidential.*
5. *Interagency or intra-agency communications which would not be available by law in litigation with the agency.*
6. *Personnel and medical files and similar files the disclosure of which would constitute a clearly unwarranted invasion of personal privacy.*
7. *Records or information compiled for law enforcement purposes, when the revelation of such records could: (a) interfere with enforcement proceedings, (b) deprive a person of a right to a fair trial or impartial adjudication, (c) constitute an unwarranted invasion of personal privacy, (d) disclose the identity of a confidential source or confidential information furnished by the confidential source, (e) disclose investigatory techniques or procedures for law enforcement investigations or prosecutions, (f) endanger the life or physical safety of law enforcement personnel.*
8. *Matters related to reports prepared by, on behalf of, or for the use of an agency responsible for the regulation or supervision of financial institutions.*
9. *Geological and geophysical information and data, including maps, concerning wells.*

Among the released documents was a list of surveillance orders issued under Section 215 of the Patriot Act, with the individual locations and their total number blacked out. After the court ruled that FOIA did not require the DOJ to release any further documents, the ACLU filed a second FOIA suit seeking an un-redacted copy of the list of Section 215 orders. In August 2004, after almost two years of litigation, the ACLU entered into an agreement with the DOJ that resulted in the disclosure of additional records, including a copy of the procedural rules of the Foreign Intelligence Surveillance Court. Unfortunately, the un-redacted copy of Section 215 orders was never released.

The most useful documents released in the FOIA litigation were lengthy lists of NSL usage. Despite that fact that all names, dates, and locations were redacted, the lists confirmed that NSLs were a heavily-used surveillance tool. Indeed, those lists became crucial evidence in a subsequent ACLU court case challenging the constitutionality of NSLs. In declaring the FBI's use of NSLs to be in violation of the First and Fourth Amendments, District Judge Victor Marrero declared:

> The evidence in this case bears out the hypothesis that NSLs work coercively in this way. The ACLU obtained, via the Freedom of Information Act ("FOIA"), and presented to the Court in this proceeding, a document listing all the NSLs the Government issued from October 2001 through January 2003. Although the entire substance of the document is redacted, it is apparent that hundreds of NSL requests were made during that period. Because §2709 has been available to the FBI since 1986 ..., the Court concludes that there must have been hundreds more NSLs issued in that long time span. The evidence suggests that, until now, none of those NSLs was ever challenged in any court.... Plaintiffs have obtained, via a FOIA request, two FBI memoranda concerning implementing and serving NSLs, yet neither memorandum discusses or even mentions the possibility that an NSL recipient could challenge the NSL in court. (*John Doe v. John Ashcroft*, Civil Action No. 04-Civ.-2614 (VM), United States District Court for the Southern District of New York, September 28, 2004)

The dramatic conclusion of Judge Marrero's opinion, examined in detail later in this chapter, declared: "The Government is therefore enjoined from issuing NSLs under §2709 or from enforcing the non-disclosure provision in this or any other case" (ibid.).

# FURTHER READINGS

"ACLU Sues for Details on Federal Snooping." *PC World* (October 24, 2002). www.pcworld.com/article/id,106338-page,1/article.html

"Freedom of Information Documents on the USA PATRIOT Act." Electronic Privacy Information Center, 2003. www.epic.org/privacy/terrorism/usapatriot/foia/

"The Government's Response." American Civil Liberties Union, 2003. www.aclu.com/patriot_foia/foia3

Implementation of the USA PATRIOT Act; Prohibition of Material Support under Sections 805 of the USA PATRIOT Act.... Hearing before the Subcommittee on Crime, Terrorism, and Homeland Security of the Committee on the Judiciary, House of Representatives, 109th Congress, 1st Session, May 10, 2005. http://judiciary.house.gov/media/pdfs/printers/109th/21139.pdf

Melanson, Philip H. *Secrecy Wars: National Security, Privacy, and the Public's Right to Know.* Washington, DC: Brassey's, 2001.

# District Court Rules NSL Gag Orders Unconstitutional

- **Documents:** *John Doe v. John Ashcroft,* United States District Court for the Southern District of New York, September 28, 2004; *John Doe v. Alberto Gonzales,* United States District Court for the District of Connecticut
- **When:** *John Doe v. John Ashcroft* decision: September 28, 2004; *John Doe v. Alberto Gonzales* decision: September 9, 2005
- **Where:** New York; Bridgeport, CT
- **Significance:** Because a violation of the gag order accompanying the issuance of an NSL incurs heavy criminal penalties, no one had been willing to publicly challenge the constitutionality of that provision until an Internet service provider in New York and a group of librarians in Connecticut undertook that challenge. Even then, the court action had to be initiated anonymously under the general name of "John Doe." The New York District Court held the NSLs provision of the Patriot Act to be unconstitutional on First and Fourth Amendment grounds; the Connecticut District Court enjoined the Justice Department from enforcing the gag order against "John Doe," representing the first legal restraint on implementation of a Patriot Act provision.

---

# DOCUMENTS

## 1. *Doe v. Ashcroft,* U.S. District Court for the Southern District of New York

Plaintiffs in this case challenge the constitutionality of 18 U.S.C. §2709 ("§2709"). That statute authorizes the Federal Bureau of Investigation ("FBI") to compel communications firms, such as internet service providers ("ISPs") or telephone companies, to produce certain customer records whenever the FBI certifies that those records are "relevant to an authorized investigation to protect against international terrorism or clandestine intelligence activities."

The FBI's demands under §2709 are issued in the form of national security letters ("NSLs"), which constitute a unique form of administrative subpoena cloaked in secrecy and pertaining to national security issues. The statute bars all NSL recipients from ever disclosing that the FBI has issued an NSL.

The lead plaintiff, called "John Doe" ("Doe") for purposes of this litigation, is described in the complaint as an internet access firm that received an NSL.... Plaintiffs contend that §2709's broad subpoena power violates the First, Fourth and Fifth Amendments of the United States Constitution, and that the non-disclosure provision violates the First Amendment. They argue that §2709 is unconstitutional on its face and as applied to the facts of this case. Plaintiffs' main complaints are that, first §2709 gives the FBI extraordinary and unchecked power to obtain private information without any form of judicial process, and, second, that §2709's non-disclosure provision burdens speech categorically and perpetually, without any case-by-case judicial consideration of whether that speech burden is justified. The parties have cross-moved for summary judgment on all claims.

For the reasons explained below, the Court grants Plaintiffs' motion. The Court concludes that §2709 violates the Fourth Amendment because, at least as currently applied, it effectively bars or substantially deters any judicial challenge to the propriety of an NSL request. In the Court's view, ready availability of judicial process to pursue such a challenge is necessary to vindicate important rights guaranteed by the Constitution or by statute. On separate grounds, the Court also concludes that the permanent ban on disclosure contained in §2709(c), which the Court is unable to sever from the remainder of the statute, operates as an unconstitutional prior restraint on speech in violation of the First Amendment....

To summarize, the court concludes that the compulsory, secret, and unreviewable production of information required by the FBI's application of 18 U.S.C. §2709 violates the Fourth Amendment, and that the non-disclosure provision of 18 U.S.C. §2709(c) violates the First Amendment. The Government is therefore enjoined from issuing NSLs under §2709 or from enforcing the non-disclosure provision in this or any other case, but enforcement of the Court's judgment will be stayed pending appeal, or if no appeal is filed, for 90 days.

SOURCE: *John Doe v. John Ashcroft*, Civil Action No. 04-Civ.-2614 (VM), United States District Court for the Southern District of New York, September 28, 2004.

---

## 2. *John Doe v. Alberto Gonzales*, United States District Court for the District of Connecticut

On August 9, 2005, the plaintiffs filed suit challenging the constitutionality of 18 U.S.C. §2709. One of the plaintiffs is John Doe, the recipient of a National Security Letter ("NSL") issued pursuant to §2709.... In this lawsuit, the plaintiffs claim, first, that §2709 violates the First Amendment by prohibiting any person from disclosing that the FBI has sought or obtained information with a NSL; second, that §2709 violates the First amendment by authorizing the FBI to order disclosure of constitutionally protected information without tailoring its demand to a demonstrably compelling need; third, that §2709 violates the First and Fourth Amendments because it fails to provide for or specify a mechanism by which a recipient can challenge the NSL's validity; fourth, that §2709 violates the First, Fourth, and Fifth Amendments by authorizing the FBI to demand disclosure of constitutionally protected information without prior notice to individuals whose information is disclosed and without requiring that the FBI justify that denial of notice on a case-by-case basis; and fifth, that §2709 violates the Fifth Amendment because it is unconstitutionally vague. With respect to all five challenges, the plaintiffs claim that the statute is unconstitutional both on its face and as applied to them. They seek declaratory and injunctive relief.

Currently pending before the court is plaintiffs' motion for preliminary relief filed on August 16, 2005. The NSL in question tracks the language of the statute in advising the recipient "the Title 18, U.S.C., Section 2709(c), prohibits any officer, employee or agent of yours from disclosing to any person that the FBI has sought or obtained access to information or records under these provisions [18 U.S.C. §2709]."....

The issue before the court in connection with the motion for preliminary injunction is whether the §2709(c) prohibition on the plaintiffs' disclosure of the identity of the recipient is unconstitutional as applied in this case such that enforcement of that prohibition ought to be enjoined pending resolution of the case on the merits....

For the reasons discussed above, the plaintiffs' motion for preliminary relief is GRANTED. The defendants are hereby enjoined from enforcing 18 U.S.C. §2709(c) against the plaintiffs with regard to Doe's identity.

SOURCE: *John Doe et al. v. Alberto Gonzales*, Civil Action No. 3:05-cv-1256 (JCH), September 9, 2005, U.S. District Court for the District of Connecticut.

---

# ANALYSIS

During the first few years following passage of the Patriot Act, librarians and booksellers complained that Patriot Act surveillance tools like Section 215 and NSLs represented a threat to Americans' right to read. But Department of Justice spokespersons responded by claiming that they had never used such provisions against American citizens. Patriot Act critics could not prove otherwise, and, in particular, librarians could provide no specific examples of Patriot Act intrusions. The inclusion of gag rules in Section 215 warrants and NSLs ensured that no librarian could publicly reveal Patriot Act surveillance without suffering heavy criminal penalties.

On October 28, 2002, *Newsweek* magazine ran a story under the headline "Librarians Keep Quiet," in which it described the frustration felt by librarians who were forced to cooperate with FBI surveillance orders but unable to reveal the visits because of the Patriot Act gag orders: "[T]he ACLU has been searching for a librarian who doesn't want to cooperate and is willing to serve as a test case in the courts....Yet despite widespread outrage among librarians, so far no one has come forward, and the statute remains untested in the courts. The search for Conan the Librarian continues" ("Librarians Keep Quiet," *Newsweek*, October 28, 2002, p. 12).

There would be almost three more years of enforced silence before two cases with anonymous plaintiffs challenged the use of NSLs and their accompanying gag orders. The first case, *John Doe v. John Ashcroft*, arose when an Internet service provider (ISP) received an NSL that requested information on a subscriber and warned the ISP not to inform "any person" that the records were sought or obtained. The ACLU brought suit challenging §2709(c) of the Patriot Act on behalf of the ISP plaintiff, who was protected from criminal charges by using the anonymous name of "John Doe."

On September 28, 2004, U.S. District Judge Victor Marrero ruled that the FBI's use of NSLs and its enforcement of the accompanying gag order violated the First and Fourth Amendments to the Constitution. In particular, the written opinion defended the right of Internet subscribers to confidentiality and anonymity:

> [T]he Court concludes that Section 2709 may, in a given case, violate a [Internet] subscriber's First Amendment privacy rights....No court has adopted the Government's argument here that anonymous internet speech or associational activity ceases to be protected because a third party ISP is in possession of the identifying

information.... The Court rejects the invitation to permit the right of internet anonymity and association to be placed at such grave risk.

Judge Marrero categorically rejected the Patriot Act's use of open-ended gag orders, declaring:

[P]ublic knowledge secures freedom. Hence, an unlimited government warrant to conceal, effectively a form of secrecy per se, has no place in our open society. Such a claim is especially inimical to democratic values for reasons borne out by painful experience. Under the mantle of secrecy, the self-preservation that normally impels our government censorship may potentially be turned on ourselves as a weapon of self-destruction.... [A] categorical and uncritical extension of non-disclosure may become the cover for spurious ends that the government may then deem too inconvenient, inexpedient, merely embarrassing, or illicit to expose to the light of the day." (*John Doe v. John Ashcroft*, Civil Action No. 04-Civ.-2614 (VM), United States District Court for the Southern District of New York, September 28, 2004)

Marrero said "enforcement of the Court's judgment will be stayed pending appeal," and the government promptly appealed the decision. While *Doe v. Ashcroft* awaited an appeals court hearing, a second anonymous case, *John Doe v. Alberto Gonzales*, arose to challenge the Patriot Act's gag order provision. The case was precipitated by an FBI visit to a Connecticut library in August 2005, during which two FBI agents delivered an NSL to library official George Christian, warning him to tell no one of the order. The letter directed Christian to surrender "all subscriber information, billing information and access logs of any person" who used a specific computer at a library branch.

Christian, who manages digital records for three dozen Connecticut libraries, said that despite the fact that he configures the system for privacy, the software provided by vendors can reveal the Web sites that patrons browse, the e-mail accounts they open, and the books they borrow. He refused to surrender these electronic records, and his employer, Library Connection Inc., filed suit for the right to publicly challenge and protest the order. As in the New York case, the threat of felony charges against the company if it went public made it necessary to file the suit anonymously. Hence, *John Doe v. Alberto Gonzales* was born, with the plaintiff "John Doe" actually representing four Library Connection officials, George Christian, Peter Chase, Barbara Bailey, and Janet Nocek.

George Christian, Library Connection's executive director, is identified in his Affidavit as "John Doe II," perhaps to distinguish him from the "John Doe" in the New York case. In his sworn statement, Christian said library patron records may contain "highly sensitive, embarrassing or personal" information. He said he wanted to challenge the FBI order, but could not even contact a lawyer because the NSL forbade him from disclosing the matter to "any person." He consulted Peter Chase, vice president of Library Connection, who advised him to call the ACLU. The anonymous suit soon followed.

In September 2005, U.S. District Judge Janet Hall ruled that the NSL gag order violated the First Amendment rights of Christian and the other Library Connection officials. In particular, she concluded: "The defendants are hereby enjoined from enforcing 18 U.S.C. §2709(c) against the plaintiffs with regard to Doe's identity." Judge Hall's ruling thus ordered an almost immediate change in FBI behavior, staying the enforcement of the order for just ten days.

The ACLU's Ann Beeson, the lead attorney in the case, said, "We are extremely pleased that the court has recognized that gagging our client from participating in the Patriot Act debate violates the First Amendment and is profoundly undemocratic. Today's ruling makes clear that the government cannot silence innocent Americans simply by invoking national security" ("FBI Ordered to Lift Patriot Act Gag on Librarian," ACLU Online, September 15, 2005. http://legalminds.lp.findlaw.com/list/news/msg00200.html).

Figure 13. Cartoon of Connecticut librarians. Cagle Cartoons, Inc., © 2006.

Despite the fact that Hall's order freed the plaintiffs to identify only *themselves*, not the targets of the FBI investigation, the government quickly appealed, thus extending the silence imposed on the Connecticut librarians. The appeals court proceedings, which lasted until May 2006, were chaotic and often contradictory, as the Second Circuit sought to combine the New York and Connecticut cases while referring to the plaintiffs as "John Doe I" and "John Doe II."

The government continued to insist that the gag orders and the broader NSL authority were essential in the war on terror. Then, suddenly, during the first week of April 2006, the government filed a sealed letter brief with the court in which it stated that it "will not oppose" the lifting of the gag order on the Connecticut librarians. The government's unexpected reversal surprised both the court and the ACLU, which declared that the government "has in essence abandoned its appeal" of the Connecticut ruling that struck down the gag order provision. Still, the government reaffirmed its intent to pursue its appeal of the New York decision, which struck down the entire NSL provision as unconstitutional.

Meanwhile, the ungagged Connecticut librarians—George Christian, Peter Chase, Janet Nocek, and Barbara Bailey—and the broader library profession celebrated their victory over the Patriot Act's nondisclosure provision (see Figure 13). George Christian declared, "As a citizen, I was shocked by the restraints the gag order imposed upon me. I am incensed that the government uses provisions of the Patriot Act to justify unrestrained and secret access to the records of libraries.... It can't help but be intimidating, and it is not something I believe the government should be allowed to do."

Peter Chase said, "It was galling for me to see the government's attorney in Connecticut... travel around the state telling people that their library records were safe, while at the same time he was enforcing a gag order preventing me from telling people that their library records were not safe."

Janet Nocek said, "Imagine the government came to you with an order demanding that you compromise your professional and personal principles. Imagine then being permanently gagged from speaking to your friends, your family or your colleagues about this wrenching experience."

Barbara Bailey said, "It was…difficult to sit among colleagues and listen to them discuss John Doe—I had to work hard to keep my mouth shut!" ("Tangled Web," *NOW*, PBS, June 2, 2006. www.pbs.org/now/shows/222/george-christian-interview.html).

The American Library Association's Intellectual Freedom Committee quickly passed a resolution, subsequently approved by the full ALA Council, declaring:

> The Intellectual Freedom Committee joins our colleagues and all others who value privacy as an eternal value in thanking George Christian, Barbara Bailey, Peter Chase, and Janet Nocek for their courageous personal and professional stand to defend intellectual freedom in libraries.
>
> Therefore, the IFC urges Council to adopt this resolution to commend the stand of our courageous colleagues, and moves the adoption of "Resolution to Commend the John Does of the Library Connection."
>
> RESOLVED, that the American Library Association strongly commend the stand of the Connecticut John Does—George Christian, Barbara Bailey, Peter Chase, and Janet Nocek—in their successful legal battle to defend the privacy of library user records; and be it further
>
> RESOLVED, that the American Library Association condemn the use of National Security Letters to demand any library records; and be it further
>
> RESOLVED, that the American Library Association reaffirm its opposition to sections of the USA PATRIOT Act that infringe on library patrons' ability to access library services without privacy safeguards. ("Resolution to Commend the John Does of the Library Connection," American Library Association, June 28, 2006. www.ala.org/ala/oif/ifissues/usactlibrarians.html)

The actual decision of the Second Circuit Court of Appeals turned out to be anticlimactic. The ruling on "Doe I" (*John Doe v. Ashcroft*) was "vacated and remanded," based largely on the changes to the Patriot Act effected in the Reauthorization Act of 2006. The reasoning went as follows:

> Because the Reauthorization Act added provisions permitting NSL recipients to challenge the issuance of NSLs in court, John Doe I no longer presses Fourth Amendment claims on this appeal. Therefore, we deem them abandoned, rendering this portion of the appeal moot. Accordingly, we vacate the Fourth Amendment portion of the Southern District of New York Opinion in Doe I.

As for the First Amendment challenge in Doe I, the court declared:

> The Reauthorization Act also added procedures for the judicial review of the terms and conditions of nondisclosure imposed on a recipient of an NSL. However, Plaintiffs argue that the revised version of §2709(c), as amended and supplemented by the Reauthorization Act, still violates John Doe I's First Amendment rights.…We do not believe that it would be prudent to resolve these novel First Amendment issues as a part of this appeal. Therefore, we also vacate the First Amendment portion of Doe I, and we remand this case so that the Southern District of New York…can address the First Amendment issues presented by the revised version of §2709(c).

On the matter of Doe II, the Second Circuit declared:

> Given the concession of the Government on appeal that John Doe II can disclose its identity, the Government no longer opposes the relief granted by the District of Connecticut in its preliminary injunction ruling. Thus, the Government has

---

## IN HISTORY

### Silencing Debate until the Patriot Act Is Reauthorized

On September 9, 2005, a federal judge lifted an NSL gag order against four Connecticut librarians who had been forced to file suit anonymously to avoid felony penalties for disclosure. The government pursued its appeal of *Doe v. Gonzales* throughout the congressional debate on reauthorization of the Patriot Act, effectively silencing any testimony on abuses in libraries.

The ACLU, which represented "John Doe," declared,

Our client is eager to share information with the public and Congress today, while our leaders are still debating Patriot Act reform. As of this hour, "John Doe" stands in silence....Even though a federal judge has ruled that our client's voice should be heard, and as the clock is ticking towards House and Senate votes on the Patriot Act, John Doe is being prevented from participation by our own government. ("Take Action," ACLU Online, http://legal minds,lp.findlaw.com/list/news/msg00200.html)

George Christian, a plaintiff who was silenced by the gag order, recalls, "This all happened during the reauthorization debate and the government was saying no one's rights were being violated."

Barbara Bailey, another silent plaintiff, complained, "We could not speak to Congress until after the renewal of the Patriot Act."

After the Patriot Act was reauthorized in March 2006, the government immediately informed the Appeals Court that it would no longer oppose lifting the gag order. Ann Beeson, the ACLU's lead attorney, said, "Our clients were gagged at a time when Congress needed to hear their voices the most. This administration has repeatedly shown that it will hide behind the cloak of nation security to silence its critics and cover up embarrassing facts" ("Gagged Librarians Break Silence on Patriot Act," *therawstory*, May 31, 2006. www.rawstory.com/news/2006/Gagged_librarians_break.html).

effectively rendered this appeal moot by its own voluntary actions.... Therefore, in light of the Government's concession on appeal that John Doe II can reveal its identity—as was required by the District of Connecticut's preliminary injunction ruling—a simple dismissal of Doe II on mootness grounds is appropriate. (*John Doe I, John Doe II v. Alberto Gonzales*, United States Court of Appeals for the Second Circuit, May 23, 2006. Docket Nos. 05-0570-cv(L), 05-4896-cv(CON))

The only matter unresolved was the First Amendment claim in Doe I, which was remanded back to the Connecticut district court for "its views on the constitutionality of the revised version of §2709(c) and the Reauthorization Act" (ibid.).

## FURTHER READINGS

Alexandrova, Larisa. "Librarians Defy the FBI," *AlterNet* (June 2, 2006). www.alternet.org/story/36953/

Christoffersen, John. "U.S. Prosecutors Drop Request for Library Records, Civil Liberties Group Says," *Associated Press* (June 26, 2006).

"Connecticut Librarians Bitterly Decry Gag Order in Patriot Act Case." *The Experiment*, May 30, 2006. www.theexperiment.org/?p=18

Willing, Richard. "With Only a Letter, FBI Can Gather Private Data; National Security Letters' Reach Expanded After 9/11," *USA Today* (July 6, 2006), p. 1A.

"With Patriot Act Debate Over, Government Drops Fight to Gag Librarians from Discussing Objections to Controversial Law." American Civil Liberties Union, April 12, 2006. www.aclu.org/natsec/gen/24995prs20060412.html

# CHA8TER

# Reauthorization and Beyond:
# The New and Improved Patriot Act

Figure 14. Signing ceremony for the USA PATRIOT Improvement and Reauthorization Act. AP Images © 2006.

# The USA PATRIOT Improvement and Reauthorization Act of 2005

- **Document:** Table of Contents and list of titles and sections
- **When:** Signed March 9, 2006
- **Where:** Washington, DC
- **Significance:** The USA PATRIOT Improvement and Reauthorization Act of 2005 (H.R. 3199), unlike the original Patriot Act bill, was the subject of intense debate, but its ultimate fate would once more be determined by White House intervention.

## DOCUMENT

### USA PATRIOT Improvement and Reauthorization Act of 2005 (H.R.3199)

SHORT TITLE; TABLE OF CONTENTS.
TITLE I—USA PATRIOT Improvement and Reauthorization Act.

Section 108. Multipoint Electronic Surveillance under Section 206 of the USA PATRIOT Act.

Section 109. Enhanced Congressional Oversight.

Section 110. Attacks against Railroad Carriers and Mass Transportation Systems.

Section 111. Forfeiture.

Section 112. Section 2332b(g)(5)(B) Amendments Relating to the Definition of Federal Crime of Terrorism.

Section 113. Amendments to Section 2516(1) of Title 18, United States Code.

Section 114. Delayed Notice Search Warrants.

Section 115. Judicial Review of National Security Letters.

Section 116. Confidentiality of National Security Letters.

Section 117. Violations of Nondisclosure Provisions of National Security Letters.

Section 118. Reports on National Security Letters.

Section 119. Audit of Use of National Security Letters.

Section 120. Definition for Forfeiture Provisions under Section 806 of the USA PATRIOT Act.

Section 121. Penal Provisions Regarding Trafficking in Contraband Cigarettes or Smokeless Tobacco.

Section 122. Prohibition of Narco-Terrorism.

Section 123. Interfering with the Operation of an Aircraft.

Section 124. Sense of Congress Relating to Lawful Political Activity.

Section 125. Removal of Civil Liability Barriers That Discourage the Donation of Fire Equipment to Volunteer Fire Companies.

Section 126. Report on Data-Mining Activities.

Section 127. Sense of Congress.

TITLE II—Terrorist Death Penalty Enhancement....

TITLE III—Reducing Crime and Terrorism at America's Seaports....

TITLE IV—Combating Terrorism Financing....

TITLE V—Miscellaneous Provisions....

TITLE VI—Secret Service....

TITLE VII—Combat Methamphetamine Epidemic Act of 2005....

SOURCE: USA PATRIOT Act Improvement and Reauthorization Act of 2005 (H.R.3199) www.congress.gov/cgi-bin/query/D?c109:6:./temp/-c109WqnJYg

---

# ANALYSIS

The national hysteria following 9/11 constrained congressional debate during the swift passage of the Patriot Act, but many members of Congress sought to cover their haste by including "sunset provisions" on sixteen of the more controversial sections of the Act. The idea was to revisit the Patriot Act after four years, allowing cooler heads to conduct a full debate and reach a sound judgment on what portions of the anti-terrorism legislation should be made permanent. The reauthorization debate was indeed lengthy and contentious, unlike the original Patriot Act debate, but the outcome was still determined by national security fears and White House intervention.

When Congress began reauthorization hearings in early 2005, it became clear that the civility and solidarity imposed by 9/11 had been replaced by a more realistic candor. Indeed, a reauthorization hearing by the House Judiciary Committee on June 10, 2005 produced such repeated criticism of Bush administration surveillance policies that Republican chairman

James Sensenbrenner simply picked up his gavel and walked out while Democrats continued to testify to dead microphones.

Representative Jerrold Nadler (D-NY) said, "I notice that my mike was turned off, but I can be heard anyway." One of the witnesses, James Zogby, said Sensenbrenner's action was "totally inappropriate—no mike on, and no record being kept" ("Panel Chairman Leaves Hearing," *Washington Post*, June 11, 2005, p. A4). In July 2005, the partisan acrimony in the Republican-controlled House produced a one-sided reauthorization bill (H.R.3199), passed along party lines and reflecting the Bush Administration's desire to maintain all Patriot Act authorities.

In contrast, the Senate worked effectively in crafting a bipartisan reauthorization bill (S.1389) that would reform the more controversial provisions of the Patriot Act while maintaining the essential anti-terrorism powers. In an amazing show of common purpose and collegiality, the Senate Judiciary Committee *unanimously* approved S.1389 and reported it out of committee, where it was *unanimously* approved by the full Senate.

The House and Senate bills were then sent to the usual conference committee to negotiate a single compromise bill, but some unusual back-room machinations produced a flawed "conference report" bill that would leave bitterness and dissatisfaction in its wake. During the January 2006 reauthorization debate, Senator Patrick Leahy described the Senate bill and subsequent conference report:

> Every single Senator—Republican and Democratic—voted last July to mend and extend the PATRIOT Act. That bipartisan solution was cast aside by the Bush administration and Republican congressional leaders when they hijacked the conference report, rewrote the bill in ways that fell short in protecting basic civil liberties and then tried to ram it through Congress as an all-or-nothing proposition. (*Congressional Record—Senate*, January 31, 2006, p. S363)

Leahy said Democratic conferees were excluded from the conference meetings at the request of the White House, and Senator Jay Rockefeller (D-WV), himself a conferee, confirmed that fact in his description of the strange conference proceedings.

> I remain disappointed…in the process followed by the House-Senate conference, which not only excluded Democratic Members from key meetings and deliberations but also excluded the public….I was one of the Senate's 10 conferees: 6 Republicans and 4 Democrats….The Senate conferees were appointed on July 29, 2005, immediately upon the Senate's passage by unanimous consent of the bill that had been unanimously reported by the Senate Judiciary Committee….[T]he House did not name its conferees until November 9. The conference met the following day, on November 10, for its one and only meeting. That meeting was devoted exclusively to 5-minute opening statements….Unfortunately, our opening statements turned out to be our closing ones, because we never met again as a conference. The flawed process of the conference produced a flawed result. (*Congressional Record—Senate*, March 2, 2006, p. S1630)

Understandably, the Senate refused to approve the conference report, setting the stage for a Patriot Act showdown: if a compromise reauthorization bill could not be approved by December 31, the Patriot Act would expire, something no member of Congress wanted. House Republicans, backed by four prominent republicans—John Sununu (NH), Larry Craig (ID), Lisa Murkowski (AL), and Chuck Hagel (NE)—had the votes to block cloture and prevent a vote on the conference report. The Republican leadership was outraged. Senate Majority Leader Bill Frist angrily declared, "The Patriot Act expires on December 31, but the terrorist threat does not. Those on the Senate floor who are filibustering the Patriot Act are killing the Patriot Act" ("4 GOP Senators Hold Firm Against Patriot Act Renewal," *Washington Post*, December 21, 2005, p. A4).

Only a temporary extension of the Patriot Act, agreed to by both parties, allowed the Patriot Act to survive into 2006, but by the end of January 2006, time was again running out on the Patriot Act. This time, Democrats were blaming Republicans for the stalemate. Senator Patrick Leahy explained his position on January 31:

> As soon as it became apparent that the conference report filed by the Republican leadership would be unacceptable to the Senate, I joined on Thursday, December 8, in urging a 3-month extension to work out a better bill. On the first day the Senate was next in session…Senator Sununu and I introduced such a bill, S.2082….That would have extended the PATRIOT Act until March 31, 2006, to allow us a chance to work out the remaining differences and improve this reauthorization legislation in ways to better protect the rights of ordinary Americans….Contrary to the false claims and misrepresentations by some, there was no effort on either side of the aisle to do away with the PATRIOT Act….There is no reason why the American people cannot have a PATRIOT Act that is both effective and that adequately protects their rights and their privacy. The only people who were threatening an expiration of the PATRIOT Act were the President and House Republicans…. They came to their senses in the days that followed. But now, as we approach the expiration of the current extension this Friday, the Republican congressional leadership has taken no further action and we risk sections of the PATRIOT Act expiring, again. (*Congressional Record—Senate*, January 31, 2006, p. S363)

At the last minute, the Republican House leadership agreed to another extension of the Patriot Act, keeping the law in effect until March 10, 2006, allowing the White House time to negotiate a deal on a compromise reauthorization bill. Indeed, in the coming weeks, negotiations with the White House produced a Senate amendment to the unpopular conference report, paving the way to congressional passage of a reauthorization bill and ending the threat of Patriot act expiration.

The Senate compromise bill, analyzed in detail in the next section, accomplished much less than its advocates had sought with respect to civil liberties protections. Senator Richard Durbin (IL), one of the Democrats who reluctantly agreed to the compromise, admitted that it fell far short of the earlier reauthorization bill passed by the Senate, but he said, "if you measure it against the original Patriot Act…we've made progress toward protecting basic civil liberties" ("A Deal on Extension of the Patriot Act," *Washington Post*, February 10, 2006, p. A5).

# FURTHER READINGS

"New Bill Even Worse Than USA PATRIOT Act," *Syracuse Post-Standard* (July 26, 2006), p. A13.

Reese, Shawn. "CRS Report for Congress: State and Local Homeland Security; Unresolved Issues for the 109th Congress, June 9, 2005." www.fas.org/sgp/crs/homesec/RL32941.pdf

"Ten Against Patriot Act Reauthorization." *The Nation* (March 3, 2006). www.thenation.com/blogs/thebeat?pid=65474

"USA PATRIOT Act." White House, March 9, 2006. www.whitehouse.gov/infocus/patriotact/

"USA PATRIOT Act Reauthorization in Brief," CRS Report for Congress (August 10, 2005). http://fpc.state.gov/documents/organization/51133.pdf

"USA PATRIOT and Terrorism Prevention Reauthorization Act of 2005." Report of the Committee on the Judiciary, House of Representatives, to Accompany H.R.3199 together with Dissenting Views. Washington, DC: Government Printing Office, 2005.

# FISA Orders, National Security Letters, and Gag Orders

- *Document:* Text of S.2271, the Additional Reauthorizing Amendments Act
- *When:* Signed March 9, 2006
- *Where:* Washington, DC
- *Significance:* The basic reauthorizing legislation, the USA PATRIOT Improvement and Reauthorization Act of 2005, was essentially the bill passed by the House. Because it included only a small number of the civil liberties provisions from the Senate bill, the Senate added the USA PATRIOT Additional Reauthorization Act of 2005 to the final legislative package.

---

## DOCUMENT

### USA PATRIOT Act Additional Reauthorizing Amendments Act (S.2271).

An Act to clarify that individuals who receive FISA orders can challenge nondisclosure requirements, that individuals who receive national security letters are not required to disclose the name of their attorney, that libraries are not wire or electronic communication service providers unless they provide specific services, and for other purposes.

*Be it enacted by the Senate and House of Representatives of the United States of America in Congress assembled,*

### Section 1. Short Title.

This Act may be cited as the "USA PATRIOT Act Additional Reauthorizing Amendments Act of 2006."

### Section 2. Definition.

As used in this Act, the term "applicable Act" means the Act entitled "An Act to extend and modify authorities needed to combat terrorism, and for other purposes." (109th Congress, 2d Session).

**Section 3. Judicial Review of FISA Orders.**

Subsection (f) of section 501 of the Foreign Intelligence Surveillance Act of 1978 (50 U.S.C. 1861), as amended by the applicable Act, is amended to read as follows:

(f)(1) In this subsection—

(A) The term "production order" means an order to produce any tangible thing under this section; and

(B) The term "nondisclosure order" means an order imposed under subsection (d).

(2)(A)(i) A person receiving a production order may challenge the legality of that order by filing a petition with the pool established by section 103(e)(1). Not less than 1 year after the date of the issuance of the production order, the recipient of a production order may challenge the nondisclosure order imposed in connection with such production order by filing a petition to modify or set aside such nondisclosure order, consistent with the requirements of subparagraph (C), with the pool established by section 103(e)(1).

(ii) The presiding judge shall immediately assign a petition under clause (i) to 1 of the judges serving in the pool established by section 103(e)(1). Not later than 72 hours after the assignment of such petition, the assigned judge shall conduct an initial review of the petition. If the assigned judge determines that the petition is frivolous, the assigned judge shall immediately deny the petition and affirm the production order or nondisclosure order. If the assigned judge determines the petition is not frivolous, the assigned judge shall promptly consider the petition in accordance with the procedures established under section 103(e)(2).

(iii) The assigned judge shall promptly provide a written statement for the record of the reasons for any determination under this subsection. Upon the request of the Government, any order setting aside a nondisclosure order shall be stayed pending review pursuant to paragraph (3).

(B) A judge considering a petition to modify or set aside a production order may grant such petition only if the judge finds that such order does not meet the requirements of this section or is otherwise unlawful. If the judge does not modify or set aside the production order, the judge shall immediately affirm such order, and order the recipient to comply therewith.

(C)(i) A judge considering a petition to modify or set aside a nondisclosure order may grant such petition only if the judge finds that there is no reason to believe that disclosure may endanger the national security of the United States, interfere with a criminal, counterterrorism, or counterintelligence investigation, interfere with diplomatic relations, or endanger the life of any person.

(ii) If, upon filing of such a petition, the Attorney General, Deputy Attorney General, an Assistant Attorney General, or the Director of the Federal Bureau of Investigation certifies that disclosure may endanger the national security of the United States or interfere with diplomatic relations, such certification shall be treated as conclusive, unless the judge finds that the certification was made in bad faith.

(iii) If the judge denies a petition to modify or set aside a nondisclosure order, the recipient of such order shall be precluded for a period of 1 year from filing another such petition with respect to such nondisclosure order.

(D) Any production or nondisclosure order not explicitly modified or set aside consistent with this subsection shall remain in full effect.

(3) A petition for review of a decision under paragraph (2) to affirm, modify, or set aside an order by the Government or any person receiving such order shall be made to the court of review established under section 103(b), which shall have jurisdiction to consider such petitions. The court of review shall provide for the records a written statement of the reasons for its decision and, on petition by the government or any person receiving such order for writ of certiorari, the record shall

be transmitted under seal to the Supreme Court of the United States, which shall have jurisdiction to review such decision.

(4) Judicial proceedings under this subsection shall be concluded as expeditiously as possible. The record of proceedings, including petitions filed, orders granted, and statements of reasons for decision, shall be maintained under security measures established by the Chief Justice of the United States, in consultation with the Attorney General and the Director of National Intelligence.

(5) All petitions under this subsection shall be filed under seal. In any proceedings under this subsection, the court shall, upon request of the government, review ex parte and in camera any Government submission, or portions thereof, which may include classified information.

**Section 4. Disclosures.**

(a) FISA—Subparagraph (C) of section 501(d)(2) of the Foreign Intelligence surveillance Act of 1978 (50 U.S.C. 1861(d)(2)), as amended by the applicable Act, is amended to read as follows:

(C) At the request of the director of the Federal Bureau of Investigation or the designee of the director, any person making or intending to made a disclosure under subparagraph (A) or (C) of paragraph (1) shall identify to the Director or such designee the person to whom such disclosure will be made or to whom such disclosure was made prior to the request.

(b) Title 18—Paragraph (4) of section 2709(c) of title 18, United States Code, as amended by the applicable Act, is amended to read as follows:

(c) (4) At the request of the Director of the Federal Bureau of Investigation or the designee of the Director, any person making or intending to make a disclosure under this section shall identify to the Director or such designee the person to whom such disclosure will be made or to whom such disclosure was made prior to the request, except that nothing in this section shall require a person to inform the Director or such designee the identity of an attorney to whom the disclosure was made or will be made to obtain legal advice or legal assistance with respect to the request under subsection (a).....

(e) National Security Act of 1947—Paragraph (4) of section 802(b) of the National Security Act of 1947 (50 U.S.C. 436(b)), as amended by the applicable Act, is amended to read as follows:

(4) At the request of the authorized investigative agency, any person making or intending to made a disclosure under this section shall identify to the requesting official of the authorized investigative agency the person to whom such disclosure will be made or to whom such disclosure was made prior to the request, except that nothing in this section shall require a person to inform the requesting official of the identity of an attorney to whom the disclosure was made or will be made to obtain legal advice or legal assistance with respect to the request under subsection (a).

**Section 5. Privacy Protections for Library Patrons.**

Section 2709 of title 18, United States Code, as amended by the applicable Act, is amended by adding at the end the following:

(f) Libraries—A library (as that term is defined in section 213(1) of the Library Services and Technology Act (20 U.S.C. 9122(1)), the services of which include access to the Internet, books, journals, magazines, newspapers, or other similar forms of communication in print or digitally by patrons for their use, review, examination, or circulation, is not a wire or electronic communication service provider for purposes of this section, unless the library is providing the services defined in section 2510(15) ("electronic communication service") of this title.

*SOURCE:* USA PATRIOT Act Additional Reauthorizing Amendments Act of 2006 (S.2271). http://thomas.loc.gov/cgi-bin/query/D?c109:4:./temp/-c109Q1jY2H

---

# ANALYSIS

Even the constrained debate during the passage of the original Patriot Act produced expressions of concern over Section 215 orders and National Security Letters (NSLs), in part because of the fears that these provisions would be used to seize library and bookstore records. These concerns, muted during the 2001 congressional debate, emerged with new vigor during the 2005 reauthorization debates. A House Judiciary committee hearing on June 8, 2005 produced both spirited criticism and resolute defense of Section 215 and NSLs.

Representative Maxine Waters (D-CA) criticized Section 215's weak requirement of simple "relevance," saying it gave the government "too much secret surveillance power." She concluded, "American citizens have the right to be eventually notified that they are under surveillance and Section 215 impedes that right by allowing the government to conduct surveillance, without the requirement of notice, for time periods that are unspecified and unchecked" (Hearing before the Committee on the Judiciary, House of Representatives, 109th Congress, First Session, June 8, 2005, p. 3).

Deputy Attorney General James Comey responded:

> Section 215 has been criticized by some because it does not exempt libraries and booksellers. The absence of such an exemption is consistent with criminal investigative practice. Prosecutors have always been able to obtain records from libraries and bookstores through grand jury subpoenas. Libraries and booksellers should not become safe havens for terrorists and spies....Concerns that section 215 allows the government to target Americans because of the books they read or websites they visit are misplaced. The provision explicitly prohibits the government from conducting an investigation of a U.S. person based solely upon protected First Amendment activity.

Comey did not explain that the prohibition against investigations based *solely* on activities protected by the First Amendment did not preclude investigations based *partly* or even *predominantly* on First Amendment activities. He was most steadfast in his defense of the simple *relevance* standard required for Section 215 orders.

> The Department is very concerned by proposals currently pending before Congress which would require the government to show 'specific and articulable facts' that the records sought through a section 215 order pertain to a foreign power or agent of a foreign power. Such a requirement would disable the government from using a section 215 order at the early stages of an investigation, which is precisely when such an order is most useful." (ibid., 10)

Representative Dan Lundgren (D-CA) was unconvinced. "[You] say, if we exempt or change 215 relative to libraries …, it's the end of the world. The roof will fall in; terrorists will make libraries safe havens. And I guess I'm skeptical of that.… People are afraid that their reading rights are in fact being chilled today.… [W]hy not require that personally identifiable information be exempt from section 215?"

Comey refused to concede that any change to Section 215 was necessary. "Something is broken…but I think it's people's understanding of 215.… I'm going to work till I have no more breath to try and fix that; rather than change 215 just because folks don't understand it" (ibid., 35–38).

In the end, Comey's arguments would carry the day in the House of Representatives, which passed a reauthorization bill that corresponded closely to the demands of the Justice Department and made no meaningful changes to Section 215 orders or NSLs. The Senate, on the other hand, embraced the need for Patriot Act reform in its reauthorization bill, S.1389, introducing numerous civil liberties protections while retaining the major anti-terrorism powers. It was now up to a "conference committee" to merge the two bills into the final reauthorization legislation. A reasonable compromise bill was within reach, until the White House intervened, producing a one-sided conference report that was rejected by the Senate. The resulting chaos, described in detail in the previous section, produced impassioned Congressional debate on the conference report, with particular focus on Section 215 and NSLs.

By February 2006, even members of the House seemed willing to reconsider some of the hard-line provisions in the conference report. Representative Robert C. Scott (D-VA) told his colleagues:

> First, we should modify the [conference] report and explicitly require that records sought under Section 215—commonly called the library provision—be connected to a foreign power or an agent of a foreign power. This is the traditional FISA standard. A looser standard invites "fishing expeditions." Second, we should explicitly state section 215 recipients have the right to challenge a gag order in court. Third, we should ensure that National Security Letters are not used as back doors for getting library circulation, medical, tax, and educational institutions records and to modify the "conclusive presumption" language which makes it virtually impossible for NSL recipients to challenge "gag" orders in court. (*Congressional Record—House*, February 1, 2006, p. H63)

Rep. Jerald Nadler (D-NY) declared:

> Section 215 should be amended to provide meaningful protection from abuse by an overzealous government seeking sensitive and personal documentation. We should replace the mere showing of relevance standard with a three-part test that was the basis of the Senate compromise. Recipients of 215 orders and of section 505 national security letters must be allowed a meaningful court challenge to the gag order, and the national security letter authority should sunset in order to guarantee Congressional oversight. (ibid., H64)

The concerns voiced in the House were translated into action in the Senate, where a set of amendments specifically targeting Section 215 and NSLs was introduced. Titled the USA PATRIOT Act Additional Reauthorizing Amendments Act of 2006 (S.2271), the bill was cosponsored by Republican Senator John Sununu, who described it during the February 15 reauthorization debate.

> First, we add a clear, explicit judicial review process for the 215 subpoena gag order.… Second, we were able to get language striking the requirement that a

recipient of a National Security Letter disclose the name of their attorney to the FBI.... Third, we added clarification to National Security Letters as they pertain to libraries. Our agreement adds a provision that makes very clear that libraries operating in their traditional role, including the lending of books, including making books available in digital form, including providing basic Internet access, are not subject to National Security Letters.

The changes introduced in S.2271 were relatively minor, leaving most of the terms of the conference report unchanged. As a result, most Republicans were willing to accept the amendments in order to pass the White House-crafted conference report. Russ Feingold (D-WI), the only senator who voted against the original Patriot Act, refused to accept S.2271. He explained:

> Some may argue that there is no harm in passing a bill that could charitably be described as trivial. But protecting the rights of law-abiding Americans is not trivial, and passage of S.2271 is the first step toward passage of the flawed PATRIOT Act conference report.... What we are seeing, I regret to say, is quite frankly, a capitulation on the intransigent and misleading rhetoric of the White House that sees any effort to protect civil liberties as a sign of weakness.... We have come too far and fought too hard to agree to reauthorize the PATRIOT Act without fixing any of the major problems with the act. A few insignificant face-saving changes don't cut it. (*Congressional Record—Senate*, February 15, 2006, p. S1327)

Despite Feingold's impassioned opposition, S.2271 passed the Senate and House, paving the way for approval of the conference report, the final version of the Reauthorization and Improvement Act (H.R. 3199). Together, H.R.3199 and S.2271 formed the full reauthorization package that would make fourteen sections of the Patriot Act permanent, sunset two others, and modify several others, primarily Section 215 and the NSLs authority. H.R.3199, the basic reauthorization law, made the following changes to Section 215 and NSLs:

- Creates a new sunset for Section 215.
- Provides greater congressional and judicial oversight of Section 215 and NSLs, including: (1) annual reports to Congress containing the total numbers of applications made for Section 215 orders; (2) the total number of such orders granted, modified, or denied for library circulation records and patron lists, books sales records or customer lists, firearms sales records, tax return records, educational records, and medical records.

## IN HISTORY

### The "Three-Prong Test" for Section 215 Orders

Much of the reauthorization debate in the Senate concerned Section 215 of the Patriot Act, with particular focus on the standard that should be met before approval of a Section 215 order. The Senate had already passed its reauthorization bill (S.1389) requiring a relatively high standard called the "three-prong standard," which required the government to meet one or more of three tests before issuing a Section 215 order. When the White House pressured the Republican leadership to remove the three-prong test from the conference report, replacing it with a test requiring only that the records sought be "relevant" to a counterintelligence investigation, a group of resolute senators, led by Russ Feingold, refused to support the conference report, insisting that the three-prong test be restored to the bill. During the February 16, 2006 Senate debate, Feingold explained:

"The Senate bill's standard is the following: No. 1, that the records pertain to a terrorist or spy; No. 2, that the records pertain to an individual in contact with or known to a suspected terrorist or spy; or No. 3, that the records are relevant to the activities of a suspected terrorist or spy" (*Congressional Record—Senate*, February 16, 2006, p. S1382).

Feingold then offered an amendment to restore the "three-prong test" to the conference report, declaring, "I urge my colleagues to support this change which we all consented to 6 months ago, and which was one of the core issues which many of us stood up for in December when we voted against cloture on the conference report" (ibid.).

The amendment was defeated, and the "relevance" standard became the permanent basis for issuing Section 215 orders.

- Requires personal approval by either the FBI Director, the FBI Deputy Director, or the Executive Assistant for National Security for Section 215 orders for library; bookstore; firearms; medical, tax, and educational records.
- Requires the Inspector General of the Justice Department to conduct an audit for the years 2002 to 2006 to determine the effectiveness, and identify any abuses, with respect to the use of Section 215 or NSLs.
- Requires the Attorney General to promulgate "minimization" standards to limit the retention and regulate the dissemination of information acquired concerning nonconsenting U.S. persons.
- Requires applications for Section 215 order to include a "statement of facts" showing reasonable grounds to believe that the materials sought are "relevant" to a terrorism or counterintelligence investigation. However, the materials sought are "presumptively relevant" if they pertain to a foreign power, an agent of a foreign power, or an individual in contact with a foreign power or agent.
- Allows recipients of a Section 215 nondisclosure order to disclose its existence to their attorney. However, on request of the FBI Director, the recipient *must* reveal to the FBI the name of the individual to whom the disclosure is made.
- Allows the recipient of an NSL to petition a U.S. district court to modify or set aside the order.
- Prohibits service providers from disclosing the issuance of an NSL *only* if the investigative agency certifies that disclosure may endanger an individual or the national security of the United States; interfere with international relations, or a criminal or intelligence investigation.

The Additional Reauthorizing Amendments Act (S.2271) adds the following restraints on Section 215 orders and NSLs:

- Exempts the identity of attorneys sought for legal advice from Section 215 and NSL nondisclosure requirements.
- Establishes a judicial review procedure for Section 215 nondisclosure orders beginning one year *after* the issuance of the order.
- Exempts libraries operating in their "traditional role" from NSL orders.

# FURTHER READINGS

Doyle, Charles. *National Security Letters in Foreign Intelligence Investigations; Legal Background and Recent Amendments*. Washington, DC: Congressional Research Service, Library of Congress, 2006.

"Foreign Intelligence Surveillance Act Orders 1979–2005." Electronic Privacy Information Center. www.epic.org/privacy/wiretap/stats/fisa_stats.html

"The USA Patriot Act." American Library Association, 2006. www.ala.org/ala/washoff/WOissues/civilliberties/theusapatriotact/usapatriotact.html

"USA PATRIOT Act Reauthorization Proposals and Related Matters in Brief," CRS Report for Congress, July 15, 2005. www.fas.org/sgp/crs/intel/RS22196.pdf

USA PATRIOT Improvement and Reauthorization Act of 2005. Conference Report (to accompany HR3199). Washington, DC: Government Printing Office, 2005.

# Roving Wiretaps and Sneak and Peek Warrants

- **Documents:** Section 108 (Multipoint Electronic Surveillance under Section 206 of the USA PATRIOT Act) and Section 114 (Delayed Notice Search Warrants under Section 213 of the USA PATRIOT Act) of the USA PATRIOT Act Improvement and Reauthorization Act of 2005 (H.R.3199)
- **When:** Signed March 9, 2006
- **Where:** Washington, DC
- **Significance:** Sections 108 and 114 of H.R.3199 amend the roving wiretap and sneak and peek provisions of the Patriot Act, two of the more controversial surveillance authorities.

---

## DOCUMENTS

### 1. Section 108: Multipoint Electronic Surveillance

*Section 108. Multipoint Electronic Surveillance under Section 206 of the USA Patriot Act.*

(a) Inclusion of Specific Facts in Application—

    (1) APPLICATION—Section 104(a)(3) of the Foreign Intelligence Surveillance Act of 1978 (50 U.S.C. 1804(a)(3)) is amended by inserting "specific" after "description of the".

    (2) ORDER—Subsection (c) of Section 105 of the Foreign Intelligence Surveillance Act of 1978 (50 U.S.C. 1805 (c)) is amended—

        (A) in paragraph (1)(A) by striking "target of the electronic surveillance" and inserting "specific target of the electronic surveillance identified or described in the application pursuant to section 104(a)(3)"; and

        (B) in paragraph (2)(B), by striking "where the Court finds" and inserting "where the Court finds, based upon specific facts provided in the application,".

(b) Additional Direction—Such subsection is further amended—

(1) by striking "An order approving" and all that follows through "specify" and inserting "(1) SPECIFICATIONS—An order approving an electronic surveillance under this section shall specify";

(2) in "paragraph (1)(F), by striking "; and" and inserting a period;

(3) in paragraph (2), by striking "direct" and inserting "DIRECTIONS—An order approving an electronic surveillance under this section shall direct"; and

(4) by adding at the end the following new paragraph:

(3) SPECIAL DIRECTIONS FOR CERTAIN ORDERS—An order approving an electronic surveillance under this section in circumstances where the nature and location of each of the facilities or places at which the surveillance will be directed is unknown shall direct the applicant to provide notice to the court within ten days after the date on which surveillance beings to be directed at any new facility or place, unless the court finds good cause to justify a longer period of up to 60 days, of—

(A) the nature and location of each new facility or place at which the electronic surveillance is directed;

(B) the facts and circumstances relied upon by the applicant to justify the applicant's belief that each new facility or place at which the electronic surveillance is directed is or was being used, or is about to be used, by the target of the surveillance;

(C) a statement of any proposed minimization procedures that differ from those contained in the original application or order, that may be necessitated by a change in the facility or place at which the electronic surveillance is directed; and

(D) the total number of electronic surveillances that have been or are being conducted under the authority of the order.

(c) Enhanced Oversight—

(1) REPORT TO CONGRESS—Section 108(a)(1) of the Foreign Intelligence Surveillance Act of 1978 (50 U.S.C. 1808(a)(1)) is amended by inserting ", and the Committee on the Judiciary of the Senate," after "Senate Select Committee on Intelligence".

(2) MODIFICATION OF SEMIANNUAL REPORT REQUIREMENT ON ACTIVITIES UNDER FOREIGN INTELLIGENCE SURVEILLANCE ACT OF 1978—Paragraph (2) of section 108(a) of the Foreign Intelligence Surveillance Act of 1978 (50 U.S.C. 1808(a)) is amended to read as follows:

"(2) Each report under the first sentence of paragraph (1) shall include a description of—

"(A) the total number of applications made for orders and extensions of orders approving electronic surveillance under this title where the nature and location of each facility or place at which the electronic surveillance will be directed is unknown;

"(B) each criminal case in which information acquired under this Act has been authorized for use at trial during the period covered by such report;

"(C) the total number of emergency employments of electronic surveillance under section 105(f) and the total number of subsequent orders approving or denying such electronic surveillance.".

SOURCE: H.R.3199, USA PATRIOT Improvement and Reauthorization Act of 2005. http://thomas.loc.gov/cgi-bin/query/F?c109:9:./temp/-c109muu6gk:e38527:

---

## 2. Section 114: Delayed Notice Search Warrants

### *Section 114. Delayed Notice Search Warrants.*

(d) Limitation on Reasonable Period for Delay—Section 3103a of title 18, United States Code, is amended—

(1) by striking subsection (b)(3) and inserting the following:
"(3) the warrant provides for the giving of such notice within a reasonable period not to exceed 30 days after the date of its execution, or on a later date certain if the facts of the case justify a longer period of delay.".

(2) by adding at the end the following:

(c) Extensions of delay—Any period of delay authorized by this section may be extended by the court for good cause shown, subject to the condition that extensions should only be granted upon an updated showing of the need for further delay and that each additional delay should be limited to periods of 90 days or less, unless the facts of the case justify a longer period of delay.

(e) Limitation on Authority to Delay Notice—Section 3103a(b)(1) of title 18 United States Code, is amended by inserting ", except if the adverse results consist only of unduly delaying a trial" after "2705".

(f) Enhanced Oversight—Section 3103a of title 18, United States Code, is further amended by adding at the end the following:

(g)(d) Reports—

(1) REPORT BY JUDGE—Not later than 30 days after the expiration of a warrant authorizing delayed notice (including any extension thereof) entered under this section, or the denial of such warrant (or request for extension), the issuing or denying judge shall report to the Administrative Office of the United States Courts—

(A) the fact that a warrant was applied for;

(B) the fact that the warrant or any extension thereof was granted as applied for, was modified, or was denied;

(C) the period of delay in the giving of notice authorized by the warrant, and the number and duration of any extensions; and

(D) the offense specified in the warrant or application.

(2) REPORT BY ADMINISTRATIVE OFFICE OF THE UNITED STATES COURTS—Beginning with the fiscal year ending September 30, 2007, the Director of the Administrative Office of the United States Courts shall transmit to Congress annually a full and complete report summarizing the data required to be filed with the Administrative Office by paragraph (1), including the number of applications for warrants and extensions of warrants authorizing delayed notice, and the number of such warrants and extensions granted or denied....

(3) REGULATIONS—The Director of the Administrative Office of the United States Courts, in consultation with the Attorney General, is authorized to issue binding regulations dealing with the content and form of the reports required to be filed under paragraph (1).

SOURCE: H.R.3199, USA PATRIOT Improvement and Reauthorization Act of 2005. http://thomas.loc.gov/cgi-bin/query/F?c109:9:./temp/-c109muu6gk:e62525:

---

# ANALYSIS

Most of the contentious debate over reauthorization of the Patriot Act centered on Section 215 and NSLs, but Section 213 (delayed notice search warrants) and Section 206 (roving wire taps) received their share of attention as well. During the June 8, 2006 hearings before the house Judiciary Committee, Deputy Attorney General James Comey defended the Justice Department's use of Section 213, popularly referred to as "sneak and peek" searches, and opposed any reduction in its authority.

Comey rejected criticism that Section 213 was being used primarily in criminal cases, telling the House Judiciary Committee that the authority was essential in the war on terrorism, despite the fact that it was used more frequently in non-terrorism contexts. He explained,

> Indeed, the use of delayed notice search warrants in non-terrorism cases is consistent with Congressional intent—section 213 was never limited to terrorism cases.... [C]ertain proposals currently before Congress would limit the discretion of a federal judge in granting the initial periods of delay other than seven days. It would allow extensions in 21-day increments, but only if the Attorney General, DAG, or Associate Attorney General personally approved the application for an extension. Requiring the government to go back to court after seven days...would unduly burden law enforcement and judicial resources. And although the provision for a 21-day extension period is better than the 7-day period previously suggested by critics, requiring personal approval by the AG, DAG, or Associate would be impractical and unnecessarily burdensome. (Hearing before the Committee on the Judiciary, House of Representatives, June 8, 2005, p. 17)

The Justice Department also opposed any change to Section 206 of the Patriot Act, which authorizes "roving" wire taps. "Before the USA PATRIOT Act, the use of roving wire taps was not available under FISA," said Deputy Attorney General Comey.

> Therefore, each time a suspect changed communication providers, investigators had to return to the FISA Court for a new order just to change the name of the facility to be monitored and the "specified person" needed to assist in monitoring the wiretap....Proposals currently pending before Congress would require the government to know the identity of the target in order to obtain a roving wiretap. This limitation would be problematic in the FISA context, in which we may be dealing with spies and terrorists trained to cloak their identities....Proposals in Congress also would require that the presence of the target at a particular telephone be "ascertained" by the person conducting the surveillance before the phone could be surveilled.... [S]uch a requirement would be exceptionally risky in a world where terrorists and spies are trained extensively in counter-surveillance measures. (ibid., 14–15)

The reforms to the Patriot Act that Deputy Attorney General Comey opposed were passionately advocated during the reauthorization debate. On March 1, 2006, Senator Patrick Leahy (D-VT) told his colleagues,

Section 213 of the PATRIOT Act authorized the Government to carry out secret searches in ordinary criminal investigations. Armed with a Section 213 search warrant, FBI agents may enter and search a home or office and not tell anyone about it until weeks or months later....Section 213 says that notice may be delayed only for "a reasonable period." The Bush administration has abused that flexible standard and used it to justify delays in notice of a year or more. Pre-PATRIOT Act case law stated that the appropriate period of delay was no more than seven days. The Senate voted to replace the "reasonable period" standard...with a basic 7-day rule, while permitting the Government to obtain additional 90-day extensions of the delay from the court. The current bill [conference report] sets a 30-day rule for the initial delay, more than three times what the Senate, and pre-PATRIOT Act courts, deemed appropriate. (*Congressional Record—Senate*, March 1, 2006, pp. S1567–68)

When Senator Feingold offered an amendment to return the legal standard for delayed notice to seven days, rather than the 30-day standard in the conference report, he asked his colleagues:

What possible rationale is there for not requiring the Government to go back to a court within 7 days and demonstrate a need for continued secrecy? Why insist that the Government get 30 days free without getting an extension? Could it be that they think that the courts usually won't agree that continued secrecy is needed after the search is conducted, so they won't get the 90-day extension? If they have to go back to a court at some point, why not go back after 7 days rather than 30?... From the point of view of the government, I don't see the big deal. But from the point of view of someone whose house has been secretly searched, there is a big difference between 1 week and a month with regard to the time you are notified that someone came into your house and you had absolutely no idea about it.

Feingold warned,

Don't be fooled for a minute into believing that this power is needed to investigate terrorism or espionage. It's not. Section 213 is a criminal provision....In fact, most sneak and peek warrants are issued for drug investigations....FISA also can apply to those investigations. And FISA search warrants are always executed in secret and never require notice. If you really don't want to give notice of a search in a terrorism investigation, you can get a FISA warrant. So any argument that limiting the sneak

---

# IN HISTORY

## Legal Precedent for Delayed Notice Search Warrants

Over the years, the courts have faced claims by the government that the circumstances of a particular investigation require conducting a search without notifying the target. For example, in some cases the government has claimed that giving notice would compromise the success of the search by causing the suspect to flee or destroy evidence.

The two leading court decisions on what was then called "surreptitious entry" held that notice of criminal search warrants could be delayed, but not omitted entirely. Both the Second Circuit in *U.S. v. Villegas* and the Ninth Circuit in *U.S. v. Freitas* held that such a warrant must provide that notice of the search will be given within seven days, unless extended by the court. The *Freitas* court said:

We take this position because surreptitious searches and seizures of intangibles strike at the very heart of the interests protected by the Fourth Amendment. The mere thought of strangers walking through and visually examining the center of our privacy interest, our home, arouses our passion for freedom as does nothing else. That passion, the true source of the Fourth Amendment, demands that surreptitious entries be closely circumscribed. (*U.S. v. Freitas*, 800 F.2d 1451 (9th Cir. (1986))

and peek power as we have proposed will interfere with sensitive terrorism investigations is a red herring. (*Congressional Record—Senate*, February 15, 2006, p. S1332)

Feingold's amendment failed to pass, leaving the 30-day delay for sneak and peek warrants in the conference report unchanged. Congress would also follow the Justice Department's recommendations on roving wiretaps, rejecting a requirement that the target of such surveillance be known.

What, then, were the changes to Sections 213 and 206 in the reauthorization legislation passed by Congress? On the "sneak and peek" provision, the Reauthorization Act required notice of a search warrant to be given no more than 30 days after the warrant's execution, a considerably longer period than the 7-day limit specified in the Senate's reauthorization bill, but considerably shorter than the 180-day limit in the House bill. In addition, the final reauthorization legislation removed the catch-all phrase "unduly delaying a trial" as a justification for delaying notice. Finally, the Reauthorization Act requires that no later than 30 days after the expiration or denial of such a warrant, the issuing or denying judge must notify the Administrative Office of the U.S. Courts of the fact that the delayed notice was applied for, granted, modified, or denied; the length of time of the delay in giving notice; and the offense specified in the warrant or application.

On the roving wire tap provision, the Reauthorization Act required that if the government begins surveillance at a new site, the nature and location of which were unknown when the original order was issued, it must provide the FISA court with the facts and circumstances justifying the applicant's belief that each new site is or was being used, or is about to be used, by the target of the surveillance; an explanation of any proposed minimization procedures that differ from those contained in the original order, if such change is necessitated by the new site; and the total number of electronic surveillances that have been or are being conducted under the roving surveillance order. The Act also added the Senate Judiciary Committee as a recipient of the semiannual FISA reports and modified the FISA reporting requirements to include a description of the total number of applications made for roving electronic surveillance orders.

# FURTHER READINGS

Anti-terrorism Investigations and the Fourth Amendment after September 11, 2001. Hearing before the Subcommittee on the Constitution of the Committee on the Judiciary, House of Representative, 108th Congress, First Session, May 20, 2003.

Implementation of the USA Patriot Act; Sections 201, 202, 223, of the Act that address criminal wiretaps, and section 213 of the Act that Addresses delayed notice. Hearing before the Subcommittee on Crime, Terrorism and Homeland Security of the Committee on the Judiciary, House of Representative, 109th Congress, First Session, May 3, 2005.

"President Signs Patriot Act Reauthorization Lacking Civil Liberties Protections." Center for Democracy and Technology, March 17, 2006. www.cdt.org/publications/policyposts/2006/6

"Stupak Calls USA PATRIOT Act Reauthorization an Open-Door Attack on Personal Liberties." News from Congressman Bart Stupak, December 15, 2005. www.house.gov/list/press/mi01_stupak/121505

Tiefer, Charles. *Veering Right: How the Bush Administration Subverts the Law for Conservative Causes.* Berkeley, CA: University of California, 2004.

# Permanence and Sunsets

- **Document:** Section 102 of the USA PATRIOT Improvement and Reauthorization Act of 2005 (H.R.3199)
- **When:** Signed March 9, 2006
- **Where:** Washington, DC
- **Significance:** Section 102 of the H.R.3199 repeals Section 224 of the Patriot Act, which applied sunsets to sixteen of the Patriot Act's sections. In its place, H.R.3199 applies two new sunset dates to Sections 206 and 215.

---

## DOCUMENT

### Sunset Provisions

Section 102. USA PATRIOT Act Sunset Provisions

(a) In General—Section 224 of the USA PATRIOT Act is repealed.

(b) Sections 206 and 215 Sunset—

(1) IN GENERAL—Effective December 31, 2009, the Foreign Intelligence Surveillance Act of 1978 is amended so that sections 501, 502, and 105(c)(2) read as they read on October 25, 2001.

(2) EXCEPTION—With respect to any particular foreign intelligence investigation that began before the date on which the provisions referred to in paragraph (1) cease to have effect, or with respect to any particular offense or potential offense that began or occurred before the date on which such provisions cease to have effect, such provisions shall continue in effect.

SOURCE: USA PATRIOT Act Additional Reauthorizing Amendments Act of 2006 (S.2271). http://thomas.loc.gov/cgi-bin/query/F?c109:9:./temp/-c109Hb0VuZ:e11397:

---

# ANALYSIS

Perhaps the most significant check on the sweeping powers of the Patriot Act was the inclusion of sunsets on sixteen of the more controversial provisions. Ironically, the author of those sunset requirements was a conservative Republican, Dick Armey. His insistence that certain Patriot Act provisions be re-examined and reauthorized, or rejected, after four years was the only impediment to a hasty congressional acceptance of unchecked and permanent executive power.

As the reauthorization debates began in Congress during 2005, Justice Department spokespersons made clear their discomfort with *any* sunsets on Patriot Act powers, and there was particular concern that new sunsets would be applied during reauthorization. Deputy Attorney General James Comey told the House Judiciary Committee,

> Mr. Chairman, I'd like to say a final word about…my concern that Congress, while reauthorizing the USA PATRIOT Act, may seek to include new sunsets…. [S]unsets are not required to conduct oversight. Congress maintains its authority and responsibility to conduct oversight, to ask questions, to demand answers, even without sunsets. My concern is that sunsets on these important tools might inhibit the culture of information sharing that we are trying to foster. Rather than encouraging and empowering our agents and prosecutors to rely upon these new tools, we send a message that a particular provision may only be temporary and chill development of the culture of information sharing. As long as congressional oversight remains robust, which I am convinced it will, there is no need for sunsets. (Hearing before the Committee on the Judiciary, House of Representatives, 109th Congress, First Session, June 8, 2005, p. 19)

When questioned by Committee members, Comey said, "I think,…especially with some of these tools, if you sunset them again we will never be able to get people to completely believe that the world has changed, particularly on information sharing. We're trying to change a culture" (ibid., 51).

But many in Congress felt that it was the culture of freedom that was being changed by unfettered surveillance programs. On March 1, 2006, during last minute Senate debate on the reauthorization conference report, Senator Leahy recalled the inclusion of sunsets in the original Patriot Act legislation and the positive role they played in subsequent congressional oversight.

"Republican House Majority Leader Dick Armey and I insisted in 2001, on a 4-year sunset for PATRIOT Act powers," Leahy told his colleagues.

> If we had not done that, we would not even be having this debate today. We would not have even looked at what happened, especially with a Congress as reluctant to do oversight, a Congress unwilling to question anything this administration does. They were forced, actually, to ask questions about what is happening under the PATRIOT Act because a conservative Member of the House—Dick Armey—and a liberal Senator—myself—put in the sunset provisions so we would be forced to look at it no matter who was President, no matter who controlled the House, no matter who controlled the Senate. And thank goodness we did because if we had not done that, I guarantee you, this Congress never would have been going through a review and renewal process over the last few months….As usual, the Republican majorities in the House and the Senate did their utmost to follow the White House's directives to prevent any sudden breakout of bipartisanship. But a ray of bipartisanship slipped through the cracks, and the bill is the better for it. It contains 4-year sunsets, not 7- or 10-year sunsets like the administration wanted. (*Congressional Record*—Senate, March 1, 2006, p. S1566)

Leahy was a reluctant supporter of the Republican-drafted conference report that would make permanent fourteen of the sixteen sections sunsetted in the original Patriot Act, adding new sunsets only for Sections 206 and 215. As debate on the conference report proceeded, Senator Feingold proposed an amendment that would add a four-year sunset to the NSL authorities that were expanded by the Patriot Act. Feingold explained,

> I would think that a sunset of the NSL authorities is justified to ensure that Congress has the opportunity to take a close look at such a broad power. And let me emphasize, the sunset in this amendment would only apply to the expansions of NSL authorities contained in the PATRIOT Act, not to pre-existing authorities.... Ideally, we could go ahead and actually fix the NSL statutes now, but sunsetting the expanded powers would at least be a step in the right direction." (*Congressional Record—Senate*, February 16, 2006, p. S1383)

Feingold's amendment failed to pass, leaving just two new sunsets in the final USA PATRIOT Reauthorization and Improvement Act. The text of the Act's sunset provisions, shown above, accomplished the following.

The brief opening statement, "Section 224 of the USA PATRIOT Act is repealed," removes all sixteen sunsets originally imposed on Patriot Act sections. Those sections were:

Section 201—Certain terrorism crimes as wiretap predicates.
Section 202—Computer fraud as wiretap predicates.
Section 203(b)—Sharing criminal wiretap information with intelligence agencies.
Section 204—Technical clarification of no conflict between Title III and FISA.
Section 206—Roving taps under FISA.
Section 209—Seizure of voice mail pursuant to warrant.
Section 212—Emergency disclosures of e-mail without a court order.
Section 214—Lowering pen register and trap and trace standards under FISA.
Section 215—Access to business records under FISA.
Section 217—Interception of computer trespasser communications without a court order.
Section 218—The "significant purpose" provision.
Section 220—Nationwide service of search warrant for electronic evidence.
Section 224—The sunset provision.
Section 225—Immunity for compliance with FISA wiretap.

The remainder of the sunset provisions in the reauthorization legislation creates new sunsets, effective December 31, 2009, on Section 206 and Section 215 of the Patriot Act, and specifies that these sunsets will not have effect on any investigations begun before the effective date of the Reauthorization Act.

Thus, after reauthorization, the Patriot Act retains sunsets on only two of its more than 150 provisions.

# FURTHER READINGS

"Let the Sun Set on Patriot." Electronic Frontier Foundation, 2006. www.eff.org/patriot/sunset
"Patriot Act Sunsets." Center for Democracy and Technology, January 27, 2004. www.cdt.org/security/20040127sunsets.pdf
Podesta, John. "USA Patriot Act: The Good, the Bad, and the Sunset," *Human Rights Magazine* (Winter 2002). www.abanet.org/irr/hr/winter02podesta.html
"The Sun Also Sets: Understanding the Patriot Act 'Sunsets.'" American Civil Liberties Union, 2005. http://action.aclu.org/reformthepatriotact/sunsets.html
"USA Patriot Act Sunset: Provisions That Expire on December 31, 2005." CRS Report for Congress, June 10, 2004. www.fas.org/iirp/crs/RL32186.pdf

# New Oversight Provisions in the Reauthorization Act

- **Document:** Section 109 of the USA PATRIOT Improvement and Reauthorization Act of 2005 (H.R.3199)
- **When** Signed March 9, 2006
- **Where:** Washington, DC
- **Significance:** Section 109 of the USA PATRIOT Improvement and Reauthorization Act of 2005 mandated addition congressional oversight of the Patriot Act. Together with other oversight requirements within particular sections of H.R.3199, these reauthorization provisions may provide a greater role for Congress during future implementation of the Patriot Act.

---

## DOCUMENT

### Section 109: Congressional Oversight

Section 109. Enhanced Congressional Oversight.

(a) Emergency Physical Searches—Section 306 of the Foreign Intelligence Surveillance Act of 1978 (50 U.S.C. 1826) is amended—

    (1) in the first sentence, by inserting ", and the Committee on the Judiciary of the Senate," after "the Senate";

    (2) in the second sentence, by striking "and the Committees on the Judiciary of the House of Representatives and the Senate" and inserting "and the Committee on the Judiciary of the House of Representatives";

    (3) in paragraph (2), by striking "and" at the end;

    (4) in paragraph (3), by striking the period at the end and inserting "; and"; and

    (5) by adding at the end the following:
        "(4) the total number of emergency physical searches authorized by the Attorney General under section 304(e) and the total number of subsequent orders approving or denying such physical searches."

(b) Emergency Pen Registers and Trap and Trace Devices—Section 406(b) of the Foreign Intelligence Surveillance Act of 1978 (50 U.S.C. 1846(b)) is amended—

   (1) in paragraph (1), by striking "and" at the end;

   (2) in paragraph (2), by striking the period at the end and inserting "; and"; and

   (3) by adding at the end the following:

   (4) the total number of pen registers and trap and trace devices whose installation and use was authorized by the Attorney General on an emergency basis under section 403, and the total number of subsequent orders approving or denying the installation and use of such pen registers and trap and trace devices.

(c) Additional Report—At the beginning and midpoint of each fiscal year, the Secretary of Homeland Security shall submit to the Committees on the Judiciary of the House of Representatives and the Senate, a written report providing a description of internal affairs operations at U.S. Citizenship and Immigration Services, including the general state of such operations and a detailed description of investigations that are being conducted (or that were conducted during the previous six months) and the resources devoted to such investigations. The first such report shall be submitted not later than April 1, 2006.

(d) Rules and Procedures for FISA Courts—Section 103 of the Foreign Intelligence Surveillance Act of 1978 (50 U.S.C. 1803) is amended by adding at the end the following:

   (f)(1) The courts established pursuant to subsections (a) and (b) may establish such rules and procedures, and take such actions, as are reasonably necessary to administer their responsibilities under this Act.

   (2) The rules and procedures established under paragraph (1), and any modifications of such rules and procedures, shall be recorded, and shall be transmitted to the following:

      (A) All of the judges on the court established pursuant to subsection (a).

      (B) All of the judges on the court of review established pursuant to subsection (b)

      (C) The Chief Justice of the United States.

      (D) The Committee on the Judiciary of the Senate.

      (E) The Select Committee on Intelligence of the Senate.

      (F) The Committee on the Judiciary of the House of Representatives.

      (G) The Permanent Select Committee on Intelligence of the House of Representatives.

   (3) The transmissions required by paragraph (2) shall be submitted in unclassified form, but may include a classified annex.

*SOURCE:* USA PATRIOT Act Additional Reauthorizing Amendments Act of 2006 (S.2271). http://thomas.loc.gov/cgi-bin/query/F?c109:9:./temp/-c109muu6gk:e38527:

# ANALYSIS

As described earlier, the conference report negotiated from the competing House and Senate reauthorization bills was considered "flawed," precipitating heated debate, a filibuster, and two last-minute extensions of the Patriot Act to avoid the expiration of many of its key provisions. The one aspect of the conference report that drew praise from most members of Congress was its emphasis on reporting and oversight.

Senator Patrick Leahy told his colleagues,

> For the first time ever, the Justice Department is going to be required to report publicly on its use of two secret surveillance tools that have come under fire from civil libertarians but also from the business community. These are the FISA business record authority and the so-called national security letters, or NSLs....The conference between the two bodies accepted my proposal that these powers be subject to detailed, comprehensive, and unclassified audits by the Justice Department's Office of the Inspector General....I proposed another sunshine provision....from a bill I introduced in the last Congress with Senators Specter and Grassley. It requires the FISA Court to publish its procedures and share their rules in an unclassified report. Also, it requires annual reporting of the use of so-called sneak-and-peek search warrants and FISA's emergency surveillance authorities. (*Congressional Record—Senate*, March 1, 2006, p. S1566)

Even Senator Russ Feingold, the most implacable opponent of the conference report, said,

> I also want to acknowledge that the conference report creates new reporting requirements for some PATRIOT Act powers, including new reporting on roving wiretaps, section 215, "sneak and peek" search warrants, and national security letters. There are also new requirements that the Inspector General of the Department of Justice conduct audits of the Government's use of national security letters and section 215. In addition, the conference report includes some other useful oversight provisions relating to FISA. It requires that Congress be informed about the FISA Court's rules and procedures and about the use of emergency authorities under FISA, and gives the Senate Judiciary committee access to certain FISA reporting that currently only goes to the Intelligence Committee. I am also glad to see that it required the Department of Justice to report to us on its data mining activities.

Feingold was quick to add,

> But adding sunsets and new reporting and oversight requirements only gets you so far. The conference report...remains deeply flawed....Simply requiring reporting on the Government's use of these overly expansive tools does not ensure that they will not be abused....Trust of Government cannot be demanded or asserted or assumed; it must be earned. And this administration has not earned our trust. It has fought reasonable safeguards for constitutional freedoms every step of the way. It has resisted congressional oversight and often misled the public about its use of the PATRIOT Act." (*Congressional Record—Senate*, February 15, 2006, p. S1332)

There were additional proposals for enhanced congressional oversight during the final days of the reauthorization debate, but the reporting provisions already in the conference report were all that appeared in the final Reauthorization and Improvement Act. Section 109 (Enhanced Congressional Oversight), the only section specifically devoted to reporting and oversight, was presented in full at the beginning of this analysis and is briefly summarized here:

- Section 109(a) enhances congressional oversight of physical searches under FISA, requiring the Attorney General to:
  
  (1) Make full reports concerning all physical searches to the Senate Judiciary Committee in addition to the House and Senate Intelligence Committees.

(2) Submit to the House Judiciary Committee a report with statistical information concerning the number of emergency physical search orders authorized or denied by the Attorney General.

- Section 109(b) requires that the Attorney General's semiannual report to the House and Senate Judiciary committees concerning the FISA use of pen registers or trap and trace devices must include statistical information regarding the emergency use of such devices.
- Section 109(c) requires an annual report from the Secretary of Homeland Security to the House and Senate Judiciary Committees providing a description of internal affairs operations at U.S. Citizenship and Immigration Services.
- Section 109(d) requires that the rules and procedures of the FISA Courts shall be recorded and transmitted to:

(1) All judges on the FISA Court and the FISA Court of Review
(2) The Chief Justice of the United States
(3) The Judiciary Committees of the House and Senate
(4) The Senate Select Committee on Intelligence
(5) The Permanent Select Committee on Intelligence of the House.

Other oversight and reporting requirements in the Reauthorization Act were contained within subparagraphs of particular sections. The new reporting requirements associated with Patriot Act sections 206, 213, 215, and NSLs were described in detail earlier in this chapter. Together, these new oversight requirements convinced many members of Congress that, despite the lack of explicit protections for civil liberties in the H.R.3199, there would now be sufficient opportunity for congressional oversight to prevent serious abuses.

But would enhanced oversight of the Patriot Act be effective? Would the White House ignore congressional attempts to confine executive power? That issue became a source of contention during the reauthorization debate. Senate Minority Leader Reid declared:

> On the same day we voted on the PATRIOT Act conference report last December …, the President had authorized a secret program to eavesdrop on American citizens without warrants required by the Foreign Intelligence Surveillance Act. That story had a clear impact on the vote that day, as it well should have. There was some question why we were even having this protracted debate over the PATRIOT Act, since the President seemed to believe he was free to ignore the laws we enact anyway. But, in fact, no one is above the law—not even the President of the United States. One lesson of the NSA spying scandal is that Congress must stand up to the President and must insist on additional checks on the powers exercised by the executive branch. (*Congressional Record—Senate*, March 2, 2006, p. S1609)

With the passage of the USA PATRIOT Reauthorization and Improvement Act, all but two provisions of the Act had been made permanent. Two new sunsets had been applied to Sections 206 and 215, and new reporting requirements had been added. With the Democratic takeover of both the House and Senate in the November 2006 elections, there was hope for more aggressive oversight of the Patriot Act, but the broad prerogatives claimed by the President had given the vast new executive powers granted through the Patriot Act a life of their own.

# FURTHER READINGS

Dinan, Stephen. "Congress Urged to Take More Power; 9/11 Panelists Push Increase in Oversight," *Washington Times* (August 4, 2004). http://washingtontimes.com/national/20040803-155712-6618r.ht

Foreman, Christopher H. "Signals from the Hill: Congressional Oversight and the Challenge of Social Regulation," *American Political Science Review*, 84, no. 1 (March 1990), pp. 302–3.

Johnson, Loch J. "The Contemporary Presidency: Presidents, Lawmakers, and Spies: Intelligence Accountability in the United States," *Presidential Studies Quarterly*, 34, no. 4 (2004), pp. 828–37.

"Patriot Act." OnlineNewsHour, April 6, 2005. www.pbs.org/newshour/bb/terrorism/jan-june05/anti-terror_4-5.html

Polek, Frank J. "The Future of the Patriot Act," *The Daily Transcript* (May 6, 2004). www.sheppardmullin.com/images/pubs/pub283.pdf

Schulhofer, Stephen J. *Rethinking the Patriot Act: Keeping America Safe and Free*. New York: Century Foundation Press, 2005.

# Minor Provision in the Reauthorization Act Causes a Major Scandal

- **Document:** Remarks by Senator Dianne Feinstein introducing S.214, a bill that would return the process by which interim U.S. Attorneys are appointed to pre-Patriot Act status
- **When:** March 19, 2007
- **Where:** U.S. Senate, Washington, DC
- **Significance:** The USA PATRIOT Improvement and Reauthorization Act of 2005 included a brief and seemingly trivial provision authorizing the Attorney General to replace U.S. Attorneys without the usual Senate confirmation process. When the Justice Department fired a number of U.S. Attorneys late in 2006 and attempted to replace them with less qualified political appointees, a scandal erupted that threatened Attorney General Alberto Gonzales' job. The U.S. Senate responded by essentially repealing the Patriot Act provision.

---

# DOCUMENT

## Senator Dianne Feinstein (D-CA) Introduces S.214

[I]n March of 2006, the Patriot Act was reauthorized and a change was made into the law, made in conference without Democratic senators present, and to the best of my knowledge, it was made without the knowledge of *any* senator, Republican or Democrat. It's my understanding that this was a request from the Justice Department that was presented by William Moschella to the staff of the Judiciary Committee, and without knowledge of the senators was put into the bill. It gave the President the authority, essentially, to appoint a U.S. Attorney without confirmation for the remainder of his term. The bill, S.214, that is before the Senate today simply returns the law to the way it was before this took place in March of 2006....

We now know that at least 8 U.S. Attorneys were forced from office and that, despite shifting rationales for why, it has become clear that politics has, in fact, played at least some role. Last week we learned that the White House was involved in this process and that discussions took place with such prominent figures as presidential advisor Carl Rove and former White House Counsel Harriet Myers.... We have learned that as many as 6 of the 8 U.S. Attorneys who were fired upon that one day were involved in public corruption cases. While we don't know what role this played in their selection, it is an unavoidable fact that raises serious questions....

Finally, in an email that discussed avoiding the Senate confirmation process, the Attorney General's Chief of Staff wrote: "There is some risk that we will lose the [Patriot Act] authority, but if we're not going to use it, what's the use of having it?"

Think about that. I believe the time has come for the administration to lose that authority. All these unanswered questions and allegations have demonstrated, at the very least, one real thing. The law must be returned to what it was prior to the reauthorization of the Patriot Act, and the bipartisan bill before the Senate would do just that, no more, no less.... [W]e are now considering legislation that would give the Attorney General authority to appoint an interim U.S. Attorney, but only for 120 days. If after that time, the President has not sent up a nominee to the Senate and had that nominee confirmed, then the authority to appoint an interim U.S. Attorney would fall to the District Court. Given all we have learned in the past few months, I believe this is the least we can do to restore the public's faith in an independent system of justice. This bill will also help prevent any future abuse or appearance of politicization of the United States Attorney positions.... These changes are in line with the way the law used to be and would simply be restoring the proper checks and balances that are needed in our system of government.

SOURCE: U.S. Senate, Debate on S.214, 110th Congress, March 19, 2007, televised live on C-SPAN2.

---

# ANALYSIS

Who could have predicted that a brief, little-noticed provision in the USA PATRIOT Improvement and Reauthorization Act, seemingly more appropriate to Justice Department housekeeping than domestic surveillance, would provoke a national political scandal that brought the Attorney General to the brink of resignation? The provision allowed the Attorney General to make interim appointments of U.S. Attorneys without the usual Senate confirmation process. Indeed, under this new Patriot Act authority these interim appointments could continue indefinitely. Given this new authority, the Bush administration prepared plans to fire a number of U.S. Attorneys who had not "exhibited loyalty" on issues ranging from immigration to the death penalty. At this time, most of the targeted prosecutors were overseeing significant public corruption investigations, some directed at Republican politicians or their supporters.

In January 2006, Kyle Sampson, chief of staff for Attorney General Alberto Gonzales, sent the first list of targeted U.S. Attorneys to the White House, and in subsequent e-mails he urged the President to bypass Congress in naming replacements. One e-mail stated, "I strongly recommend that as a matter of administration, we utilize new statutory provisions that authorize the AG to make USA appointments." Recognizing the controversial nature of such action, Sampson added, "There is some risk that we'll lose the [Patriot Act] authority, but if we don't ever exercise it then what's the point of having it?" ("Documents Show White House Involvement in Prosecutors' Dismissals," *Washington Post*, March 13, 2007, p. A6).

Eight U.S. Attorneys were fired late in 2006, with little explanation from Justice Department officials, who later told Congress that the dismissals were performance-related. Documents subsequently released by the Justice Department made it clear that most of the fired prosecutors had received excellent performance reviews, and some of them alleged intimidation and threats of retaliation from the department if they refused to resign. Even Republicans were shocked to discover that U.S. Attorney Patrick Fitzgerald was among the prosecutors listed as "not distinguished" on the Justice Department's chart of incumbents who might be removed. Fitzgerald was so listed at the very time he was leading the Central Intelligence Agency (CIA) leak investigation that resulted in the perjury conviction of vice presidential aide Scooter Libby.

A *Washington Post* editorial accused the Bush administration of using the Patriot Act provision to circumvent the requirement that U.S. Attorneys be confirmed by the Senate, concluding: "The best way to prevent that would be to return the law to its previous state" ("Strange Justice," *Washington Post*, March 3, 2007, p. A14). Indeed, such legislation was already being prepared by Democrats in Congress. Senator Diane Feinstein (D-CA) proposed S.214, a bill that would return to the pre-Patriot Act process of appointing and confirming U.S. Attorneys. The bill drew bipartisan support, including Senator Arlen Specter (R-PA), the ranking Republican on the Senate Judiciary Committee.

During the debate on S.214, freshman Senator Sheldon Whitehouse (D-RI), himself a former U.S. Attorney, declared:

> Having served as Rhode Island's States Attorney, I would like to share some thoughts based on that experience. First, I want to say that even if everything the administration has said about their firings of the U.S. Attorneys were true, and we certainly have cause to doubt that,...there is still a real concern here, a concern that merits the attention of this body over the independence of the United States Attorneys....Even if the mass firings, the purge of U.S. Attorneys had been done just to punish policy disputes, the firings would still defeat that healthy check and balance....The message of these firings by the Bush administration is this: You serve at our whim, you displease us at your peril, and sudden firing awaits you if you cross us....
>
> What truth lies behind the bodyguard of lies? Is it this, that U.S. Attorneys who prosecuted public corruption cases against Republicans, or those who didn't bring public

## IN HISTORY

### Historical Precedent for Firing and Replacing U.S. Attorneys

Throughout the congressional and public debate over the firings of eight U.S. Attorneys, the Justice Department frequently pointed out that U.S. Attorneys were political appointees who "serve at the pleasure of the President." Indeed, officials noted that it was common for new presidents to remove virtually all of the 93 U.S. Attorneys who had been appointed by the previous administration, replacing them with new appointees. Since this is basically true, how could the firings have been controversial? The problem, it seems, concerns *when* the U.S. Attorneys are fired, the reasons for the firing, and the process for replacing them.

The Congressional Research Service (CRS) analyzed the history of firings of U.S. Attorneys and found that only two U.S. Attorneys out of 486 confirmed by the Senate over the past twenty-five years have been fired in the middle of a presidential term for reasons unrelated to misconduct. Thus, when the Bush Administration fired its *own* appointees, everyone, including Congress, noticed. But what of the replacement process?

Historically, as far back as the Civil War, the statutes gave the courts the authority to appoint an interim U.S. Attorney. That authority was first vested with the Circuit Courts in March of 1863. Then, in 1898, the authority was switched to the District Courts, where it remained for almost 100 years, until 1986 when the statute was changed during the Reagan Administration to give the interim appointment authority to the Attorney General. If, after 120 days, a nominee had not been confirmed, the district courts would appoint an interim U.S. Attorney. The one thing that remained unchanged throughout these changing procedures was the need for Senate confirmation.

Finally, in 2006, as part of the Patriot Act reauthorization, a provision was inserted that gave the Attorney General the authority to appoint an interim U.S. Attorney for an indefinite period and without Senate confirmation. This unprecedented extension of executive authority was immediately, and successfully, challenged by Congress.

corruption cases against Democrats, were terminated with extreme political prejudice?...I hope we will all support Sen. Feinstein's commendable legislation, S.214, to close the Patriot Act loophole that may have invigorated the Bush administration in its unprecedented assault on the United States Attorney corps." (U.S. Senate, Debate on S.214, 110th Congress, March 20, 2007, televised live on C-SPAN2)

Two major Republican amendments were proposed to S.214, both intended to reduce the role of the courts in the appointment process. Democrats insisted that since S.214 was designed simply to return the law on interim appointments of U.S. Attorneys to its pre-Patriot Act status, any attempt to add new provisions would be inappropriate. In the end, the Senate rejected the amendments and voted overwhelmingly, 94 to 2, to pass Senator Feinstein's bill.

Meanwhile, the House companion bill, H.R. 580, proceeded toward markup with strong bipartisan support. Introduced by Representative Howard Berman (D-CA), Chairman of the Judiciary Subcommittee on Courts, H.R. 580 would also return the law on interim appointments to its pre-Patriot Act status. In decrying the "unprecedented firing of 8 U.S. Attorneys," Berman declared,

> The language that granted this new power to the Attorney General was slipped into the PATRIOT Act reauthorization at the request of the Department of Justice at a time when Republican negotiators were excluding Democrats. This "lockout" at the end of the process was part of the reason that the majority of House Democrats opposed the reauthorization of the PATRIOT Act. My bill will reset the system of checks and balances in the U.S. Attorney confirmation process. ("Rep. Berman Calls for Quick House Action on Bill to Protect Appointment Process for U.S. Attorneys," press release, Congressman Howard Berman, March 6, 2007. www. house.gov/apps/list/press/ca28_berman/billattorney.html)

On March 26, 2007, H.R. 580 was passed by a vote of 329 to 78. Thus, Congress had sent a stinging, bipartisan message to the Justice Department and the Bush Administration that at least one provision of the Patriot Act was ill-advised and unacceptable. But the repeal of this bothersome Patriot Act provision did not end the controversy. Congress immediately issued subpoenas to administration officials, including Carl Rove, President Bush's top political adviser, Harriet Myers, the former White House counsel, and Kyle Sampson, former chief of staff to Attorney General Alberto Gonzales. The White House said the subpoenas intruded on executive branch prerogatives and offered instead to allow informal "interviews" with White House officials. Those interviewed would not be under oath and there would be no transcripts of the interviews. Democrats insisted that the witnesses be under oath and that their testimony be public. A constitutional conflict appeared unavoidable.

Kyle Sampson, who was no longer employed by the Justice Department, decided on his own to appear before the Senate Judiciary Committee to give his version of the firings of U.S. Attorneys. Sampson, who was probably more closely involved with the controversial firings than any other administration official, was cooperative and candid in his responses to questions. In particular, his answers to Ranking Member Senator Arlen Specter acknowledged that even the Justice Department could not defend the Patriot Act provision that generated the firings.

> **Specter:** Would you agree Mr. Sampson that on this state of the record, where you have a request by the Justice Department for this new procedure under the Patriot Act and you have the plan set forth,...that the Department of Justice had it in mind at the outset to get the law changed and then to use it for replacing U.S. Attorneys who were asked to resign, and use the shenanigans or "bad faith," as you yourself characterized it, to run out the clock and have all of these U.S. Attorneys serve out the balance of the President's term without Senate involvement or Senate confirmation?
>
> **Sampson:** It was a bad idea. It was recommended by staff, including me, and it wasn't adopted by the principals.
>
> **Specter:** Was the modification in the Patriot Act a bad idea too, to circumvent the U.S. Senate?

*Sampson:* I can understand how that would raise a question for a U.S. Senator....I think it was well-intentioned at the time.

*Specter:* That's all very interesting, but was it a bad idea?

*Sampson:* In hindsight, it seems like a bad idea. (U.S. Senate, Judiciary Committee, Hearings on Firing of U.S. Attorneys, 110th Congress, March 29, 2007, televised live on C-SPAN2)

# FURTHER READINGS

Baker, Nancy B. *Conflicting Loyalties: Law and Politics in the Attorney General's Office, 1789–1990.* Lawrence, KS: University of Kansas Press, 1992.

Emert, Phyllis Raybin. *Attorneys General: Enforcing the Law.* Minneapolis, MN: Oliver Press, 2005.

McElroy, Lisa Tucker. *Alberto Gonzales: Attorney General.* Brookfield, CT: Millbrook Press, 2006.

Minutaglio, Bill. *The President's Counselor: The Rise to Power of Alberto Gonzales.* New York: Harper Collins, 2006.

Seymour, Whitney North. *United States Attorney: An Inside View of "Justice" in America under the Nixon Administration.* New York: Morrow, 1975.

# Inspector General's Report Reveals FBI Abuse of National Security Letters

- **Documents:** Inspector General report documenting FBI abuse of the National Security Letter (NSL) authority; statement by Senator Patrick Leahy, Chairman, Judiciary Committee, at FBI oversight hearings
- **When:** Report dated March 2007; hearings occurred March 27, 2007
- **Where:** Washington, DC
- **Significance:** The Inspector General's audit of the use of NSLs was mandated by a provision in the USA PATRIOT Improvement and Reauthorization Act. The report revealed massive FBI incompetence and abuse in the use of NSLs, and Congress quickly moved to consider new oversight requirements on the use of NSLs; the FBI oversight hearings on March 27, 2007 revealed a growing congressional sense that the unprecedented powers granted to the executive branch in the Patriot Act needed to be restricted.

## DOCUMENTS

### 1. Inspector General's Report on FBI Use of NSLs

As required by the Patriot Reauthorization Act, our review...examined instances of improper or illegal use of national security letters. First, our review examined national security letter violations that the FBI was required to report to the President's Intelligence Oversight Board (IOB). Executive Order 12863 directs the IOB to inform the President of any activities that the IOB believes "may be unlawful or contrary to Executive order or presidential directive." The FBI identified 26 possible violations involving the use of national security letter authorities from 2003 through 2005, of which 19 were reported to the IOB. These 19 involved the issuance of NSLs without proper authorization, improper requests under statutes cited in the national security letters, and unauthorized collection of telephone or Internet e-mail transactional records, including records containing data beyond the time period requested in the national security letters. Of these 26 possible violations, 22 were the result of FBI errors, while 4 were caused by mistakes made by recipients of the national security letters.

Second, in addition to the violations reported by the FBI, we reviewed documents relating to national security letters in a sample of FBI investigative files in four FBI field offices. In our review of 77 FBI investigative files, we found that 17 of these files—22 percent—contained one or more possible violations relating to national security letters that were not identified by the FBI. These possible violations included infractions that were similar to those identified by the FBI and considered as possible IOB violations, but also included instances in which the FBI issued national security letters for different information than what had been approved by the field supervisor. Based on our review and the significant percentage of files that contained unreported possible violations (22 percent), we believe that a significant number of NSL-related possible violations are not being identified or reported by the FBI.

Third, we identified many instances in which the FBI obtained telephone toll billing records and subscriber information from 3 telephone companies pursuant to more than 700 "exigent letters" signed by personnel in the Counterterrorism Division without first issuing national security letters. We concluded that the FBI's acquisition of this information circumvented the ECPA [Electronic Communications Privacy Act] NSL statute and violated the Attorney General's Guidelines for FBI National Security Investigations and Foreign Intelligence Collection (NSI Guidelines) and internal FBI policy. These matters were compounded by the fact that the FBI used the exigent letters in non-emergency circumstances, failed to ensure that there were duly authorized investigations to which the requests could be tied, and failed to ensure that NSLs were issued promptly after the fact, pursuant to existing or new counterterrorism investigations. In addition, the exigent letters inaccurately represented that the FBI had already requested subpoenas for the information when, in fact, it had not.

Fourth, we determined that in circumstances during 2003 through 2005 FBI Headquarters Counterterrorism Division generated over 300 national security letters exclusive from "control files" rather than from "investigative files" in violation of FBI policy. In these instances, FBI agents did not generate and supervisors did not approve documentation demonstrating that the factual predicate required by the Electronic Communications Privacy Act, the Attorney General's Guidelines for FBI National Security Investigations and Foreign Intelligence Collection, and internal FBI policy had been established. When NSLs are issued from control files rather than from investigative files, internal and external reviews cannot determine whether the requests are tied to investigations that establish the required evidentiary predicate for issuing the national security letters.

Fifth, we examined FBI investigative files in four field offices to determine whether FBI case agents and supervisors adhered to FBI policies designed to ensure appropriate supervisory review of the use of national security letter authorities. We found that 60 percent of the investigative files we examined contained one or more violations of FBI internal control policies relating to national security letters. These included failures to document supervisory review of national security letter approval memoranda and failures to include required information such as the authorizing statute, the status of the investigative subject, or the number or types of records requested in NSL approval memoranda. Moreover, because the FBI does not retain copies of signed national security letters, we were unable to conduct a comprehensive audit of the FBI's compliance with its internal control policies and the statutory certifications required for national security letters.

Our review describes several other "noteworthy facts or circumstances" we identified. For example, we found that the FBI has not provided clear guidance describing how case agents and supervisors should apply the Attorney General Guidelines' requirement to use the "least intrusive collection techniques feasible" in their use and sequencing of national security letters. In addition, we found confusion among FBI attorneys and communication providers over the meaning of the phrase "telephone toll billing records information" in the ECPA NSL statute. We also saw indications that some Chief Division Counsel and Assistant Division Counsel are reluctant to provide an independent review of national security letters requests because these attorneys report to the Special Agents in Charge who have already approved the underlying investigation.

SOURCE: U.S. Department of Justice, Office of the Inspector General. *A Review of the Federal Bureau of Investigation's Use of National Security Letters*. March 2007, pp. 122–24. http://cryptome.org/fbi-nsl/fbi-nsl.html

---

### 2. Statement of Senator Patrick Leahy, Chairman, Committee on the Judiciary

From the FBI's illegal and improper use of National Security Letters (NSLs), to the Bureau's failure to be accountable for and secure its own computers and weapons, to the politically motivated dismissal of eight of the Nation's U.S. Attorneys, there are growing concerns about the competence of the FBI and the independence of the Department of Justice. This pattern of abuse and mismanagement causes me, and many others on both sides of the aisle, to wonder whether the FBI and Department of Justice have been faithful trustees of the great trust that the Congress and American people have placed in them to keep our Nation safe, while respecting the privacy rights and civil liberties of all Americans.

And it is more than just the FBI that deserves scrutiny for the abuses and lack of competence that have come to light just in recent weeks. Last year the Administration sought new powers in the PATRIOT Act to appoint U.S. Attorneys without Senate confirmation, and to more freely use National Security Letters. The Administration got these powers, and they have badly bungled both....

In the recent reauthorization of the [Patriot] Act, one of my priorities...was to retain sunset provisions and to supplement them with new "sunshine" provisions, to require the Justice Department to report to the Congress and to the American people on how several of the Act's powers are being used. The Inspector General's audit and report on National Security Letters was one of these new requirements we added to the law, and the troubling findings of that audit are why we are here today.

I am deeply disturbed by the Justice Department Inspector General's report finding widespread illegal and improper use of NSLs to obtain Americans' phone and financial records.... Even more troubling is that the violations the Inspector General uncovered are probably just the tip of the iceberg. When he appeared before Congress last week, Inspector General Glenn Fine testified that there could be thousands of additional violations among the tens of thousands of NSLs that the FBI is now using each year....

The FBI is again at a crossroads. Because of these, and other, shortcomings, some are calling on Congress to take away the FBI's domestic intelligence functions altogether and to create a separate domestic intelligence agency like Britain's M15. Last week the leading Republican on this oversight Committee questioned whether Director Mueller is up to the job....The time has come for demonstrable progress by the Bureau on a learning curve that has gone on and on for far too long.

SOURCE: U.S. Senate, Committee on the Judiciary. Statement of Senator Patrick Leahy, Chairman, Committee on the Judiciary, Hearing on FBI Oversight, March 27, 2007. http://judiciary.senate.gov/member_statement.cfm?id=2569&wit_id=2629

---

# ANALYSIS

During 2007, two concurrent Patriot Act scandals could be traced to particular provisions in the USA PATRIOT Improvement and Reauthorization Act. As we saw in the previous

---

## IN HISTORY

### Did Reauthorization Fix the NSL Gag Order Problem?

The Patriot Act reauthorization included a provision allowing NSL gag orders to be challenged in court, a right that civil libertarians had advocated for some time. When FBI Director Robert Mueller was called before Congress to defend the use of NSLs in the wake of the March 2007 Inspector General's report, he reassured committee members that "the latest iteration [reauthorization] of the Patriot Act gives the person the opportunity to go to court and challenge the gag order." Yet the problems posed by gag orders persisted.

Representative Jerrold Nadler (D-NY) explained why:

> Until we made a minor change in the [Patriot Act] law last year, if you got a National Security Letter you couldn't even tell your attorney.…[Y]ou can go to court now…but the law provides that the government's mere assertion that it would [cause harm to the United States] is conclusive, which means that they don't have to offer any evidence, and the judge has no discretion to say that's absurd or that's wrong. If the government simply says that revealing this information would do harm, that's the end of the question.… The provision is meaningless. ("Washington Journal," C-SPAN, March 20, 2007)

Evidence of the continuing power of the Patriot Act to gag those who receive NSLs was seen on March 23, 2007, when the *Washington Post* published an unsigned op-ed article by an Internet service provider who described the difficulties he suffered under a three-year-old NSL gag order. The author, who was forced to remain anonymous because the Patriot Act would make his public statement a felonious act, said the Inspector General's report of FBI abuses encouraged him to go public. He explained, "The [NSL] letter ordered me to provide sensitive information about one of my clients.…The letter came with a gag provision that prohibited me from telling anyone, including my client, that the FBI was seeking this information."

Rather than turn over the information, the author contacted lawyers at the American Civil Liberties Union and filed a lawsuit challenging the constitutionality of the NSL power. The FBI eventually decided that it no longer needed the information, but maintained the gag order nonetheless. In fact, the government returned to court to defend the gag letters. The author complains,

> I resent being conscripted as a secret informer for the government and being made to mislead those who are close to me, especially because I have doubts about the legitimacy of the underlying investigation. I found it particularly difficult to be silent about my concerns while Congress was debating the reauthorization of the Patriot Act. ("My National Security Gag Order," *Washington Post*, March 23, 2007, p. A17)

---

section, the controversy over the firings of U.S. Attorneys had its origin in the reauthorization provision that allowed those attorneys to be replaced by the Attorney General without the usual Senate confirmation. The scandal over the FBI's abuse of NSLs was not *caused* by any provision of the reauthorization act, but the abuse was *exposed* as the result of a provision requiring an Inspector General's audit of the FBI's use of NSLs. Many members of Congress would later make the case that the *absence* of any meaningful restraints on the use of NSLs in the reauthorization bill contributed to the FBI's abuse of that tool, but it was the new oversight requirement that directly created the scandal.

Like the concurrent scandal over the firings of U.S. Attorneys, the revelations of FBI abuse of NSLs brought calls for changes to the Patriot Act, with particular emphasis on tightening the loose "relevance standard" by which NSLs are authorized under the Patriot Act. But restricting the DOJ's anti-terrorism powers would prove much more difficult than reducing the Attorney General's authority to fire and replace DOJ employees. In his testimony before the Senate Judiciary Committee on March 28, 2007, FBI Director Mueller acknowledged the seriousness of the Bureau's abuse of its NSL authority, but he firmly declared:

> I do not believe, however, that the statute itself should be changed. The relevance standard established by the Patriot Act for the issuance of National Security Letters is unrelated to the problems identified by the Inspector General. As the Inspector General testified, the problems were generally the product of, and I quote, "mistakes, carelessness, confusion, sloppiness, lack of training, lack of adequate guidance, and lack of adequate oversight." In short, the statute did not cause the errors. The FBI's implementation of the statute did. ("Oversight of the Federal Bureau of Investigation," Senate Judiciary Committee, March 27, 2007, Webcast available at http:// judiciary.senate.gov/hearing.cfm?id=2569)

Despite Mueller's strong defense of the NSL provision in the Patriot Act, Democratic members of the Senate Judiciary Committee expressed their concern. Senator Richard Durbin (D-IL) told Mueller that he disagreed with the claim that the abuses described by the Inspector General revealed nothing more than "a management problem." Durbin concluded,

> I believe there are some fundamental weaknesses and difficulties in the law, that we've given such a broad power to the Department and through the FBI that it is really open to abuse, and as a consequence, abuses occurred and now have been documented.... Would you support revising the Patriot Act to require the government to show a need before a gag order is imposed for a National Security Letter?

Mueller responded, "I probably would not" (U.S. Senate, Committee on the Judiciary, Hearing on FBI Oversight, March 28 2007. Televised live on C-SPAN).

Despite documented evidence of FBI abuse of the National Security Letter authority, Attorney General Gonzales told Congress that no "verified case of civil liberties abuse" had occurred since passage of the Patriot Act. When later challenged on this claim, Gonzales told the Senate Judiciary Committee that he defined "abuse" to mean "intentional, deliberate misuse" of the Patriot Act, and since he believed that all FBI violations were unintentional, they were not really abuses.

Even this bit of tortured semantics soon crumbled before new evidence. In July 2007, the *Washington Post* reported that the FBI had sent Gonzales at least half a dozen reports of legal or procedural violations before his congressional testimony. One of those violations stood out because it was indisputably intentional. The FBI's own report to Gonzales told of an agent who gathered financial records without proper authority or approval, violating both bureau policy and federal law. The FBI concluded, "In this instance the conduct...was willful and intentional." Thus, even by the attorney general's definition, it was abuse.

Gonzales's credibility had all but disappeared, and Congress would no longer give the FBI a blank check for its use of NSLs.

When the Justice Department's Inspector General appeared before a House subcommittee, Representative Dan Lundgren (R-CA) told him that FBI promises to improve their management of NSLs may not be enough. "I don't think...you're going to have to worry about improving your procedures for NSLs, because you probably won't have NSL authority," he said (Lehrer NewsHour, public television, March 20, 2007).

Representative William Sensenbrenner (R-WI), the former Republican Chairman of the House Judiciary Committee that oversaw the use of the Patriot Act, declared,

> I am shocked. I think that the Justice Department has overreached. There is something seriously wrong with the internal management of the Justice Department, and that better be fixed, because if it isn't, support for the internal part of the war upon terrorism is going to evaporate rapidly.

Sensenbrenner warned that the FBI's abuse of NSLs would force a strong reaction by Congress, and he concluded: "I think the use of NSLs is going to have to be restricted by statute, and very frankly, I think there ought to be some heads that roll here" ("Privacy Abuses: FBI Mistakes and Misuse of the Patriot Act," Lehrer NewsHour, public television, March 9, 2007).

Heads would indeed roll. Alberto Gonzales's Justice Department began to crumble under the weight of two concurrent Patriot Act scandals and a succession of bumbling, dissembling appearances before Congress by the attorney general. On April 6, 2007, Monica Goodling, senior counselor to Gonzales, submitted her resignation, just two weeks after she had refused to answer questions from Congress about the firing of U.S. Attorneys. Goodling's departure came just a month after the resignations of Kyle Sampson, Gonzales's chief of staff, and Michael Battle, the Justice Department official who had carried out the firings. When Paul McNulty, Gonzales's deputy, resigned on May 15, bipartisan calls for the attorney general's resignation began to emerge.

Even Republican icon Newt Gingrich declared, "I cannot imagine how [Attorney General Gonzales] is going to be effective for the rest of this administration.... I think the country, in fact, would be much better served to have a new team at the Justice Department, across the board" ("Gonzales Should Go: Newt Gingrich," *Washington Post*, April 9, 2007, p. A2).

Despite unflagging support from the White House, Gonzales finally announced his resignation on August 28, 2007.

# FURTHER READINGS

*Alberto Gonzales v. John Doe*. United States Court of Appeals for the Second Circuit, Brief of Electronic Frontier Foundation et al. in Support of Appellees and Affirmation of Judgment Below. August 3, 2005. www.eff.org/patriot/NSL_EFF_brief.pdf

Doyle, Charles. "National Security Letters in Foreign Intelligence Investigations: A Glimpse of the Legal Background and Recent Amendments," Congressional Research Service Reports and Issue Briefs, September 25, 2006.

Hentoff, Nat. "National Security Letters Abused," *Washington Times* (March 26, 2007). http://washingtontimes.com/op_ed/20070325-100601-7793r.html

United States Senate, Committee on the Judiciary. Testimony of Alberto Gonzales, Attorney General of the United States, U.S. Department of Justice, January 6, 2005. http://judiciary.senate.gov/testimony.cfm?id=1345&witid=3936

Weiner, Lauren M. "Special Delivery: Where Do National Security Letters Fit into the Fourth Amendment?" *Fordham Urban Law Journal*, 33, no. 5 (2007), p. 1453.

# Patriot Act Resources: Electronic, Print, and Video

## WEB SITES

There is a vast amount of information available online pertaining to the USA PATRIOT Act and its introduction as a response to the September 11 attacks. Below are selected official U.S. government Web sites, international Web sites, and nongovernmental information from think tanks, nonprofit organizations, online archives, and other sources.

### Federal Agencies and Departments

#### Central Intelligence Agency

www.cia.gov

The Central Intelligence Agency (CIA) is responsible for detecting and preventing acts of international terrorism, including those aimed at the U.S. homeland. Since passage of the Patriot Act, the CIA and other intelligence agencies have worked more closely with domestic law enforcement in counter-terrorism investigations.

#### CIA *World Factbook*

http://www.cia.gov/cia/publications/factbook/

The *World Factbook* is a well-known source of information on 266 nations and regions.

Director of Central Intelligence Agency George J. Tenet's Testimony before the Joint Inquiry into Terrorist Attacks against the United States, June 18, 2002.

http://www.cia.gov/cia/public_affairs/speeches/2002/ dci_testimony_06182002.html

#### War on Terrorism

http://cia.gov/terrorism/index.html

This site provides a collection of links, documents, and speeches on the CIA's war on terrorism.

## *Department of Defense*

www.defenselink.mil/

> This Department of Defense (DoD) site offers information on U.S. military operations and the military's role in homeland security.

DoD News Transcripts

www.defenselink.mil/transcripts/

> This site provides transcripts of briefings and interviews with DoD personnel.

Pentagon Releases Videotape of Osama bin Laden, December 13, 2001

www.defenselink.mil/news/Dec2001/b12132001_bt630-01.html

War on Terrorism

www.defendamerica.mil/

## *Department of Homeland Security*

www.dhs.gov/dhspublic/

> The Department of Homeland Security (DHS) was created in 2003 to lead the national effort to "prevent and deter terrorist attacks, protect against and respond to threats and hazards to the United States, and ensure safe and secure borders." The DHS includes:

> Coast Guard: www.uscg.mil/uscg.shtm

> Customs Service (now U.S. Customs & Border Protection, CBP: www.CBP.gov/

> Domestic Emergency Support Teams: www.fema.gov/rrr/conplan/conpinle.shtm Energy Security and Assurance Program

> Environmental Measurements Laboratory: www.eml.doe.gov/

> Federal Computer Incident Response Center (now U.S. Computer Emergency Readiness Team, US-CERT): www.us-cert.gov/federal/

> Federal Emergency Management Agency: www.fema.gov

> Federal Law Enforcement Training Center: www.fletc.gov/

> Federal Protective Service (now part of Immigration and Customs Enforcement, ICE, the investigative bureau of the Border and Transportation Security Directorate of the DHS): www.ice.gov/

> Immigration and Naturalization Service (now U.S. Citizenship and Immigration Services, USCIS): uscis.gov/graphics/index.htm

> National BW Defense Analysis Center (now Chemical and Biological Defense Information Analysis Center, CBIAC): www.cbiac.apgea.army.mil/

> National Communications System: www.ncs.gov/

> National Domestic Preparedness Office (now part of Office for Domestic Preparedness, ODP): www.ojp.usdoj.gov/odp/

> Nuclear Incident Response Team: www.llnl.gov/nai/rdiv/nucinc.html

> Office for Domestic Preparedness: www.ojp.usdoj.gov/odp/

> Plum Island Animal Disease Center: www.ars.usda.gov/plum/

> Secret Service: www.secretservice.gov/

Strategic National Stockpile and the National Disaster Medical System: www.bt.cdc.gov/stockpile/index.asp

Transportation Security Administration: www.tsa.gov/public/index.jsp

## Department of Justice

www.usdoj.gov

The Department of Justice (DOJ) is the primary law enforcement agency in the United States. Since passage of the USA PATRIOT Act in 2001, the distinction between domestic law enforcement and international counter-terrorism has been blurred. The sharing of investigative information between all law enforcement and intelligence agencies was mandated by the Patriot Act. The DOJ is involved in the domestic surveillance, arrest, detention, and trial of suspected terrorists, and new FBI guidelines have made counter-terrorism the most important function of the department. Typical information displayed on the DOJ Web site includes:

OIG Testimony Concerning Section 1001 of the USA PATRIOT Act.

www.usdoj.gov/opa/oig/testimony/0505b.htm

Fact Sheet: USA PATRIOT Improvement and Reauthorization Act of 2005

www.usdoj.gov/opa/pr/2006/March/06_opa_113.html

Foreign Intelligence Surveillance Act 2005 Annual Report, Department of Justice.

www.fas.org/irp/agency/doj/fisa/2005rept.html

Patriot Act Hearing, House Subcommittee on the Constitution, May 20, 2003.

www.usdoj.gov/opa/pr/2003/June/03_opa_323.html

The Justice Department's Office of the Inspector General (OIG) has reporting and oversight responsibility for the operation of the DOJ. In particular, the Patriot Act established a set of new reporting obligations, and those reports are available on:

www.usdoj.gov/oig/reports/index.html

Examples of Patriot Act-mandated OIG reports available on this site include:

A Review of the Federal Bureau of Investigation of National Security Letters, March 2007;
A Review of the Federal Bureau of Investigation's Use of Section 215 Orders for Business Records, March 2007.

The Department of Justice also maintains a Web site devoted exclusively to the USA PATRIOT Act:

www.lifeandliberty.gov/

This DOJ site summarizes the PATRIOT Act and provides links to related sites.

## Department of the Treasury, Office of Foreign Assets Control

www.treas.gov/offices/eotffc/ofac/

Under the Patriot Act, seizure of assets from charities and other organizations suspected of supporting terrorism has become common. The Office of Foreign Assets Control (OFAC) of the U.S. Department of the Treasury "administers and enforces economic and trade sanctions based on national security goals, against targeted foreign countries, terrorists, international drug traffickers, and proliferators of weapons of mass destruction." Similarly, the Office of Terrorism and Financial Intelligence (TFI) safeguards "U.S. and international financial systems from abuse by terrorist financing, money laundering, and other financial crime." Its Web site is www. treasury.gov/offices/enforcement/

### Federal Bureau of Investigation

www.fbi.gov/

The Federal Bureau of Investigation (FBI) is responsible for preventing terrorist attacks on U.S. soil, coordinating the federal response to a terrorist crisis, investigating crimes including terrorist incidents, and apprehending suspects. New FBI Guidelines issued after 9/11 made the *prevention* of terrorism the highest priority of the Bureau. Typical post-9/11 content on the FBI's Web site includes:

The USA PATRIOT Act

www.fbi.gov/aboutus/transformation/patriot_act.htm

The Emergency Disclosure Provision of the USA PATRIOT Act

www.fbi.gov/page2/may05/hulon050905.htm

Testimony of Director Robert Mueller on Patriot Act

www.fbi.gov/congress/congress04/mueller052004.htm

Freedom of Information Act (FOIA)

foia.fbi.gov/

Most Wanted Terrorists

www.fbi.gov/mostwant/terrorists/fugitives.htm

Terrorism in the United States

www.fbi.gov/publications/terror/terroris.htm

War on Terrorism Page

www.fbi.gov/terrorinfo/counterrorism/waronterrorhome.htm

### FirstGov

www.firstgov.gov/

FirstGov.gov is the official U.S. gateway to all government information available online. This site provides online information, services, and resources.

### Government Accountability Office (formerly General Accounting Office)

www.gao.gov/

The Government Accountability Office (GAO) "studies how the federal government spends taxpayer dollars. The GAO evaluates federal programs, audits federal expenditures, and issues legal opinions."

## *Intelligence Community Agencies*

www.intelligence.gov/1-members_nima.shtml

The intelligence community (IC) is a large, complex collection of U.S. agencies organizations. The IC is engaged in intelligence collection for the president, the National Security Council, the secretaries of State and Defense, and other executive branch officials. The IC also produces and disseminates intelligence and information. The following agencies and organizations are members of the IC:

Air Force Intelligence: www.intelligence.gov/l-members_airforce.shtml

Army Intelligence: www.intelligence.gov/l-members_army.shtml

Central Intelligence Agency: www.cia.gov

Coast Guard Intelligence: www.intelligence.gov/1-members_coastguard.shtml

Defense Intelligence Agency (The DIA provides military intelligence to the Secretary of Defense and the chairman of the Joint Chiefs of Staff. It also provides intelligence on foreign weapon systems.): www.dia.mil/

Department of Energy, Office of Intelligence (The Department of Energy's Office Intelligence is the IC's technical intelligence resource in the areas of "nuclear weapons and nonproliferation; energy security; science and technology; and nuclear energy, safety, and waste."): www.intelligence.gov/1-members_energy.shtml

Department of Homeland Security, Information Analysis and Infrastructure Protection (The DHS's Information Analysis and Infrastructure Protection directorate, IAIP, is a member of the IC. IAIP administers the Homeland Security Advisory System.): www.dhs.gov/dhspublic/display?theme=52&content=207

Department of State, Bureau of Intelligence and Research (The State Department's Bureau of Intelligence and Research is a member of the IC and "functions as the 'eyes and ears' of the State Department," providing intelligence support to senior policymakers and working-level officials.): www.intelligence.gov/1-members_state.shtml

Department of the Treasury (The Department of the Treasury is not in its entirety part of the IC but does contain an office dedicated to intelligence, the Office of Intelligence Support [OIS], which is responsible for providing intelligence to the department.): www.intelligence.gov/l-members_treasury.shtml

Federal Bureau of Investigation: www.fbigov/

Marine Corps Intelligence: www.intelligence.gov/l-members_marines.shtml

National Geospatial-Intelligence Agency (The NGA, formerly the National Imagery and Mapping Agency [NIMA], is a major intelligence and combat support agency of the Department of Defense. It supports U.S. national policymakers and military forces by providing geospatial intelligence, which is intelligence gathered from the merging of imagery, maps, charts, and environmental data.): www.nima.mil/ portal/ site/ngaOl/

National Reconnaissance Office (The NRO designs, builds, and operates U.S. reconnaissance satellites.): www.nro.gov

National Security Agency/Central Security Service: www.nsa.gov

Navy Intelligence: www.intelligence.gov/l-members_navy.shtml

### National Archives and Records Administration

http://www.archives.gov/index.html

The National Archives and Records Administration (NARA) is a public trust that provides continuing access to essential documents.

### National Security Agency/Central Security Service

www.nsa.gov/about/index.cfm

The National Security Agency/Central Security Service (NSA/CSS) "is America's cryptologic organization. It coordinates, directs, and performs highly specialized activities to protect U.S. information systems and produce foreign intelligence information."

### State Department

www.state.gov

The U.S. Department of State is the lead foreign affairs agency of the United States.

Countering Terrorism

www.state.gov/s/ct/c4291.htm

This site contains links to official State Department statements, policies, photos, and audio clips.

Counterterrorism Office

www.state.gov/s/CT/

The State Department's Counterterrorism Office makes available a number of resources on this site, including the Most Wanted Terrorists list, U.S. Counterterrorism Policy, and International Terrorism: American Hostages. Its Web site includes documents such as:

Foreign Terrorist Organizations

www.state.gov/s/ct/rls/fs/

The most recent list of foreign terrorist organizations (FTOs) is found on this site.

Open Forum Proceedings

www.state.gov/s/p/of/proc/

Patterns of Global Terrorism

www.state.gov/s/ct/rls/pgtrpt/

The annual *Patterns of Global Terrorism* is a congressionally mandated report from the U.S. State Department. It is intended to provide a complete record of countries and groups that are involved in international terrorism.

### Transportation Security Administration

www.tsa.gov

The Transportation Security Administration (TSA) protects U.S. transportation systems.

## White House

The White House is the seat of the executive branch, within which function the president, his cabinet, staff, and advisors. The White House Web site, www.whitehouse. gov, contains documents such as:

President Pledges to Work with Congress to Re-Authorize Patriot Act

www.whitehouse.gov/news/releases/2005/12/20051222-11.html

President Appreciates Senate Extension of Patriot Act

www.whitehouse.gov/news/releases/2005/12/20051221.html

Fact Sheet: Safeguarding America: President Bush Signs Patriot Act Reauthorization

www.whitehouse.gov/news/releases/2006/03/20060309-7.html

Fact Sheet: Giving Law Enforcement the Tools They Need to Safeguard Our Homeland

www.whitehouse.gov/news/releases/2005/07/20050720-3.html

The White House: Patriot Act Signing

www.whitehouse.gov/news/releases/2001/09/20010911-16.html

White House, September 11, 2001

www.whitehouse.gov/news/releases/2001/10/20011026-5.html

National Strategy for Homeland Security, July 16, 2002

www.whitehouse.gov/homeland/book/index.html

News and Policies

www.whitehouse.gov/news/

The full texts of the president's remarks, orders, proclamations, addresses, and other statements are available on the White House News and Policies page. Examples include:

President Bush Signs Homeland Security Act, November 25, 2002

www.whitehouse.gov/news/releases/2002/11/20021125-6.html

Executive Order 13224: Blocking Property and Prohibiting Transactions with Persons Who Commit, Threaten to Commit, or Support Terrorism, September 24, 2001: www.whitehouse.gov/news/releases/2001/09/20010924-l.html

Executive Order 1322S: Establishing the Office of Homeland Security and the Homeland Security Council, October S, 2001: www.whitehouse.gov/news/releases/2001/10/20011008-2.html

Homeland Security Presidential Directive 2: Combating Terrorism through Immigration Policies, October 29, 2001: www.whitehouse.gov/news/releases/2001/10/20011030-2.html

Military Order: Detention, Treatment and Trial of Certain Non-citizens in the War against Terrorism, November 13, 2001: www.whitehouse.gov/news/releases/2001/11/20011113-27.html

Homeland Security Presidential Directive 3: Homeland Security Advisory System, March 11, 2002: www.whitehouse.gov/news/releases/2002/03/20020312-S.html

Securing the Homeland, Strengthening the Nation

www.whitehouse.gov/homeland/homeland_security-book.html

## U.S. Congress

Congress is the legislative branch of the federal government, consisting of two chambers, the House of Representatives and the Senate. The full Congress has a Web site: www.congress.gov, and each chamber has its own site.

### *House of Representatives*

www.house.gov

Typical documents on this Web site include:

House Judiciary Committee, letter to Attorney General John Ashcroft, June 13, 2002. www.house.gov/judiciary/ashcroft061302.html

Miller Urges Repeal of USA PATRIOT Act

www.house.gov/georgemiller/rel92403.html

Representative Smith Votes against Flawed Patriot Act Conference Report

www.house.gov/list/press/wa09_smith/morenews/20051214bpr.html

A number of House members closely associated with USA PATRIOT Act have relevant documents on their Web sites. These include:

Representative James Sensenbrenner, former chair, House Judiciary Committee: www.sensenbrenner.house.gov

Representative John Conyers, former ranking member and current chair, House Judiciary Committee: www.house.gov/conyers

### *Senate*

www.senate.gov

Documents related to the Patriot Act appear on this Web site, but most such documents appear under the names of individual senators. Examples include:

USA PATRIOT Act: U.S. Senator John E. Sununu

http://sununu.senate.gov/usa_patriot_act.htm

Coleman Announces Extension of Patriot Act

http://coleman.senate.gov/index.cfm?FuseAction=PressReleases.Details&PressRelease_id=2

Civil Rights and Civil Liberties—Fixing the USA PATRIOT Act

http://feingold.senate.gov/issues/patriot.html

Chambliss Supports Passage of Patriot Act Renewal

http://chambliss.senate.gov/public/index.cfm?FuseAction=NewsCenter.PressReleases&ContentR

Senate Members closely associated with USA PATRIOT Act include:

Senator Patrick Leahy, chair, Senate Judiciary Committee: www.leahy.senate.gov
Senator Arlen Specter, former chair, Senate Judiciary Committee: www.specter.senate.gov

## Laws, Commissions, and Reports Related to the USA PATRIOT Act

### Laws

USA PATRIOT Act: Public Law No: 10-56, October 26, 2001

http://frwebgate.access.gpo.gov/cgi-bin/getdoc.cgi?dbname=107cong_public_laws&do-cid=f:publ056.1 07.pdf

> This site provides the text of the USA PATRIOT Act.

USA PATRIOT Act Additional Reauthorizing Amendments Act of 2006 (S.2271)

http://thomas.loc.gov/egi-bin/query/D?c109:4:./temp/-c109QljY2H

Benjamin Franklin True Patriot Act

www.theorater.com/bills/hr3171.html

Freedom to Read Protection Act

http://thomas.loc.gov/egi-bin/query/z?c108:H.R.1157

USA PATRIOT Improvement and Reauthorization Act of 2005 (H.R.3199)

www.congress.gov/egi-bin/query/D?c109:6:./temp/-c109WqnJYg

### Public Laws

www.gpoaccess.gov/plaws/index.html

> NARA's Office of the Federal Register (OFR) makes available on this site the text of public and private laws. A database of laws related to terrorism enacted from the 104th Congress to the present can be searched. Documents are available as ASCII text and PDF format

Public Law No: 107-40, September 18, 2001

http://thomas.loc.gov/cgi-bin/bdquery/z?dl07:SJ00023: TOM:/bss/dl07 query.html

> This law authorizes the use of U.S. Armed Forces against those responsible for the September 11 attacks.

Public Law No: 107-42, September 22, 2001

http://thomas.1oc.gov/cgi-bin/bdquery/z?dl07:HR02926: TOM:/bss/dl0

### Commission and Committee Reports

The most frequent and significant committee reports on the Patriot Act have come from the Judiciary Committees of the House and Senate. Those reports are available at the following Web sites:

http://judiciary.house.gov
http://judiciary.senate.gov

> Some other commission and committee reports related to the Patriot Act and domestic terrorism generally are:

Hart-Rudman Commission: U.S. Commission on National Security in the 21st Century

http://www.fas.org/man/ docs/nwc/

This site reports on the threat of mass casualty terrorism to the United States and stresses the need for an Office of Homeland Security.

Joint Inquiry: *Report of the Joint Inquiry into Intelligence Community Activities before and after the Terrorist Attacks of September 11, 2001*

www.gpoaccess.gov/serialset/creports/911.html

In 2002, the Senate Select Committee on Intelligence and the House Permanent Select Committee on Intelligence agreed to conduct a Joint Inquiry into the activities of the U.S. intelligence community in connection with the September 11 attacks. This report presents the Joint Inquiry's findings and conclusions, and a series of recommendations.

National Commission on Terrorism (Bremer Commission): *Countering the Changing Threat of International Terrorism*

http://www.access.gpo.gov/nct/

In 2000, the National Commission on Terrorism evaluated U.S. laws, policies, and practices for preventing and punishing terrorism directed at American citizens.

9/11 Commission: National Commission on Terrorist Attacks upon the United States

http://9-11commission.gov/ and www.gpoaccess.gov/911/ (report)

The National Commission on Terrorist Attacks upon the United States (also known as the 9/11 Commission) was a bipartisan commission created in 2002 to provide a full and complete account of the circumstances surrounding the September 11 attacks, "including preparedness for and the immediate response to the attacks. The commission was also mandated to provide recommendations designed to guard against future attacks." The final report was released July 22, 2004.

U.S. Senate Select Committee on Intelligence

http://intelligence.senate.gov/statutes.htm

This site lists some of the laws and precedents the U.S. government is using to combat the domestic war on terrorism.

## Libraries

### *American Library Association*

www.ala.org/

The American Library Association (ALA) site provides links to several Patriot Act and terrorism resources. Typical information on its Web site includes:

The USA PATRIOT Act in the Library

www.ala.org/ala/oif/ifissues/usapatriotactlibrary.htm

USA PATRIOT Act and Intellectual Freedom

www.ala.org/ala/oif/oifissues/usapatriotact.htm

The USA PATRIOT Act & Libraries

www.ala.org/ala/washoff/Woissues/civilliberties/theusapatriotact/usapatriotact.htm

Guidelines for Librarians on the USA PATRIOT Act

www.ala.org/ala/washoff/Woissues/civilliberties/theusapatriotact/patstep.pdf

Resolution on the USA PATRIOT Act Reauthorization

www.ala.org/ContentManagement/ContentDisplay.cfm&ContentID=114304

USA Patriot Act Search Warrant

www.ala.org/?Section=ifissues&Template=/ContentManagement/ContentDisplay.
cfm&amp

Resolution on the USA PATRIOT Act and Libraries

www.ala.org/ala/oif/statementspols/ifresolutions/usapatriotactlibraries.htm

USA PATRIOT Act Resolutions

www.ala.org/ala/oif/ifgroups/stateifchairs/stateifcinaction/usapatriotact.htm

USA PATRIOT Act

www.ala.org/washoff/patriot.html

> This American Library Association (ALA) site provides links to various full-text analy-
> ses of the USA PATRIOT Act and to related organizations such as the American
> Bar Association.

## *Library of Congress*

www.loc.gov

September 11 Digital Archive

http://911digitalarchive.org/

> This site provides access to material acquired by the Library of Congress (LOC) related
> to September 11, including prints, photographs, drawings, poems, eyewitness
> accounts and personal reactions, headlines, books, magazines, songs, maps, video-
> tapes, and films.

## Nongovernmental Organizations and Research Institutes

### *American Civil Liberties Union (ACLU)*

www.aclu.org

> The American Civil Liberties Union is the premier civil liberties organization, whose
> mission is to preserve First Amendment rights, the right to equal protection under
> the law, the right to due process, and the right to privacy. Typical of the informa-
> tion on the ACLU Web site are the following:

Revised ACLU Interested Person's Memo on the Security and Freedom Ensured
(SAFE) Act

www.aclu.org/safefree/general/18464leg20040616.html

Seeking Truth from Justice: PATRIOT Propaganda

www.aclu.org/safefree/resources/16825pub20030709.html

Safe and Free: USA PATRIOT Act

www.aclu.org/safefree/patriot/index.html

Assessing the So-Called USA PATRIOT Act

www.aclu.org/FilesPDFs/what%20the%20patriot%20act%20means%20to%20you.pdf

ACLU Letter to the House of Representatives Opposing Reauthorization of the USA PATRIOT Act

www.aclu.org/safefree/general/19915leg20050720.html

Legal Papers Relating to August 2002 FOIA Request

www.aclu.org/safefree/patriot_foia/2003/reply_sj_040403.pdf

How the USA PATRIOT Act Redefines Domestic Terrorism

www.aclu.org/safefree/natsec/emergpowers/14444leg20021206.html

### Avalon Project at Yale Law School: Documents on Terrorism

www.yale.edu/lawweb/avalon/terrorism/terror.htm

> The Avalon Project digitizes and displays online documents related to law, politics, history, and diplomacy. The terrorism section contains documents related to terrorism legislation, including:

Treasury Announced USA PATRIOT Act....

www.yale.edu/lawweb/avalon/sept_11/treas_029.htm

Remarks by the President at Signing of the USA PATRIOT Act

www.yale.edu/lawweb/avalon/sept_11/president_075.htm

Hearing on the "Financial War on Terrorism"

www.yale.edu/lawweb/avalon/sept_11/chertoff_022.htm

### C-Span.org. Response to Terrorism

www.c-span.orgfhomepage.asp?Cat=Current_Event&Code-terr&ShowVidNum=6&Roe CaeCD=91LResp&RoeHT=&RoeWD=&ShowVidDays=30&ShowVidDesc=&Archive Days=30

> C-Span.org has links to and video of government, media, and academic perspectives on the war on terrorism, including the Patriot Act.

### Cato Institute

www.cato.org/index.html

> The Cato Institute "is a nonprofit, public policy research foundation" devoted to libertarianism and limited government. It has criticized the Patriot Act for its expansion of government authority over the lives and property of American citizens. Typical content on its Web site includes:

What's Up with the Patriot Act?

www.cato.org/events030414pf.html

USA PATRIOT Act and Domestic Detention Policy

www.cato.org/pubs

The USA PATRIOT Act: Renew, Revise, or Repeal?

www.cato.org/event.php?eventid=2285

Text of the USA PATRIOT Act

www.cato.org/current/terrorism/patriot_act_text.html

Terrorism Page

www.cato.org/current/terrorism/index.html

## *Center for Defense Information, Terrorism Project*

www.cdi.org/program/index.dm?programid=39

The Center for Defense Information (CDI) "is a nonpartisan, nonprofit organization committed to independent research on the social, economic, environmental, political, and military components of global security." The Terrorism Project site features many CDI articles on terrorism issues.

## *Center for Democracy and Technology (CDT)*

www.cdt.org

The Center for Democracy and Technology analyzes the effects of modern technology, particularly information technology, on politics and society. The Patriot Act has been a focus of the CDT because of the increased surveillance of the Internet under anti-terrorism legislation. Typical content on the CDT Web site includes:

USA Patriot Act and Other Security Issues

www.cdt.org/security/010911response.php

Setting the Record Straight: An Analysis of the Justice Department's PATRIOT Act Web Site

www.cdt.org/security/usapatriot/031027cdt.shtml

CDT/PATRIOT Act Overview

www.cdt.org/security/usapatriot/overview2005.php

Analysis of the USA PATRIOT Act by CDT and Others

www.cdt.org/security/usapatriot/analysis.shtml

Summary and Analysis of Key Sections of USA PATRIOT Act

www.cdt.org/security/011031summary.shtml

## *Center for Nonproliferation Studies, Monterey Institute of International Studies*

http://cns.miis.edu/iridex.htm

The Center for Nonproliferation Studies (CNS), Monterey Institute of International Studies, is a nongovernmental organization "devoted exclusively to research and training on nonproliferation issues." This site features information on weapons of mass destruction and terrorist interest in these weapons.

## Council on Foreign Relations

www.cfr.org/

The Council on Foreign Relations (CFR) "is an independent, national membership organization and a nonpartisan center for scholars" that seeks to improve the understanding of U.S. foreign policy and international affairs. Documents on its Web site include:

Essential Documents, USA PATRIOT Act

www.cfr.org/search.html

CFR's List of Must-Reads

www.cfr.org/reg_issues.php?id=131111

This site provides an up-to-date list of books, reports, and articles on terrorism worldwide.

Terrorism: Questions and Answers

www.terrorismanswers.org/home/

This online encyclopedia of terrorism is provided by the CFR.

## Electronic Frontier Foundation (EFF)

www.eff.org

The Electronic Frontier Foundation is a leading research and lobbying organization on information technology and open access to the Internet. Its concerns over the surveillance provisions of the Patriot Act have made it both a critic and litigator. Typical information on its Web site includes:

USA PATRIOT Act

www.eff.org/patriot

Analysis of USA PATRIOT Act

www.eff.org/privacy/surveillance/Terrorism/20011031_eff_usa_patriot_analysis.html

Let the Sun Set on Patriot

www.eff.org/patriot/sunset/

Patriot II Draft Legislation

www.eff.org/Censorship/Terrorism_militias/patriot2draft.html

Patriot Act II Analysis

www.eff.org/Censorship/Terrorism_militias/patriot-act-II-analysis.php

## Federation of American Scientists

www.fas.org/index.html

The Federation of American Scientists (FAS) is an organization "dedicated to ending the worldwide arms race and avoiding the use of nuclear weapons for any purpose."

The FAS maintains a digital library and links related to the Patriot Act, global terrorism, and the September 11 attacks. Typical information on its Web site includes:

The USA PATRIOT Act: A Sketch

www.fas.org/irp/crs/intel/RS21203.pdf

The Patriot Act: A Legal Analysis

www.fas.org/irp/crs/RL31377.pdf

USA PATRIOT and Improvement and Reauthorization Act of 2005: A Legal Analysis

www.fas.org/sgp/crs/intel/RL33332.pdf

USA PATRIOT Act Sunset: A Sketch

www.fas.org/sgp/crs/intel/RS21704.pdf

Libraries and the USA PATRIOT Act

www.fas.org/sgp/crs/intel/RS21441.pdf

USA PATRIOT Act Reauthorization Proposals and Related Matters

www.fas.org/sgp/crs/intel/RS22196.pdf

USA PATRIOT Act: Background and Comparison of House and Senate

www.fas.org/sgp/crs/intel/RL33027.pdf

National Strategy for Combating Terrorism, February 14, 2003

www.fas.org/irp/threat/ctstrategy.pdf

America's War on Terrorism

www.fas.org/terrorism/index.html

Intelligence Resource Program, Terrorism Page

www.fas.org/irp/threat/terror.htm

### National Security Archive

www.gwu.edu/-nsarchiv/

> This nongovernment research institute at George Washington University collects and publishes declassified international affairs documents acquired through the Freedom of Information Act (FOIA). Its site contains important documents related to the fight against al Qaeda. Archived documents include a large set of FOIA documents on the FBI's Library Awareness Program and the September 11th sourcebooks.

### OMB Watch

www.ombwatch.org

> OMB Watch monitors the activity of the federal government generally and the Office of Management and Budget in particular. Typical documents on its Web site include:

Muslim Charities and the War on Terror

www.ombwatch.org/pdfs/muslim_charities.pdf#search=%22OMB

## *RAND Corporation*

www.rand.org

> The RAND Corporation is a nonprofit research institution that seeks to improve policy and decision making through research and analysis. It "provides analysis and solutions that address the challenges facing the public and private sectors around the world." Prominent among the materials on the RAND Web site is its Terrorism Page: http://rand.org/research_areas/terrorism/

## United Nations

The United Nations is an international organization composed of member states (nations). It was founded in 1946 to maintain international peace and security, and promote cooperation in solving economic, social, cultural, and humanitarian problems. As of April 2004, there were 191 member states. Its Web site, www.un.org, contains documents such as:

Counter-Terrorism Committee (established pursuant to Resolution 1373)

> www.un.org/Docs/sc/committees/13 73/

Definitions of Terrorism

> www.unodc.org/unodc/terrorism- definitions.html

U.N. Action against Terrorism

> www.un.org/terrorism/

> > This site pulls together all the major U.N. responses to terrorism, including resolutions, reports, and other actions by the General Assembly, the Security Council, and the Secretary-General.

U.N. Security Council

> www.un.org/Docs/sc/unsc_background.html

U.N. Security Council Resolution 1373: Adopts Steps and Strategies to Combat International Terrorism, September 28, 2001

> www.un.org/News/Press/docs/2001/sc7158.doc.htm

U.N. Security Council Unanimously Adopts Resolution 1368, September 12, 2001

> www.un.org/News/Press/docs/ZO01/SC7143.doc.htm

U.N. Treaties against International Terrorism

> www.un.org/News/dh/latest/intreaterror.htm

# BIBLIOGRAPHY

Abele, Robert P. *A User's Guide to the USA PATRIOT Act and Beyond.* Lanham, MD: University Press of America, 2005.

Aberbach, Joel T. *Keeping a Watchful Eye: The Politics of Congressional Oversight.* Washington, DC: Brookings Institution, 1990.

Adams, James A. *Electronic Surveillance: Commentaries and Statutes.* Notre Dame, IN: National Institute for Trial Advocacy, 2003.

Akbar, M.J. *The Shade of Swords: Jihad and the Conflict between Islam and Christianity*. London and New York: Routledge, 2002.

Baker, Stewart A. *Patriot Debates: Experts Debate the USA PATRIOT Act*. Chicago, IL: American Bar Association, 2005.

Balkin, Karen. *The War on Terrorism: Opposing Viewpoints*. Detroit, MI: Greenhaven Press, 2005.

Ball, Howard. *The USA PATRIOT Act of 2001: Balancing Civil Liberties and National Security: A Reference Handbook*. Santa Barbara, CA: ABC-CLIO, 2004.

Benjamin, Daniel, and Steven Simon. The Age of Sacred Terror. New York: Random House, 2002.

Bodansky, Yossef. *Bin Ladin: The Man Who Declared War on America*. New York: Random House, 2001.

Bovard, James. *Terrorism and Tyranny: Trampling Freedom, Justice, and Peace to Rid the World of Evil*. New York: Palgrave Macmillan, 2003.

Carafano, James Jay. *Winning the Long War: Lessons from the Cold War for Defeating Terrorism and Preserving Freedom*. Washington, DC: Heritage Foundation, 2005.

Clarke, Richard A. *Against All Enemies: Inside America's War on Terror*. New York: Free Press, 2004.

Cohen, H. Rodgin. *New Responsibilities & Obligations under the Money Laundering Abatement & Financial Anti-terrorism Act of 2001*. New York: Practicing Law Institute, 2002.

Collins, Aukai. *My Jihad: The True Story of an American Mujahid's Amazing Journey from Usama Bin Laden's Training Camps to Counterterrorism with the FBI and CIA*. Guilford, CT: Lyons, 2002.

Denton, Robert E. *Language, Symbols, and the Media: Communications in the Aftermath of the World Trade Center Attack*. New Brunswick, NJ: Transaction Publishers, 2004.

Der Spiegel. *Inside 9-11: What Really Happened*. Translated by Paul de Angelis and Elisabeth Kaestner. New York: St. Martin's, 2001.

Ehrenfeld, Rachel. *Funding Evil: How Terrorism Is Financed-and How to Stop It*. Chicago, IL: Bonus Books, 2003.

El-Ayouty, Yassin, ed. *Perspectives on 9/11*. Westport, CT: Praeger, 2004.

Emerson, Steven. *American Jihad: The Terrorists Living among Us*. New York: Free Press, 2002.

Etzioni, Amitai. *How Patriot Is the Patriot Act?: Freedom versus Security in the Age of Terrorism*. New York: Routledge, 2004.

Etzioni, Amitai. *Rights vs. Public Safety after 9/11: America in the Age of Terrorism*. Lanham, MD: Rowman & Littlefield, 2003.

Ewing, Alphonse B. *The USA PATRIOT Act*. New York: Novinka Books, 2002.

Farnam, Julie. *U.S. Immigration Laws under the Threat of Terrorism*. New York: Algora Pub., 2005.

Foerstel, Herbert N. *Refuge of a Scoundrel: The Patriot Act in Libraries*. Westport, CT: Libraries Unlimited, 2004.

Friedman, Lauri S. *The Patriot Act*. Detroit, MI: Greenhaven Press, 2006.

Gerdes, Louise L. *The Patriot Act: Opposing Viewpoints*. Detroit, MI: Greenhaven Press, 2005.

Gertz, Bill. *Breakdown: How America's Intelligence Failures Led to September 11*. Washington, DC: Regnery Publishing, 2002.

Goldstein, Joshua S. *The Real Price of War: How You Pay for the War on Terror*. New York: New York University Press, 2004.

Greenwald, Robert. *Unconstitutional: The War on Our Civil Liberties*. New York: Disinformation Co., 2006.

Gunaratna, Rohan. *Inside al Qaeda: Global Network of Terror*. New York: Columbia University Press, 2002.

Henderson, Harry. *Terrorist Challenge to America*. New York: Facts on File, 2003.

Heymann, Philip B. *Terrorism, Freedom, and Security: Winning without War*. Cambridge, MA: MIT Press, 2003.

Hiro, Dilip. *War without End: The Rise of Islamist Terrorism and the Global Response*. London and New York: Routledge, 2002.

*Homeland Security Statutes*. Rockville, MD: Government Institutes, ABS Consulting, 2003.

Katz, Samuel M. *Relentless Pursuit: The DSS and the Manhunt for the Al-Qaeda Terrorists*. New York: Forge, 2002.

Kepel, Gilles. *Jihad: The Trail of Political Islam*. Translated by Anthony F. Roberts. Cambridge, MA: Harvard University Press, 2002

Laqueur, Walter. *No End to War: Terrorism in the Twenty-first Century*. New York: Continuum, 2003.

Lewis, Bernard. *The Crisis of Islam: Holy War and Unholy Terror*. New York: Modem Library, 2003.

Mack, Raneta Lawson. *Equal Justice in the Balance: America's Legal Responses to the Emerging Terrorist Threat*. Ann Arbor, MI: University of Michigan Press, 2004.

Mamdani, Mahmood. *Good Muslim, Bad Muslim: America, the Cold War, and the Roots of Terror*. New York: Pantheon, 2004.

Martin, Gus, ed. *The New Era of Terrorism: Selected Readings*. Thousand Oaks, CA: Sage, 2004.

Michaels, C. William. *No Greater Threat: America after September 11 and the Rise of a National Security State*. New York: Algora Pub., 2005.

Miller, John, and Michael Stone. *Inside the 9/11 Plot, and Why the FBI and CIA Failed to Stop It: The Cell*. New York: Hyperion, 2002.

Moore, Michael. *The Official Fahrenheit 9/11 Reader*. New York: Simon & Schuster Paperbacks, 2006.

Musch, Donald J. *Civil Liberties and Foreign Intelligence Surveillance Act*. Dobbs Ferry, NY: Oceana Publications, 2003.

Nakaya, Andrea C. *Homeland Security*. Detroit, MI: Greenhaven Press, 2005.

Nanda, Ved P. *Law in the War on International Terrorism*. Ardsley, NY: Transnational Publishers, 2005.

Northouse, Clayton. *Protecting What Matters: Technology, Security, and Liberty Since 9/11*. Washington, DC: Computer Ethics Institute, 2006.

*Oversight of the USA PATRIOT Act: Hearing before the Committee on the Judiciary*. United States Senate, 109th Congress, 1st Session, April 5, and May 10, 2005. Washington: U.S. Government Printing Office, 2005.

Piszkiewicz, Dennis. *Terrorism's War with America: A History*. Westport, CT: Praeger, 2003.

*Report from the Field: The USA PATRIOT Act at Work*. Washington, DC: U.S. Department of Justice, 2004.

Ritz, Michael W. *The Homeland Security Papers: Stemming the Tide of Terror*. Maxwell Air Force Base, AL: USAF Counterproliferation Center, 2004.

Sageman, Marc. *Understanding Terror Networks*. Philadelphia, PA: University of Pennsylvania Press, 2004.

Sammon, Bill. *Fighting Back: The War on Terrorism from Inside the Bush White House*. New York: Regnery, 2002.

Scheppler, Bill. *The USA PATRIOT Act: Anti-terror Legislation in Response to 9/11*. New York: Rosen Publishing, 2006.

Schulhofer, Stephen J. *Rethinking the Patriot Act: Keeping America Safe and Free*. New York: Century Foundation Press, 2005.

*Selected Federal Asset Forfeiture Statutes: Including Statutes Amended by the Criminal Law Technical Amendment of 2002, the Homeland Security Act of 2002, the USA PATRIOT Act of 2001, and CAFRA*. Washington, DC: U.S. Department of Justice, 2004.

*The 9/11 Commission Report: Final Report of the National Commission on Terrorist Attacks upon the United States*. Authorized edition. New York: Norton, 2004.

*USA PATRIOT Act: A Review for the Purpose of Reauthorization*. Hearing before the Committee on the Judiciary, House of Representatives, 109th Congres, 1st Session, April 6, 2005. Washington: U.S. Government Printing Office, 2005.

*The USA PATRIOT Act in Practice: Shedding Light on the FISA Process*. Hearing before the Committee on the Judiciary, United States Senate, 107th Congress, 2d Session, September 10, 2002. Washington: U.S. Government Printing Office, 2003.

Torr, James D. *The Patriot Act*. Detroit, MI: Lucent Books/Thomson Gale, 2006.

Van Bergen, Jennifer. *The Twilight of Democracy: The Bush Plan for America*. Monroe, ME: Common Courage Press, 2005.

Williams, Mary E., ed. *The Terrorist Attack on America*. Current Controversies series. Farmington Hills, MI: Greenhaven, 2003.

Wright, Robin. *Sacred Rage: The Wrath of Militant*. Updated Edition. New York: Simon& Schuster, 2001.

# FILMS AND VIDEO

*Distorted Morality: A War on Terrorism?* 172 min. Oakland, CA: AK Press, 2003.

*Fahrenheit 9/11*. Dir. Michael Moore. 122 min. Lions Gate Films, 2004.

*Liberty and Security in an Age of Terrorism*. Video. Thompson, Molly. Princeton, NJ: Films for the Humanities &Sciences, 2004.

*In Memoriam: New York, 9/11/01*. 60 min. Home Box Office, 2002.

*In Search of Al Qaeda*. Dir. Martin Smith. 60 min. Alexandria, VA: PBS Video, 2002.

*In Search of bin Laden*. Dir. Martin Smith. 56 min. Alexandria, VA: PBS Video, 2001.

*The Patriot Act*. Video. Ted Koppel. Princeton, NJ: Films for the Humanities & Sciences, 2004.

Susman, Thomas M. *Safeguarding Our Patrons' Privacy: What Every Librarian Needs to Know about the USA PATRIOT Act and Related Anti-terrorism Measures*. Video Recording.

*One Day in September*. Dir. Kevin Macdonald. 94 min. Arthur Cohn Prod., 2000.

*September 11,2001: A Turning Point in Our History*. 30 min. Austin, TX: Holt, Rinehart and Winston, 2001.

*WTC: The First 24 Hours, 9.11.2001*. Dir. Etienne Sauret. 40 min. New York: Docurama, 2001.

# Index

**About the Author**

HERBERT N. FOERSTEL is the former head of branch libraries at the University of Maryland, a board member of the Freedom to Read Foundation, and the editor of the Maryland Library Association's newspaper. He is the author of many books on free press issues, including *Refuge of a Scoundrel: The Patriot Act in Libraries* (Libraries Unlimited, 2004) and *Killing the Messenger: Journalists at Risk in Modern Warfare* (Praeger, 2006).